HOPE I GET
OLD
BEFORE I DIE

www.penguin.co.uk

Also by David Hepworth

1971: Never a Dull Moment

Uncommon People: The Rise and Fall of the Rock Stars

Nothing is Real: The Beatles Were Underrated and
Other Sweeping Statements About Pop

A Fabulous Creation: How the LP Saved Our Lives

The Rock & Roll A Level

Overpaid, Oversexed and Over There: How a Few
Skinny Brits with Bad Teeth Rocked America

Abbey Road: The Inside Story of the World's Most
Famous Recording Studio

HOPE I GET OLD BEFORE I DIE

WHY ROCK STARS NEVER RETIRE

DAVID HEPWORTH

bantam

TRANSWORLD PUBLISHERS

Penguin Random House, One Embassy Gardens, 8 Viaduct Gardens, London SW11 7BW
www.penguin.co.uk

Transworld is part of the Penguin Random House group of companies
whose addresses can be found at global.penguinrandomhouse.com

Penguin
Random House
UK

First published in Great Britain in 2024 by Bantam
an imprint of Transworld Publishers

A CIP catalogue record for this book is available from the British Library.

ISBN
9781787632783

Text design by Couper Street Type Co.

Typeset in 11.5/15.75 pt Minion Pro by Jouve (UK), Milton Keynes
Printed and bound in Great Britain by Clays Ltd, Elcograf S.p.A.

The authorized representative in the EEA is Penguin Random House Ireland,
Morrison Chambers, 32 Nassau Street, Dublin DO2 YH68.

Penguin Random House is committed to a sustainable future
for our business, our readers and our planet. This book is made
from Forest Stewardship Council® certified paper.

For Joseph David Robert Hepworth

'The older you get, the older you wanna get'
                                    – Keith Richards

Contents

Introduction: Rock's Third Act   **xi**

1   The Age of Spectacle Begins   **1**

2   Rock Enters Its Middle Years   **11**

3   What a Long Strange Dip It's Been   **21**

4   The Feuding Families of Rock   **31**

5   The Tour That Changed Everything   **45**

6   You Can't Take It With You   **57**

7   No Goin' Back for the Byrds   **71**

8   Eric Clapton's Tragic Hit   **83**

9   Nick Lowe's Indian Summer   **93**

10   The Rock Generation Takes Power   **101**

11   The Only Act Bigger Than the Beatles   **109**

12   Even the Sex Pistols Kiss and Make Up   **119**

13   Elton in the Abbey   **127**

14   Madonna Makes New Hits from Old Flops   **137**

15   Eternal Life on the Internet   **147**

16   Social Media Puts an End to Rock Star Mystique   **157**

17   Classic Rock as Costume Drama   **167**

CONTENTS

18 The Not Entirely Lonesome Death of John Entwistle   **179**

19 Rock Goes to Las Vegas Again   **189**

20 Led Zeppelin's Hot Ticket   **199**

21 Glen Campbell Forgets   **209**

22 Wilko in the Valley of the Shadow   **219**

23 Billy Joel's Saturday Night   **229**

24 All the Old Dudes   **239**

25 That Difficult Last Album   **253**

26 Bob Dylan's Nobel Prize   **261**

27 Toto and the Human Jukebox   **271**

28 If Anybody Can Save the Guitar . . .   **283**

29 Liz Phair is Still in the Game   **293**

30 Christine McVie's Last Hurrah   **301**

31 The Bitter Years of John Fogerty   **311**

32 Goodbye *Goodbye Yellow Brick Road*   **323**

33 The Old Boys of Summer   **331**

34 Sound Investments   **341**

35 The Immortality Business   **353**

36 And in the End . . .   **367**

Playlist   **381**

Bibliography   **392**

Sources   **394**

Acknowledgements   **396**

Picture Acknowledgements   **397**

Index   **399**

Introduction:
ROCK'S THIRD ACT

O n the evening of 13 July 1985, when Paul McCartney was brought before the crowd at London's Wembley Stadium in order to close the British end of the Live Aid fundraiser to help relieve famine in Ethiopia by singing his sixteen-year-old anthem 'Let It Be', he was greeted in the manner of a venerable ancient briefly stepping down from rock's notional Mount Rushmore in order to bestow his blessing on the kids who were gathered that day, largely for old times' sake. At the time it seemed faintly ridiculous to regard a veteran like McCartney as being in the same bracket as the relative youngsters who had planned the day. In fact he had only recently celebrated his forty-third birthday.

On 25 June 2022, when the same Paul McCartney was introduced to an even larger crowd at the Glastonbury Festival in Somerset and simultaneously to the watching millions on TV, an occasion he instigated by singing his fifty-eight-year-old composition 'Can't Buy Me Love' – or at least singing along with the crowd, who seemed wholly familiar with the words despite the fact that only a minority of them had been born when it was released – he was seized on as one of the few things a twenty-first-century festival audience, who had grown up in a wilderness of specialisms and sub-cultures, could possibly be expected to agree upon. This occasion took place only a week after he had celebrated his eightieth birthday. This time there was no thought of apologizing for the years. This time the years were the point.

How did pop music, which was once supposed to be exclusively about the shock of the new, come to have such a comfortable relationship with its past? What happened between the two dates in the paragraphs above to make such a thing possible? This is what this book sets out to explore. How did the likes of McCartney and hundreds of lesser lights manage to maintain and grow their mystique into their Second and Third ages? How did we end up with rock gods in their eighties? How did they keep it up? There are thousands of volumes devoted to the subject of how your favourite artists got their big break. This one's about how some of them managed to keep on working longer than the rest of us for the simple reason that they wanted to, and the more important reason that we wanted them to. It turned out they would be addicted to providing what we turned out to be addicted to consuming. They liked to feel young and we liked to feel that they still were. This was a two-way street. The pull was every bit as important as the push.

As he continued profitably to ply the trade he had taken up as a teenager into his seventies, Keith Richards was wont to greet audiences with the words 'It's good to be here – it's good to be anywhere' as though he recognized that his continued employment was a privilege not always available to other performers, particularly those who became famous in their youth. Keeping on keeping on is nothing like as easy for actors, and for athletes it is clearly impossible. Even the bewigged judge in London's ancient courts, which had once been cited as an example of a job you could continue to perform well into your dotage, is now compelled to retire at the age of seventy-five. Hence it is one of the richer ironies with which this subject is ringed that the oiks who were once arraigned before such justices for relieving themselves on garage doors or misappropriating copyrighted chord sequences gaily sailed past all the mandatory retirement ages like the bunnies who advertise batteries and continued hoovering up the cash and gliding on the thermals of acclaim long after their lordships had handed in their gavels. It turned out that there was no such statute of limitations for these formerly snake-hipped glory boys. Of all the jobs that would turn out to last a lifetime, that of rock star was by some distance the least likely.

When the eighty-year-old McCartney headlined Glastonbury he further armoured himself against any charges of being old and in the way by ensuring he was backed up by representatives of more than one generation of relative youngsters, the seventy-two-year-old Bruce Springsteen and the fifty-three-year-old spring chicken Dave Grohl. None of these veterans were having to fight for attention. They were taking advantage of the fact that their stocks appeared to have risen once again. One of the biggest music stories of July 2023 was the unexpected return to live performance of seventy-nine-year-old Joni Mitchell, who appeared to sing and play at what was supposed to be a tribute to her legacy and then promptly announced that she was so bucked by the experience she now had a taste for doing more. The eighty-two-year-old Bob Dylan had no need to return because he had clearly never gone away. Touring was now his natural condition. Tendinitis might mean that he had long since stopped playing the guitar, the keyboard behind which he was stationed on stage was making no audible contribution to the band's sound, and he appeared to employ the microphone as much for stability as audibility, but he clearly intended to be up there on stage as long as he possibly could. As the old saying goes, being a musician is not a job, it's an incurable disease.

This book's intention is to consider these lions of rock in winter, to reflect on what it means to perform songs originally aimed at wild youth in front of audiences of grandparents, to bear witness to the gradual transformation of a music which used to be exclusively for the young into the very thing it was supposed to be an alternative to, and to look at rock stars in their Third Age as closely as books like this have traditionally looked at their First. How did it all happen? How did a career which was supposed to last about as long as a boxer's end up continuing as long as a pope's? How did Mick Jagger, for instance, who said in his early thirties that he couldn't possibly imagine still doing the same job at the inconceivably distant age of forty, end up performing the same function beyond the age of eighty? How did all these scrawny scourges of the establishment end up with knighthoods? How did the tie-dyed denizens of Woodstock Nation, who were once viewed as a threat to the American way of life, crown their careers by being garlanded by presidents? How did the Baby Boomers, who had used their sheer weight of numbers and their shrewd avoidance of getting involved in wars to advance the illusion that they had also invented sex, rebellion and fun, manage to remain relevant long enough to effectively write their own obituaries?

This was after all not the way anybody imagined it was going to turn out. When in 1965 the twenty-year-old Pete Townshend had put the line 'hope I die before I get old' in the mouth of Roger Daltrey on his anthem 'My Generation', nobody argued because his was clearly the generation with which they identified. By the time, thirty years later, that Keith Richards got around to observing that the older you got the older you wanted to get, the same people found themselves agreeing more fervently with the latter sentiment than they had ever done with the former. A hundred years after George Bernard Shaw had complained that youth was wasted on the young, middle-aged rock fans were turning up in their thousands to demonstrate that they appreciated its true value.

As they moved through middle age and beyond, the bands of

former boys kept going just as they had begun, for a variety of reasons, but mainly because they could. And we are the reason they could. Despite the dire predictions of our head teachers and our parents, the Baby Boomers and those who came after had the privilege of growing up without having to conform to traditional expectations. That meant we didn't have to give up on the heroes and heroines of our teenage years. This was extremely good news for them because as we got older and waxed prosperous we had much more money to send in their direction than was ever the case when we were kids. Unlike preceding generations it seems we never put away our youthful devotion as we grew older, and as the years went by we expressed that devotion in terms ever more financially beneficial to its objects. In many ways we seemed to grow more attached to them as the years went by because they provided a kind of anchor; we preferred to think that no matter how many years they had been citizens in good standing of Planet Showbiz they still somehow stood for us; furthermore we still liked to think that if we got the chance to meet them for a drink they would warm to us every bit as much as we would warm to them. They began as our fantasy friends and they have remained the firmest of fantasy friends right to the end.

This journey was not sunny and benign for everyone. It was not always like *The Golden Girls* with a soundtrack provided by Martin Scorsese. Some fell by the wayside, others among thieves. The long haul was not without stresses and strains. There were unseemly squabbles between people who had been effectively shackled together since they were teenagers and now had to pretend to like each other in order to cover their grandchildren's school fees. The tensions between the members who had big houses because their names had turned up among the writing credits and their minimum-wage mates grew more testing as time went by. Advancing years did not in any way reduce these people's competitive nature. Very often it turned out that a life spent in the spotlight had not in any way sated their hunger for approbation. If anything it sharpened it. It turned out that the more famous they had been, the more famous they seemed determined to remain.

And all the time the world in which they lived and moved was being roiled by change, technological and cultural, to an extent that rattled everything which had seemed certain. Like every previous generation they had lived long enough to see that things mutated again and again, but their unique position as Children of the Revolution meant that they were the only people who were precluded from mentioning it, lest they appear to be on the wrong side. They had risen to fame saying the first thing that came into their heads and found that their fame had endured into an age when the first thing that came into your head was the very last thing you allowed anywhere near your tongue. By the end of the period covered by this history a handful of them were quietly resting some of their most-loved material on the grounds that the present might find it, in the new lingua franca, 'problematic'. The Rolling Stones were touring in 2024 but they wouldn't be doing 'Brown Sugar', which, while understandable, rather made you wonder what could possibly be the point of having a Rolling Stones if they couldn't offend somebody.

What follows, then, is a story of Rock's Third Act. It's an act which at the time of writing has lasted almost forty years. In that period of time many things have been turned on their heads. The past has become hip while the future seems oddly passé. The trade in pop records as physical product vanished and then re-emerged as a sub-division of the traffic in antiques. Former icons of the counter-culture have lent their names to best-selling items of confectionery. Ex-streetfighting men now do their act for corporate clients in exchange for sums of money which would once have equalled a lifetime's earnings. Songwriters have sold their catalogues to investment companies that regard old pop songs as one of the few reliable hedges against uncertainty. The only certainties have been inverted. Former firebrands gripped and grinned with long-time fans who were surprised suddenly to find themselves heads of government. No state occasion could be considered complete without the benediction provided by a star from decades earlier turning up to recapitulate an old favourite. The Nobel Prize in Literature was handed out to an elderly man whose proud boast was that he could bash out a lyric in minutes. There were new dimensions of unlikelihood. A man of pensionable age in tight trousers was invited to perform a solo on the electric guitar from the roof of Buckingham Palace. The star turn at the most notable state funeral of our time was a piano player formerly known as Reg who went on to marry a man.

Rock's Third Act is a story that has never been told, partly because it is still going on. Like all the best stories about rock it is simultaneously ludicrous, possessed of a strange, unquiet dignity, and has as much to say about us out there in the dark as it has about those on the other side of the red rope.

For the purpose of this telling, the story begins on Saturday, 13 July 1985. Long ago, in a vanished world.

Freddie Mercury's show-stopping Live Aid performance turned a generation of older TV viewers into concert-goers.

1

THE AGE OF SPECTACLE BEGINS

The Live Aid concert on 13 July 1985, which began the day at Wembley Stadium in London and closed in the evening at JFK Stadium in Philadelphia, was an event almost as close to the end of the Second World War as it is to the present time.

At that moment in popular music history – which was a mere thirty years after Little Richard's unleashing of 'Tutti Frutti' but a full thirty-nine removed from the present day – the CD was yet to fully enter our lives, the internet was entirely beyond the imagination of all but a few scientists, and nobody present in London or Philadelphia on that day could possibly have realized that a whole way of doing things would very quickly be utterly overtaken by technology in a way that would render the memory of it difficult to recapture.

Revolutionary though it would prove to be, Live Aid was concert-going the old way. The audience in London that day turned up clutching paper tickets which had cost them £25. In Philadelphia they were $35. This was 40 per cent more than people were used to paying at the time but it was considered acceptable because it was made clear that most of the cost was in the way of a charitable donation.

The people who worked behind the scenes on the shows were still doing things the way they would have done them in the previous decade. The massive logistical challenge that was Live Aid – two enormous, interlocking, star-studded shows separated by thousands of miles but linked by television signals sent by satellite – was accomplished without the use of a single mobile phone for the simple reason that such things were unknown at the time to anybody but insanely early adopters or people working in distant oil fields.

The technicians working that day may have had some inkling of how that technology would soon change their work but the audience, in their stone-washed jeans, 'Frankie Say' T-shirts and Cyndi Lauper hair-stacks, didn't have a clue what they were going to get and weren't aware that they were about to enjoy one of the last unmediated experiences which music would offer. Because there was no mobile phone communication that day there was none of the social media traffic which would, within their lifetimes, come to shape responses to all events even as they were going on. None of us who were inside Wembley Stadium that day had any idea of the reverberations of what had been taking place there until we got home in the early hours of the following morning.

The set-up in Wembley was so pre-technological that Bob Geldof and all the other guests who filled the gaps by talking to broadcasters like me could only be interviewed if they first climbed via a series of catwalks up to a perspex box suspended in the eaves of the old stadium, the same box from which tweedy old commentators would pronounce on the goalscoring feats of footballers with perms. Wembley at the time was an old stadium which had been built for a pre-war world. Only a couple of months earlier it had been the venue for an FA Cup Final between two teams featuring only two players not born in the British Isles and only one of colour. It was mere weeks since the disaster at the Heysel Stadium in Brussels had killed thirty-nine people who had simply turned up to see a football match. In the Who's crew that day were people who had been present at the concert in Cincinnati when eleven fans had been killed in a crush. In 1985 Health and Safety was not yet a joke for the simple reason that Health and Safety was not yet a thing.

The crowd that made its way to Wembley that day on the London Underground were only just getting used to the idea that they were no longer permitted to light up on the journey. Pubs, restaurants and places of work were still wreathed in a haze of tobacco smoke. Magazine offices, such as the one I worked in at the time, were soundtracked by the clacking of manual typewriters and pierced by the sound of telephones that actually rang. In 1985 everything that had to be put together was put together by hand. Without spray fixative and Letraset, without ink bought by the barrel and paper delivered by fleets of trucks, without motorcycle messengers and switchboards, without turntables and reel-to-reel tape machines, the media of the time couldn't possibly function. As for consumer comforts, the Live Aid crowd, an ecumenical bunch who were different in character from the highly partisan fans who would have been in attendance if any one of the acts had been headlining singly, trooped towards the stadium without one waxed cup of fancy coffee between them.

Live Aid was devised as a demonstration of compassion and a fundraiser. For the concert business it turned out to be something else as well: an unpaid advertisement for an entirely new beginning for rock and roll, one in which music would be combined with the gestural arts which have always been an essential component of the pop music racket and mounted on an unprecedented scale in front of huge audiences who had been drawn there as much by the human need to feel part of something vast as the love of the music. Though nobody knew it at the time, Live Aid announced the dawning of the Age of Spectacle.

I didn't begin to realize this until I got home late that night. I had returned via a post-show party in the unlikely surroundings of a

Mayfair niterie at which representatives of the British bands that had performed at Wembley uncharitably barracked the efforts of the Philadelphia performers, which were being relayed into the club via a big screen, thus ensuring that I didn't leave with too wide-eyed an impression of the proceedings. In fact it confirmed my conviction that few things occur in the world of rock or show business which aren't at least partly about career. What I learned when I got home and in the days ahead was that as far as the wider world was concerned, on that one day the rock business had been suddenly transformed from a nest of vipers in which nobody's motives were ever above question into a greater force for good than any of the established religions. My wife, who has had the good grace not to get too caught up in either the ups or the downs of the way I ended up earning my living, was sitting up in bed, still trying to process the events of the day. I was surprised first of all that she had watched it. I couldn't help but be impressed by how impressed she had been. 'Well, *that* was something,' she said.

This was my first inkling of the way Live Aid had landed with the people who really mattered, who were of course not the acts, not the organizers and certainly not the people in the stadium; the people who mattered were the TV viewers. My wife was clearly not the only person who felt that way. She told me that parents and in-laws had been on the phone. She explained how she'd been contacted by friends and distant relatives saying they'd got neighbours over and were glued to their TVs as though this was a latter-day coronation. It appeared that the TV audience had grown throughout the day as people phoned each other on land lines and suggested that if they hadn't already done so they really should switch on. The following day I spoke to no less a figure than the cricketing titan Viv Richards, the captain of West Indies and Somerset, who complained that his team had found it impossible to concentrate the previous day because of the competing attractions of what was going on at

THE AGE OF SPECTACLE BEGINS

Wembley Stadium. Batsmen were quite happy to be dismissed so that they could get back to the dressing room where they could resume their position in front of the TV.

This was most significant. It seemed that rock and roll, which had been going on its own sweet way without the majority of the population much caring, had suddenly come to the attention of people who were by no means rock and roll people. These were not people who needed to know who was playing drums with Led Zeppelin or who was in the current line-up of the Pretenders. These were regular people. Barbecuing people. Car-washing people. Floating voters. People from the suburbs. People who were, although they didn't know it yet, suddenly being seduced by the appeal of an entertainment experience they had never taken a great deal of notice of before. They had been beguiled by the picturesque combination of big-name bands playing their big-name hits under cloudless skies. In the space of one day, this quite turned their heads.

If you wish to be specific about it, the Age of Spectacle began just after half past six that evening. It was at that point that Queen, a band that had been together for fifteen years, took to the stage. Queen were the turn that went down best on the day and that was because of Freddie Mercury. Freddie was the hit of the day because Freddie, being conversant with the theory and practice of showbiz, fully understood that Live Aid was most of all a TV spectacular and as such was aimed at an audience at home, and an audience at home was certainly not in the market for a few tracks from Queen's new album. Therefore his performance of their key crowd-pleasers was addressed directly to cameraman Bob Wilson, one of the unsung BBC craftsmen who were decked out in white specially for the occasion so that they could thread their way in and out of the performers without spoiling the picture. The heavy camera on Bob's strong shoulder sent the images to the big screen, which was the way that most people in Wembley saw the proceedings. Wilson got so near at one point that Mercury, emboldened by how swimmingly it appeared to be going, lunged for his testes. Certainly at one point Mercury, relishing his role as de facto executive producer of the entire event for the period when he was on stage, led Wilson to centre stage and made him point his camera at the crowd as they imitated the singer as he clapped his hands above his head on 'Radio Ga Ga', and thus could be said to have directed the defining image of the day.

There couldn't have been a better person to usher in this new age because Freddie truly knew spectacle. Six months earlier his band had played in front of three hundred thousand people in Rio de Janeiro and he understood that performing outdoors was all about the broadest of broad gestures, all about wrenching the crowd's attention away from the competing attractions of the sky, the people in their immediate vicinity and the smell of the hotdog van and making them feel they were part of something bigger. The few years that acts like Queen had on relative greenhorns like U2 really showed that day. When Bono wandered off stage to commune with fans during their act the rest of the band lost sight of him entirely, leaving the stage at the end assuming it had been a disaster and they would never work again. In 1985 even the mega-stars were mega-show virgins. The hottest act of 1985, Bruce Springsteen, didn't even feature that day. He had only just played his very first open-air show a few weeks before at Slane Castle in Ireland and had found the experience so traumatic he had a serious argument with his manager in the dressing room at half-time. The root of his unease was his assumption that he would never be the kind of act who would play shows where he couldn't look the audience in the eye. It had been one of the key tenets of punk rock that only sell-outs would agree to perform such shows. This view did not come under much challenge because the kind of acts that clung to it as an article of faith were not often invited to betray it. In the Age of Spectacle they would all be invited to betray it, and all of them would. If they felt bad about that they could take some comfort from the front pages of the newspapers in the week following Live Aid when the headline writers were beginning to describe them in terms not ordinarily employed to characterize famous musicians doing their usual job in front of a worldwide TV audience.

They were heroes.

2

In 1986 record buyers lined up to invest in some reassuringly expensive old recordings from the former future of rock and roll.

BRUCE SPRINGSTEEN
& THE E STREET BAND
LIVE/1975-85

ROCK ENTERS ITS MIDDLE YEARS

The majority of the stars who had featured on the Band Aid record in 1984 were acts, like the Boomtown Rats, Ultravox, Duran Duran and Culture Club, that had come up in that boom in pop singles which followed on the heels of the so-called New Wave. This latter movement had positioned itself firmly as the Year Zero of popular music. In their philosophy the young were the pure in heart and the old were guilty until proved innocent. This notion took such a firm hold that it was not always apparent that there wasn't a great deal in age terms between the members of the Stranglers, for instance, and the members of Fairport Convention (Hugh Cornwell and Richard Thompson having gone to school together), that Ian Dury and the Blockheads featured among their number players who had been full-grown men during the first Summer of Love, or that Debbie Harry was born in the same year as Eric Clapton. Everybody was doing everything in their power to appear to be on the side of the future rather than the past.

Live Aid seemed to put an end to that. Its youngsters were mostly in their thirties. Many of its veterans were still looking at forty. There wasn't much difference between the two generations except in terms of experience. After Live Aid there was much talk of back-stage fraternization between the seniors and the middle-schoolers. There were fewer references to the former being old and in the way. There were no longer any kids, they were all adults. There wasn't just one generation gap, there were lots. At Live Aid, Mick Jagger was closing in on his forty-second birthday; David Bowie, who had started at an earlier age, was a positively statesmanlike thirty-eight. Bob Dylan was forty-four. Tina Turner, bless her creaking bones, was all of forty-five. At the time she appeared at the concert she was celebrating more than six months on the British chart with an unlikely comeback album called *Private Dancer* and a single called 'What's Love Got To Do With It', in the course of which she made the most of the songwriting and production input of the middle-schoolers. To many of the younger people watching on TV at the time Tina may have appeared to be a game old girl who was enjoying a well-earned lap of honour. In fact she was just getting started.

Something similar could be said of Paul McCartney. In September 1986 he appeared on the cover of a new music magazine called Q, which I had been involved in launching. We managed to secure McCartney not so much because we were guaranteed to give him a fair crack of the whip as because at the time most other media weren't all that interested. His most recent public outing, the musical film *Give My Regards to Broad Street*, had endured a painful period in the critical barrel and the media climate of the times was such that nobody was inclined to give a forty-four-year-old apparent has-been an even break.

Whether he meant to or not, McCartney's interview in Q marked the beginning of his campaign to claw back some of the credit for the Beatles, credit which in the immediate wake of John Lennon's death in 1980 had been largely given to the man who had styled himself a working-class hero. This interview was the first place where he sought to make it clear that while John had been living out in the stockbroker belt succumbing to his post-touring depression, McCartney had been the one out on the town, doing the avant-garde thing. 'He was one great guy but part of his greatness was he wasn't a saint,' he said. Asked how he felt when the microphone had failed at Live Aid the previous year he confessed it had been embarrassing but he was honoured to have taken part. 'The event itself was so great, but it wasn't for my ego. It was like having been at the battle of Agincourt.'

While it had previously been axiomatic that the best thing a music magazine could offer was the hot new thing, in the years after Live Aid it was evident that there was a market for the hot old thing. Q successfully lined up the grand old men as cover stars because they gave good copy and the magazine found that they sold well. Already at this point it was becoming clear that the fame which had been won in the days when fame was rare had additional value in these MTV days when renown was suddenly cheap. In one 1986 issue there was an interview with Rod Stewart, who was in the middle of an Italian tour. The chat began with an almost accusatory 'you're forty-one', but there was no indication that he was doing anything different as a consequence. At this point in the early middle age of the people who had made their bones in the late 1960s and early 1970s, there was as yet not the smallest sign of the exercise or diet regimes it would take to keep an ageing frame in shape for the demands of touring. Indeed the piece stated that Rod and his then twenty-six-year-old paramour, Kelly Emberg, began every day with forty minutes under a sun-ray lamp and made plain that during the rest of the day he held back from neither Barolo nor osso buco.

Like everyone else he was asked about Live Aid. Rod explained he wished he had played it but his band weren't available. There was a picture of him with his Hollywood neighbours, who included Gregory Peck and Gene Kelly. At the time he was looking back on what seemed to have been a long career of twenty years and reflecting that if it all ended tomorrow he would have no regrets.

In the third issue, Elton John provided a piece which could have served as the template for many of the interviews that would be given by the stars of the seventies as they rescued their own careers from the jaws of self-inflicted harm, reflected on how low they had been at their worst and then modestly proffered their new album or tour or book or incarnation. The basic shape of the rock star interview of this time could be distilled into the following four sentences: 'I flew high. I fucked up. I'm back. Can you forgive me?' Whether or not any of the people giving these interviews were aware that they were asking for an extension on Rod Stewart's twenty years, whether or not they were consciously asking us to remain as attached to them in their later years as we had been in their first, that seemed to be the effect these chats had. At the same time they would make a modest bid to be rated among their heroes and offer some reassurance that they weren't entirely cut off from what was happening at the present time in the shape of a reference to some new album they had really been enjoying.

What was beginning to happen at the time increasingly seemed to be the recent past. On 10 November 1986 crowds began queueing outside Tower Records' flagship store in Manhattan in the dawn light, long before the trucks came up Broadway and disappeared with a much-ballyhooed cargo into the shop's loading bay. As fast as they could be unloaded the individual items of that cargo were placed on display in the superstore, which had opened an hour early in honour of just this one release. As fast as they could be stacked up eager hands snatched the shrink-wrapped copies and took them to one of the six tills that had been specially opened to deal with the demand. The price was $25, which many thought an outrageous amount to charge for what were after all old songs. Retailers called it the biggest day in the history of the record business. For once they were probably right.

The boxed set, which opened to reveal five discs, three cassettes or three of the still relatively new-fangled CDs, was a forty-track compilation of songs by Bruce Springsteen and the E Street Band which had been recorded live between 1975 and 1985, the earliest shows at the Roxy, a former strip club in West Hollywood which could just about squeeze in five hundred souls, and the later ones at Giants Stadium in New Jersey, which could accommodate more than eighty thousand. In the interval between them the local boy had made an apparently fairytale transition from seven-stone weakling to national hero. That word again.

The scale of that transformation became a story in itself. The man who had once been the special darling of the rock press was now a story big enough and broad enough for the TV news and the serious papers. Hence the *New York Times*, which in 1986 was printing and selling a million paper copies every single day, had a reporter standing by when Tower opened their tills early. All three shoppers they quoted admitted they had come out to buy the new record early out of some sense of their duty as consumers, one because her husband wouldn't forgive her if she didn't bring one home, another because he'd been frightened that if he didn't get to the shop early they would sell out, and another, a middle-aged surgeon, 'probably because of the hype'. All three were indicators of a new mainstream audience for what came to be called heritage rock and an early manifestation of what would come to be known as FOMO.

In the United States it went to number one and stayed there for eight weeks, which was unprecedented for a boxed set, a format which at the time was seen as appealing to hardcore collectors rather than impulse shoppers at the mall. By March the following year the box had abruptly stopped selling and many shops, which had been taken in by their own initial enthusiasm, were looking at overstocks they would find difficult to move. This time record retailers were saying 'it went up like a skyrocket and came down just as fast'. As time went on it seemed unlikely that many of the people who had bought it really appreciated the record the way Springsteen had hoped, as he explained to me in a suite at the Parker Meridien Hotel where he turned up to be interviewed for British TV wearing a Triumph motorcycle T-shirt. He had agonized – didn't he always? – about how to make this record, which comprised performances from a ten-year period, read like a story of his life. That's why, he said, he wanted to finish it with his version of Tom Waits' 'Jersey Girl' in order to signal that he had finally reached some sense of contentment.

This was the version of himself Springsteen was outlining at the time. He had married actress Julianne Phillips in May 1985 and there didn't seem any reason why that shouldn't lead to a domestic outcome to match the fairytale career. Now that he had finally made it to the top of the mountain, at the very advanced age of thirty-five, it was surely the time to bring the rest of his life into line. It would not prove to be as easy as that. When a member of our New York film crew commented that the golden couple's marital unhappiness was already the gossip of Manhattan I chose to ignore it, particularly since not so much as a comma on the subject had found its way into the press. It wasn't long before it turned out to be true. The two separated and then filed for divorce in 1988, with both parties pronouncing themselves satisfied with the terms of a settlement which under California law could have given her as much as half of the considerable amount he had earned during their time together. The settlement was reached quickly and both parties have been careful not to say anything controversial about their time together in the years since.

Middle age and domesticity clearly brought its own struggles, particularly for those whose working lives involved levels of excitement we civilians could not possibly imagine. Springsteen's next album, *Tunnel Of Love*, was to be about the challenges of the personal life, which often come a distant second to the ones rock stars are acting out as they strut and fret on the boards. On the cover he wore a tie and leaned against a fancy car wearing the rueful look of a disappointed bridegroom. There was only one sleeve note. It read: 'Thanks Juli.' It was clearly all grist to the mill. As the writer Nora Ephron put it, everything's copy.

3

Solid citizens enjoy a scoop of Cherry Garcia ice cream, a flavour named for the previously alternative Grateful Dead.

WHAT A LONG
STRANGE DIP
IT'S BEEN

In the middle of February 1987, when the American republic was celebrating the birthday of its first president, George Washington, a Vermont-based ice-cream company which burnished its folksy, small-town image by trading under the name Ben & Jerry's unveiled a new flavour. Featuring chocolate flakes and Bing cherries, it honoured another American folk hero and was to be marketed under the name Cherry Garcia.

The company claimed they got the idea of naming a flavour after Jerry Garcia, the leader of the San Francisco group the Grateful Dead – a figure who would once have been identified as a leading light of the counter-culture, a man so restlessly curious about the consciousness-altering properties of illegal drugs that his nickname was 'Captain Trips' – from a correspondent who signed herself 'a Deadhead from Maine'. The acolyte turned out to be an ice-cream enthusiast named Jane Williamson. Jane had intuited what would ultimately be accepted as the core truth of rock and roll merchandising: the acts that make the most money from merchandising are the ones that appear to be least bothered about that money; simultaneously the fans most ready to invest their money in said merchandising are the very ones who most pride themselves on their lack of interest in such material matters. 'You know it makes sense,' Williamson wrote to the company. 'Dead paraphernalia always sells.'

In this she was entirely correct. The Grateful Dead had begun in 1965 as a mere jug band. It wasn't until 1976 that they officially became a corporation with the members of the band making up its board of directors. This in itself was an indication they were in it for the long haul. Eschewing some of the corporate cash-grabs that did so much to tarnish the images of bands like the Rolling Stones, the Grateful Dead wished nonetheless to participate fully in the value they had created. The people at Ben & Jerry's ice cream were about to discover this.

Having shipped a few pints of their creamy new line to the Grateful Dead's PR and heard in return that Jerry was pleased to be associated with anything so long as it wasn't engine oil, they assumed they had all the blessing they needed. That was apparently not the case. Having operated on the 'don't ask permission, ask forgiveness' principle, they couldn't be entirely surprised to find they received a cease-and-desist letter from the Dead's lawyers which made it clear that the corporation would not be mollified until a royalty had been negotiated. Since Cherry Garcia immediately became one of Ben & Jerry's three most popular flavours this proved to be a steady income.

This addition to the revenue line may not have been transformational for either the band or the gelatiers but it was a small but potent symbol of how a band which in the sixties had stood for benign chaos now stood for benign continuity. Ben & Jerry's even produced a T-shirt bearing the legend 'what a long strange dip it's been' in honour of the band's slogan 'what a long strange trip it's been'. It was what conventional marketeers would call a win-win. For the confectioners it provided a way of introducing the intangible quality of credibility into the fast-melting world of ice cream. In return it achieved the previously impossible feat of connecting the Grateful Dead with middle America. Now it wasn't just stoners with the munchies who were going home with pints of the stuff, it was also soccer moms. They had always warmed to Garcia's Buddha-like appearance. Now, finally, there was a Grateful Dead product they could actually consume. Cherry Garcia softened and sweetened the image of the Grateful Dead. They were talked about on the morning chat shows. This group whose name alone had once been enough to give respectable folk the vapours was now being embraced as an American institution.

The Grateful Dead seemed to be enjoying a second wind. The album they released in 1987, *In The Dark*, did markedly better than its predecessors. This was thanks to two things with which the Grateful Dead had never previously concerned themselves: a hit single and a video. This last was always a challenge for the grand old men of Haight-Ashbury. MTV might well furnish older acts with an opportunity to reach a new audience but it was also merciless in exposing the weathered fabric of their middle-aged bodies to scrutiny that was often pitiless. Greying men who had been in the business of show for twenty years without spending very long in make-up suddenly found they were passing whole days in trailers, trying on racks of clothes provided by stylists and sometimes even following the instructions of choreographers. Some took steps to meet the challenge. The Texas blues band ZZ Top, who were nothing like as old as the Dead, had taken the step of making sure that in future they would be characters in the background in their own videos, ceding the foreground to leggy models and their universally familiar hot rod.

The lead single from the Grateful Dead's record, a song called 'Touch Of Grey', was about, of all things, ageing, and therefore it was decided that the video should take the subject matter on the chin by depicting the band, the oldest member of which was no more than forty-seven at the time, in the form of animatronic skeletons. The camera's POV was behind the band, making the video's real stars the bunch of extras playing the audience, who were of course younger, more diverse and considerably smilier than the dusty old Deadheads. 'Touch Of Grey' was not merely tolerated by MTV but actively embraced in the name of broadening the channel's base. It put on a whole day of Grateful Dead programming under the name 'The Day of the Dead'. Says Grateful Dead chronicler Dennis McNally, 'it was the Dead's peculiar luck to produce "Touch Of Grey" at precisely the time that MTV's hierarchy decreed that some old guys would be nice'. McNally remembers telling the band the news that they had a top ten record for the first time in their career. When Garcia said 'I'm appalled', he was only partly joking.

The overdubbed applause that apparently arose from the audience as the skeletons gave way to the flesh-and-blood middle-aged members of the actual band is the kind of cheap trick that would have been beneath them in the days gone by. But there was no doubt they were enjoying being on top for the first time in a long time. In July 1987 the cover of *Rolling Stone* hailed 'the new dawn of the Grateful Dead'. According to the magazine, for whom records have always had to have novelistic pretensions to being *about* something, *In The Dark* was 'about ageing, decline, rebirth and recommitment'. The final track of *In The Dark* is arguably their finest recorded moment. The words of 'Black Muddy River' were supplied by lyricist Robert Hunter but the performance was entirely the work of Jerry Garcia. Hunter said later it was a song about feeling old at the advanced age of forty-five but nonetheless recognizing the necessity of perseverance and, as Winston Churchill would have recommended, keeping buggering on. That's certainly how it sounded when the band played it. Many of their audience, who had quietly undergone their own problems, heard it exactly that way, as a celebration of a virtue new to rock and roll: the power of putting one foot in front of the other.

Some long-established Deadheads derisively referred to the newbies who had been attracted by the first hit single in the band's history as 'Touchheads'. The critic Dave Marsh was quoted as describing the band as 'nostalgia mongers offering facile reminiscence to an audience with no memory of its own'. Which may have been true, but it seemed beside the point. Bands like the Grateful Dead were playing music for people who hadn't been there when their legend was established. That was the whole point. That was the only way to keep going. As Garcia said, 'It's like we have a new beginning. It's more fun now than it's ever been.' He further argued that longevity is always a good idea when it comes to music because being in a band 'is closer than any other relationship in life'. Of course there was also the money, which enabled Robert Hunter to buy a new house and Captain Trips to treat himself to a top-of-the-range BMW 750 with sixteen cylinders.

The MTV treatment may have let daylight in on magic but it also brought them a bigger audience than ever before, and these were people who had been sold on the idea of rock as community as unthinkingly as the Walkman had sold them on the idea of exercise. This meant a band that had travelled under the radar of mass attention since coming out of Haight-Ashbury in the mid-sixties suddenly had to deal with an entirely new and potentially corrupting force: popularity. Their concerts began to be overwhelmed by fans who were unable to get a ticket but nonetheless drove out of town, parked up, held up their home-made signs saying what they would do for a ticket, smoked their weed, played their boom boxes and deluged facilities that had not been built with such crowds in mind. The people who suffered most were the Grateful Dead themselves as some venues decided the band would be better off taking their chaos to another town.

The one thing the Grateful Dead didn't have to worry about was lack of demand. They featured on the cover of the business magazine *Forbes*, which applauded the way they had managed to cultivate their base without hit records. They were more of a company than any of the acts tarred with the 'corporate rock' brush. They had a staff of thirty-five, and these people didn't just sit around all day getting high, as they might have done twenty years before. The band was at the centre of a community and it was aware of the responsibilities that went with that. They had a hot line which took six thousand calls a day. They didn't just have a mailing list of their fans, they had a computerized mailing list, which in 1987 was quite something. You could even buy a Grateful Dead golf shirt. Nobody else in the music business, from teenage sensations through hair metal acts to the Rolling Stones, had tended their garden quite as well as the Grateful Dead did. When the technology eventually came along which would allow them to communicate more often they were more ready than anyone.

As their album was being recorded, released and publicized, the band were off the road as Jerry Garcia effectively taught himself how to play all over again. This was as a result of the latest of a number of health emergencies, not all of which were related to drugs. As a consequence of this latest crisis he fell into a diabetic coma and, as he later recalled, 'felt the vegetable kingdom was talking to me'. He made his reappearance to great acclaim at a Grateful Dead show in the Bay Area in December. The audience, suddenly alive to the grand narrative about life, death and survival which seemed to find such perfect expression in this odd old band embarking on their psychedelic excursions alongside such old warhorses as 'Not Fade Away', were poised to roar their approval of any line in any song which seemed to be in favour of keeping on and cheered Garcia for being alive when he simply had no right to be. The song they started with was 'Touch Of Grey'. According to McNally, 'the place went nuts'.

Jerry Garcia finally died in 1995 at the age of fifty-three. The Grateful Dead are now no more – if, that is, you don't count the records, videos and streams that continue to pour forth in greater profusion than at any point in the past, the feverish trade in relics and associated objects of veneration, the keenness of all kinds of commercial operations to license their still unsinkably good name, the regular rumours of major film and TV projects telling various versions of their story, the multifarious former members who still gather to play some of their tunes, the endorsements that continue to pour forth from famous fans like Stephen King and George R. R. Martin, tenants of the White House such as Bill Clinton and Al Gore and even right-wing provocateurs Tucker Carlson and Ann Coulter; then there are the nine thousand recordings of Grateful Dead concerts which are available, with the band's blessing, on the Internet Archive, to be pored over by successive generations of rock and roll purists as they reach the age when they suddenly find that nothing quite touches the spot like the often shambolic charms of the Grateful Dead. All that is still out there. As is Cherry Garcia.

As a result of that second career, they have ended up occupying a position which nobody who encountered them in the early days, when they were seen as a direct contravention of everything society held dear, could possibly have predicted. Continuity. Reassurance. Americana. Ice cream.

4

George Harrison, Bob Dylan, Little Richard and Beach Boy Mike Love grapple with formality at the Rock and Roll Hall of Fame.

THE FEUDING
FAMILIES OF
ROCK

The notion of a Hall of Fame derives from the ancient Norse tradition of ancestor worship. This proposes that somewhere beyond the bounds of time and space there exists a place where the warriors of the past can achieve a very select kind of immortality. In this place, organized along the lines of heaven but with a more rigorous door policy, the greats of different eras can gather and unite, carouse, drink each other's health in nectar and tell stories of their deeds back in the day. They named this place Valhalla.

When the Rock and Roll Hall of Fame was launched in the United States in 1986 it arrived just at the point when mainstream media was increasingly incapable of deciding for itself what was and what was not significant in pop music. Thus the idea of a rock and roll Valhalla provided institutions like the press with a new way of navigating what had become a bewildering and complex landscape. When Little Richard and Jerry Lee Lewis were among the first admitted to the Hall of Fame in 1986 there was little point expecting the mass audience to remember 'Tutti Frutti' or 'Great Balls Of Fire' but they were happy to strew any number of garlands at their feet once they could be reassured they were Hall of Famers; this was an idea they had become familiar with via sport, where it provided a way of squaring away the past and rendering it intelligible to the present and easy for the future.

Much as with Valhalla, it was believed that all the great warriors belonged to a greater family of warriors in the Rock and Roll Hall of Fame. It was hoped that everyone would celebrate the idea that there was a fraternity binding famous musicians and that they would take the opportunity of their annual gathering and investiture to set aside the petty enmities of the past and any of the jealousies of their youth in order to pal around with those whose downfall they had previously plotted, finding common cause in an overextended version of 'Gloria' or 'Let It Rock', and having their pictures taken making nice with each other.

Live Aid had seemed to leave everyone – promoters, broadcasters, the editors of the photo-dominated regions of print media, and most particularly the fans who had been fans for more than twenty years – with a powerful appetite for pictorial evidence of the families of rock in attitudes of reconciliation and reunion. As the 1980s turned into the 1990s it increasingly seemed that no occasion would be complete without an image of the old comrades with their arms around each other as they accepted the acclaim of their people at the end of the show. In addition it was starting to appear that for certain musicians their sheer presence was every bit as important as any actual musical services they might be expected to provide. Like royalty, who have a similarly symbolic role, their simply being there seemed to have an almost mystical power to make some people, and hence the event itself, feel complete.

This was what Jann Wenner of *Rolling Stone*, the founder of the event, was talking about when he described the inaugural evening on 23 January 1986 at the Waldorf Hotel in New York as being 'one of the greatest nights in rock and roll history'. He was being optimistic. Anyone who thought that the rock fraternity would adapt as readily to the requirements of a dignified awards show as the acting fraternity had done decades earlier was in for a disappointment. The first stumbling block was the requirement for formal wear. This was an occasion aimed at making rock respectable, a transition which would presumably have a benefit when it came to the many dealings that were taking place all the time between legislators and the music business at boardroom level, and it would make some of the practitioners feel a little taller when it came to standing alongside the typers of books, the daubers of canvases, the speakers of words and other erstwhile craftsmen who seemed to have earned the right to call themselves 'artists' if they looked the part. Hence there had to be a dress code.

The dressing-up was a significant challenge, involving as it did compromises between standard gentlemen's evening wear (which is all about uniformity) and rock and roll costume (which pretends the wearer is entirely above all forms of uniform), some of which were not entirely happy. Keith Richards, for instance, took the stage that night in a tuxedo which he then removed to reveal a leopard-print jacket. Some old habits refused to die in the face of this quest for respectability. The tone of the remarks artists were called upon to make about each other from the stage stayed on the safe side of generous, Pete Townshend saying of the Stones 'don't try and grow old gracefully – it wouldn't suit you'.

The arrival of the Hall of Fame was ideally timed for a greying star system. Nobody is more desirous of being declared a Hall of Famer than the pop star who has known what it is like to have been loved and then apparently discarded. Once you are a Hall of Famer you are no longer past it. Such late-career elevation might even lead to bookings for live work or interest from a record company. Once you are installed in that august host, nobody will be ill-mannered enough to ask how long it has been since your last hit. The Hall of Fame was a perfect way of cultivating reverence for old pop stars among people who had, in many cases, entirely forgotten them or never really twigged what had made them so loved in the first place. It was eagerly seized upon by those organs of the media that had only the foggiest idea of the specifics of pop music but had accepted unquestioningly the idea that it was important stuff. At times this new reverence could make you pine for the old days when people over forty were against this music on principle and would be only too happy to tell you why.

By 20 January 1988 everybody seemed to know what was expected of them. The big names certainly knew why they were there that night. Mick Jagger and Bruce Springsteen sang 'I Saw Her Standing There'. George Harrison backed Bob Dylan on 'All Along The Watchtower'. Springsteen, who was beginning a distinguished second career as the only man in the music business with the knack of writing and delivering a gracious speech, made a nice one about Dylan. He talked about sitting in the car with his mother at the age of fifteen when the opening downbeat of 'Like A Rolling Stone' 'kicked open the door to your mind'. Each generation paid tribute to its predecessor, but not quite so elegantly. Elton John hailed the Beach Boys. Billy Joel toasted the Drifters. Continuity was the watchword. Wasn't this a grand old party and weren't they all proud to belong?

Viewed from another angle, it was a carnival of social awkwardness such as only the music business can contrive. While old footballers at reunions get drunk and envelop in bear hugs even those they have spent years kicking lumps off, and all actors, who know they will eventually work with all other actors, follow the wisdom of the old saw 'big smile, short memory', musicians never really know how to behave at awards ceremonies. They crave formal recognition while at the same time hating themselves for craving formal recognition. If they are called to the stage they always pretend this is entirely unexpected, despite the fact that they have been mentally gaming the precise situation for weeks. The line between being entirely forgotten and being a legend overdue for rediscovery is a thin one and the Rock and Roll Hall of Fame offered a once-in-a-lifetime opportunity to pass through the final red rope and presumably to remain there for the rest of your working life.

As an event it combined the highly competitive features of an industry prize-giving with the considerable possibilities for humiliation that abound at every high-school reunion. This was even more difficult to negotiate when the musicians had first become famous, as most of them had, as members of groups. All groups have history. That history is always far more complicated for the people on the inside than would ever be apparent to people on the outside. By the time they are in their forties their faces are road maps describing all that history. This is why the Rock and Roll Hall of Fame soon became one of the more fissile occasions in the social calendar. Putting the remaining members of groups who initially fell together in their teens then fell out in their twenties into a room and expecting the quiet joys of brotherhood to salve the old enmities was like throwing a surprise get-together for the crime families of a particularly violent city and being taken aback when things didn't go swimmingly.

Every step required negotiation. On this occasion Diana Ross refused to turn up to collect the award for the Supremes along with the only other living original member, Mary Wilson, because the latter had been the first to go into print with her memoir, *Dreamgirl*, and therefore was the first to claim the group's narrative and sort the characters into heroes and villains, painting Diana as a diva whose eyes were always on the prize of a solo career and the late Florence Ballard as a saint.

John Fogerty was there that evening in his own right rather than in the way everybody would have most welcomed him, as a member of Creedence Clearwater Revival. The last time he had had anything to do with the other three, one of whom was his actual brother, was at the latter's wedding in 1980. By 1988 Tom Fogerty had moved to Arizona where a botched blood transfusion meant that he got infected with AIDS. He died in 1990. Speaking at his funeral, John said, 'We wanted to grow up and be rock and roll stars. We did half of that. We didn't necessarily grow up.'

In January 1988 George Harrison and Ringo Starr looked less than whelmed to be representing the Beatles alongside Yoko Ono, with Sean and Julian Lennon by her side. Paul McCartney wasn't there because the other three were involved in a legal action against him. He issued a statement saying he hadn't turned up because 'I would feel like a complete hypocrite waving and smiling with them at a fake reunion'.

In the light of such no-shows, which rather undermined the Rock and Roll Hall of Fame's claim to celebrate the great brotherhood of musicians, the speech made that evening by Mike Love of the Beach Boys could be described as on point. Had it been delivered by Brian Wilson, the member the world thought could do no wrong, it may well have landed. Because it was delivered by Mike Love, the member the world had decided could do no right, it blew up in the speaker's face. After twenty years all groups have, by common consent, one member who is seen by the outside world as something of a saint and another who has horns. This answers a deep human need to divide the world into black hats and white.

They were introduced by Elton John, happy to follow in the long tradition of rock stars, the only professionals on God's earth who take to a stage without having really thought about what they're going to say, believing that preparation is for the little people and that divine inspiration will somehow supply them with words equal to the occasion.

Ladies and gentlemen, the Beach Boys.

Of all the bands that emerged from the garage in the sixties, the gap between the blithe optimism of the Beach Boys' great music – music that still beat in the hearts of their legions of fans – and the reality of them as bitter middle-aged men seems the widest. When they took the stage at the Waldorf they exhibited the awkward body language of criminal conspirators forced to share the same dock while intent on saving their own skins. The Rock and Roll Hall of Fame was a project born in sentiment and one of the things that fans most want to believe about their favourite bands deep in their sentimental hearts is that they love one another. The problem is, so often they don't. This can be even more the case if they happen to be an actual family. The friction between the members which was manageable when they were adolescents is made intolerable by the fact that they remain yoked together unwillingly in middle age. The jealousy of each other's talents is brought into focus every time they realize that absolutely nobody in the world is interested in them as individuals.

Tolstoy, who observed that while all happy families are alike, all unhappy families are unhappy in their own way, really should have met the Beach Boys. There's a book, he would undoubtedly have muttered into his beard. He might have got quite a few chapters out of how their tensions as a family were made more painful by their dependence on each other for the making of a living, and furthermore by the widespread perception that they owed it all to one family member, Brian Wilson, a member whose emotional, mental and physical state was the most fragile and who seemed to be more revered the less he apparently did to deserve it.

As if that wasn't enough, there was a ghost on the Waldorf stage. Even the great novelist probably wouldn't have dared to have their most handsome and charismatic member, the drummer Dennis Wilson, make friends with the Manson Family, the most notorious murder gang of the age. Furthermore he might have thought twice before including the section where Dennis married the unacknowledged young daughter of the band's singer, his cousin Mike Love. If he ultimately came up with a sequence where the former golden boy, under the influence of drink and drugs, dived to his death in the harbour at Marina Del Rey in 1983 while in search of trinkets he had thrown over the side of his now repossessed yacht, he might well have thought he had done an over-colourful job in fashioning a portrait of the way even the luckiest human beings are capable of being their own worst enemies.

(In 1977 Dennis Wilson had been the first member of the Beach Boys to put out a solo album on the group's label Brother. This record, *Pacific Ocean Blue*, opened with a track that was outstanding and then rather petered out. On the back of an expensive promotional campaign it managed to crawl into the Top 100 and then fell away, never to be spoken of until the twenty-first century. For fifteen years it was entirely unavailable. It was only in 2008, when the cult of Dennis Wilson as a priest of the church of beautiful losers established itself – a status that owed more than the record's many disciples allow to the massive picture of the bearded surfer on the album's cover, a picture in which he looks like Brad Pitt in a Tarantino film – that it re-emerged as a boxed set and became one of those records of the seventies which weren't celebrated until thirty years later.)

However, Tolstoy wouldn't have been able to resist the big scene at the Waldorf where the wheels came off before an audience of their peers. Brian was first to the microphone, reading a speech which proposed that the people in the room shared his simple desire to make people happy. Carl went second, saying Dennis should have lived to see this. Then came Mike Love, traditionally the least modest of the band, which was surprising because he had a good deal to be modest about. On this occasion Mike was wearing a dinner jacket and a trucker's cap, a sartorial combination which is always a cry for help.

Love had begun losing his hair from quite early on in the Beach Boys career. For a lead singer this was far more irksome than it would have been had he been safely sited behind the drums or holding a guitar. It was made additionally irksome by the fact that the rest of the group seemed to have quite enough of the stuff. To cover the embarrassment he clearly felt when standing out front singing about 'California Girls', he took to gradually opening the buttons on his shirt to reveal luxuriant chest hair while concealing his tonsorial fall-out beneath a series of increasingly jaunty caps such as might be sported by the weekend sailor. This process of flaunting the hair he had on his chest while concealing the comparative lack of the stuff on his head reached its *reductio ad absurdum* when he took to the stage at Wembley Stadium in the summer of 1975 wearing nothing above the waist but a jewelled turban.

Love launched into his speech, which was apparently extempore and clearly affected by drink taken. The substance of his remarks was what a shame it was that the generation that had once preached universal love could not find it within themselves to get over their petty problems and celebrate their greater achievements. In this he certainly had a point. All the bands that promoted universal love seemed to feel that this shouldn't interfere with their right to dislike each other heartily. By now jamming rather than speaking, Love called upon Muhammad Ali to take a bow, said what a shame it was that Paul McCartney wasn't there because he was in dispute with Ringo and George, and suggested that the Beach Boys and the Rolling Stones should somehow vie with each other in a transatlantic battle to see who had the most lead in their pencil but predicting this would never happen as long as Mick Jagger and Bruce Springsteen were too 'chickenshit' to take the stage with the Beach Boys.

Love's speech was brought to a premature end by that time-honoured show business indignity, the band striking up behind him. It turned out to be the event of the evening, but not in the way he had calculated. Elton John returned to the microphone to say 'thank fuck he didn't mention me'. This got a big laugh, illustrating the great truth of all formal gatherings of rock business people: the deployment of this one Anglo-Saxon word within any sentence is guaranteed to bring the house down. At the climax of the show, when Bob Dylan picked up his award after a speech by Bruce Springsteen that, unlike Love's, had been carefully composed and delivered, the erstwhile spokesman for a generation finished by saying, 'I'd like to thank Mike Love for not mentioning me.' He added that while peace, love and harmony were important, so was forgiveness. Then again, Bob had never been in a band, so he didn't have quite so much to forgive.

Later that year Mick Jagger, who had been putting his toe in the water of a solo career to test the level of interest, went on tour on his own for the first time. He did so, as these things are customarily done, far away from the glare of the media, on a tour of Australia and the Far East. Commenting from afar on this threat to the longevity of the Rolling Stones, Keith Richards, Mick's companion in Valhalla, unkindly referred to his singer's act as 'a jerk-off band'. Mick never did it again. Like so many other members of bands that had come up in the sixties and seventies he was forced to face the fact that audiences only truly loved him when he was among friends. Both his old friends and theirs. Preferably with their arms around each other.

5

With their 1989 Steel Wheels tour, the
Rolling Stones put scale at the centre
of live music, eventually sending ticket
prices into the stratosphere.

THE TOUR THAT CHANGED EVERYTHING

n early 1986, while loitering at Elstree Studios as the Rolling Stones were filming a video for a song from their new album *Dirty Work*, I was granted two minutes with the famously reluctant interviewee Charlie Watts. This was for a film to mark the band's upcoming and unprecedented feat of having survived for twenty-five years. Seeking some common ground I asked Charlie if he ever got used to all the hanging around involved in being a member of the Rolling Stones. 'No. In fact I should imagine that over the last twenty-five years I must have spent five years playing and twenty years hanging around.'

After much work by more than one film editor over the years this was then abbreviated into 'Five years playing, twenty years hanging around,' which was as snappy as the famously taciturn Charlie Watts ever got. What nobody knew at the time was that the drummer, whose public image was as the one member of the group far too grounded ever to succumb to drugs, was actually in the midst of a period of heroin addiction. There were some in the Stones camp, aware of the secrets too closely held for the gossip columns, who were relieved when the press were distracted from the subject of Charlie by the far more lubricious tale of his rhythm section colleague Bill Wyman, who had surprised even the rest of the band by turning up at a work function with his new girlfriend, Mandy Smith. Smith was fifteen, if you were being generous. Furthermore her

47

hair-to-weight ratio gave her the appearance of a doll. When they got married in June 1989 the media found the match titillating rather than scandalous. Indeed before they went on their honeymoon they were guests on Terry Wogan's early evening chat show, at the time the BBC's flagship family entertainment programme.

The Rolling Stones were in the midst of a period during which both Mick Jagger and Keith Richards still entertained the possibility that they might enjoy some kind of independent musical existence beyond the band they had begun back in 1962. Jagger had refused to commit to a tour behind *Dirty Work* and in 1988 became the first member of the Rolling Stones to go out on his own. He got through it unscathed but it was clear that while the market for Mick Jagger singing 'Gimme Shelter' with elite session players was limited at best, the market for Mick Jagger singing the same songs with the Rolling Stones was potentially bigger than ever. It was likely to remain buoyant regardless of the fact that *Dirty Work* had been the first Rolling Stones record since the seventies to fail to get to the number-one slot in the American albums chart.

Hence in 1989 they decided to go back on the road. This time it wouldn't be in support of a record; this time it would be in support of making a lot of money – to be more precise, as much money as a band had ever made. The resulting outing would take touring to another level and have far-reaching consequences not merely for them but ultimately for the whole business of live entertainment. This time they weren't going to see how it went. This time they planned to take any uncertainty out of matters by ensuring at the outset that they would be guaranteed a sum of money no band had ever been vouchsafed before. The only way they could do that was by in turn guaranteeing ticket buyers something they had never been able to buy before. This new model of live entertainment became possible thanks to a Canadian promoter and businessman called Michael Cohl.

THE TOUR THAT CHANGED EVERYTHING

Cohl had worked in sport and theatre as well as music and had come to an important conclusion which would revolutionize the presentation of live music for good: the production values of a musical show mattered every bit as much as the music. In 1988 he had gone to New York to visit the Stones' key adviser, Prince Rupert Loewenstein, who told him that he doubted the Rolling Stones would ever tour again. Cohl decided to test their resolve by naming a sum far higher than Loewenstein would have considered at all likely. It was this figure that got Mick and Keith back on speaking terms. It was this that got Cohl invited to pitch his plan to the band. In the summer of 1988 the Stones summoned their counsellors to Montserrat. These counsellors in turn invited two men who had widely differing notions of promoting a tour.

One, representing the old world, was Bill Graham, the gruff, charismatic former alternative theatre impresario who had built the rock concert experience in the late sixties in San Francisco and New York and had been involved in all the Stones' American tours since. He had also looked after Mick Jagger's solo tour in Japan and Australia. The other, pitching for the future, was Cohl. Cohl had never trifled with the alternative society. He came from a different school. Because he was backed by a Canadian company that was the owner of one of the largest breweries in the world, the kind of industrial behemoth that could lose the costs of even the grandest rock tour down the back of a sofa, he came with a cheque worth twice the amount Graham was proposing to pay.

Bill Graham spent an entire day arguing his case for continuing to use local promoters, for doing things the way they had always done them and for making sure that everything around the tour would match the hip standards Mick particularly would demand. He was eventually told that, even though they loved him dearly and had the greatest respect for his rock and roll credentials, his projected earnings were millions out. Make that tens of millions out.

The reason he was tens of millions out was that he was looking at this as a rock and roll tour such as he had mounted in the seventies. Cohl's company, on the other hand, were looking at it as something a great deal bigger and more lucrative than that. Cohl's idea was that if his deal with the Stones included the rights to sell sponsorship around the tour, to make unprecedented sums selling merchandise to people who bought tickets for the tour and to do deals with broadcasters for the exploitation of the shows through pay-per-view channels, he could write them a cheque nobody else would be able to write. The fact that his backers would use the tour as the spearhead of a major sales push for their newly acquired beer, which just happened to be called Rolling Rock, did no harm at all.

Cohl persuaded Jagger that things had moved on so much in the years since the Stones had last toured that he was in danger of viewing the world of 1989 through the spectacles of the previous decade. Even worse, his band were acting small-time. He was able to point to another company under his umbrella which was a major seller of merchandise. Walking into his first meeting with Jagger and Richards wearing a leather jacket with a Def Leppard logo on its back might have been considered a risky flourish. Jagger looked at it and said to Keith, 'That's what I'm talking about.' He knew that no matter how well received their new record might be, it wasn't nearly as important to the success of the tour as the ducats the band would rake in if they took an aggressive approach to putting their most valuable asset – the lips-and-tongue logo which had been designed by an art student in 1970 in an age when nobody would have dreamed of placing the words 'band' and 'brand' in the same thought – on everything from stickers to knickers.

When Cohl flew to Montserrat, where the band were finishing their album *Steel Wheels*, he was in a position to offer them a package they had never been offered before. The precise sum was never disclosed but estimates start at $60 million and go up as far as $75 million. He signed the contract, handed over the cheque and got on the plane back home. During the flight he turned to his partner and said, 'I think we've done it this time. We're bankrupt. I know it. We're going to be famous idiots.'

That didn't turn out to be the case. The Steel Wheels tour, which began in Philadelphia on 31 August 1989, drew over three million fans in North America and earned revenues of more than $100 million. It did this by setting an average ticket price that was higher than the rest of the market, by doing everything in its power to ensure that every person who attended spent at least $10 on merchandise, and also by selling the Rolling Stones' diffusion range of T-shirts, jackets, baseball caps and even skateboards through department stores to people who would never have attended a concert or bought a record. It seemed more than likely that the person shelling out $450 for the leather jacket with studded epaulettes would be the kind of person who was more at home in the golf club than the mosh pit, but that was a simple recognition of the fact that the demographic profile of the audience had changed since Hyde Park in 1969. The band didn't eat in transport cafés any more. The Steel Wheels tour changed the nature of live music in much the same way that the English Premier League, which started in 1992, utterly changed football.

The tour was approached in a very different way from the last one, which had been seven years earlier, when MTV was a scrappy start-up, concerts were put on by local promoters and the world was a very different place. This time far more effort went into the staging. There had been a time, when the venues were of a certain size and the people had a roof over their heads, when the mere sight of stage lights glinting on a band's back line would be enough to stiffen an audience's sinews and summon up its blood. In this new Age of Spectacle this was no longer enough. The audiences trooping into the stadium hours before the headliners were due on stage, in sufficient time to be able to buy the T-shirts and drink the beer which would help pay back Michael Cohl's cheque, were faced by something such as they might have seen in a Broadway theatre. The set resembled an abandoned chemical plant and came with walkways and stairways leading to different levels. This ensured that those customers too far out there in the dark to be able to see the facial expressions of the performers would at least be able to make out that there were people out there making facial expressions. It further guaranteed that customers would be happy paying high ticket prices. If they weren't particularly struck by anything happening musically they could at least come out whistling the sets.

The Steel Wheels tour didn't simply set new standards in terms of the amount of money it managed to turn over. It was also the first turn of the wheel which would see the live performance of rock and roll change from an occasion that was primarily about the things you could hear to an occasion that was above all about things you could see. In the years that would follow the amount of money spent on staging and lighting and whizz bangs would rise in nervous parallel with the ticket prices, which would in turn respond to the amount of money it took to get famous musicians, who were beginning to pass from their forties into their fifties, out of the house and out on the road for six months at a time.

The people at the sharp end of these undertakings were now middle-aged men with the financial obligations that come with families and the tastes that tend to develop when you spend a lot of your time with wealthy people. At this stage it was by no means clear that there would be another Rolling Stones tour after this one. Trying to impress on Bill Graham why his offer could never match the one the Stones were taking, Mick Jagger repeatedly said he had to think of the members of the band, the ones who couldn't rely on regular income from having written songs. The Cohl offer would see them each making $15 million. It would be an imprudent Stone who didn't think that could be his very last payday.

It wasn't just the Stones. In the same year the Who, whose Pete Townshend had sworn he would never tour America again, did just that. He realized during the pre-tour negotiation that 'America was going to insist on sending me home very, very rich. And that's a good feeling.' Bassist John Entwistle made no secret of the fact that, although he was a wealthy man with a massive house in the country, he had a tendency to spend whatever money he earned and therefore, he told *Rolling Stone*, 'I need the money from this tour very much'. In order to guarantee the show would be of a scale that could justify the unprecedented sums of money at stake, the core group, which critic Chris Charlesworth had once pointed out achieved such a level of intensity that they seemed to grow a fifth member, were now supplemented by twelve additional musicians as they presented something that seemed more like a musical theatre celebration of the Who than a show by a rock group.

At the end of the Steel Wheels tour, which had morphed into the Urban Jungle tour upon moving to Europe in 1990, Bill Wyman told the rest of the Stones that for him this would be the last time. In the previous decade he had tired of waiting for Mick and Keith to stop indulging themselves in solo careers which were clearly never going to amount to anything, patch things up and decide whether or not to tour. 'I need to be able to plan,' he told me many years later. He had a life of his own and he wished to get on with it without having to wait upon these quarrelling princelings.

They evidently thought he was joking because four years later, when they wanted to start rehearsing for their next tour, Wyman got the usual call announcing that the firm were going back to work and would he kindly make himself available. It was only then that he reminded them he had told them back in 1990 that he would no longer be there for them. The other members of the band, by then every bit as wedded to the idea of the Rolling Stones as an institution as immutable as the royal family, from whom the only permissible escape is death, simply could not process this unprecedented information. Did this mean he was leaving? No, countered Bill, it meant he had already left; they had simply failed to notice. There had obviously been no machinery to process this most momentous of resignations. There was no contract he had to renew, no HR department to put him through an exit interview, no P60 to be filed. He was simply an ex-Stone.

After pouting for a short while, the rest were about as sentimental over his departure as you might expect. They moved to replace him with Darryl Jones, who had by 2024 been playing live with the Rolling Stones for longer than Bill Wyman did. However he is not and never can be a member of the band. A band is not simply an association of musicians. It's also a picture in which the members grow into their roles, which is why bands so often replace departed members with new members who look the same. The Rolling Stones couldn't possibly replace the hangdog mien of Bill Wyman in that picture, and to be fair to them nor did they try. When they lined up for photo shoots after his departure it was as a four-piece, which looked fundamentally reduced. After the death of Charlie Watts in 2021 there were just three, which no longer looked like the Rolling Stones at all. At the time of writing they are girding their loins to tour once again, more than forty years after it had appeared they had done it for, to coin a phrase, the last time.

6

Roger Waters gathered a star-studded cast (including Joni Mitchell) for a performance of The Wall at the Berlin Wall in 1990, but he was no Pink Floyd.

**YOU CAN'T
TAKE IT WITH
YOU**

Not everything in the lives of bands entering their third decade was about money. Many of their conflicts were related to the way they felt. However, the generation of musicians who had been born in the 1940s were no more accustomed to talking about their feelings than the rest of what was still a tight-lipped generation. The lifestyles they adopted may have seemed far removed from those of their parents, the political views they espoused may have appeared calculated to provoke their elders and betters, their approach to personal morality in such matters as sex may have placed them beyond the pale as far as polite society was concerned, but in one important respect, beneath all the hair, beyond the loon pants and the 'Keep on Truckin' decals, regardless of what they chose to put in their bodies and what they occasionally chose to put in other people's, they remained in one respect substantially of the same mind as parents who had endured the poverty of the Depression, the privations of the war, the corset and hair oil. That respect being that no matter how bad things might appear they really didn't believe it did much good to talk about them.

This vow of silence seemed particularly to apply within bands. When John Lennon began bringing Yoko Ono along to every Beatles session in 1969 he didn't clear it with the rest of the group beforehand, presumably because he wouldn't have been able to find the words with which to broach the subject. Had he done so the other three probably wouldn't have known how to respond. In bands there was no forum for the discussion of policy in such matters. Bands were governed not by rules but by the ghosts of un-recorded precedent, understandings reached in bars late at night, and haunted by the things that were once said in heated moments and could never be withdrawn. In the early stages of a joint career that doesn't matter; in a band's ascent phase all the energies of indi-vidual members go into driving the project forward. Once they are up there where the air is rare they begin to be pulled in differ-ent directions. This applied just as much to a group like Pink Floyd, the members of which came from material comfort and had been educated in such a way that it ought to have been possible for them at least to give their desires names, as it was for, say, the Troggs. As their drummer, Nick Mason, was to observe years later, 'Although we possessed a remarkable ability to enrage and upset each other, while still maintaining a straight face, we never ac-quired the skill of talking to each other about important issues.'

The more important the issue the less was likely to be said. For instance, they were taken by surprise by their discovery at the end of the 1970s that Norton Warburg, the company that was supposed to be taking the huge sums they had earned from *The Dark Side Of The Moon* and investing them to ensure that even if they wanted to they didn't actually need to work any longer, had lost them a great deal of money. Furthermore it had left them with the *billet doux* which so often appears in the wake of a large-scale fraud – a massive tax bill, with no means to pay it. This experience, which hinted that even apparently gold-plated bands from university towns could find themselves facing sudden penury, rattled the group's confidence. 'We saw ourselves as educated, middle class, in control of every-thing,' reflected Mason later. 'We had been utterly wrong.'

Thus it was clear that even the mighty Pink Floyd, who had been used by the shock troops of punk as shorthand for the establishment, were at the mercy of events rather than master of them. Faced with this crisis they did not waste any time. Within just two weeks they had packed up their lives and moved to France for a year out. During this period three out of four members of the band were divorced from the women who had been there when they were nobody special. Keyboard player Rick Wright preferred to stay on his boat in Greece with his new wife. Sticking to the policy of avoiding face-to-face meetings, particularly when they were important, Roger Waters, who was in the process of turning a band that had been allegedly a democracy into a company of which he was the CEO, did not actually tell his old college mate that his services would no longer be required. He got the band's manager to do it. Interestingly, Wright's firing was not one of the experiences directly explored in *The Wall*, the work that was engaging Waters at the time. Since he declared it to be his grand statement about how human beings fail to communicate effectively, this was surely a missed opportunity.

The Wall was recorded in France with the pressure on. It had to be a hit if they were going to be able to pay off their tax bills. Fortunately, when it came out in 1979 it was a bigger success than anyone had dared predict. This was thanks in no small measure to the fact that their American producer had insisted on its single clocking in at precisely one hundred beats per minute, the required rhythmic interval to make 'Another Brick In The Wall' appealing to disco dancers. The last-minute addition during the final mix of the voices of a children's choir, for which the engineer was dispatched down the road to record with the pupils of an Islington school, had the effect of making Waters' most acerbic assault on the complacency he invariably saw all around him come up cosy enough to be number one at Christmas. Nothing subverts the most subversive of plans more than having one's mouth stopped with gold.

Waters supplied most of the songs on *The Wall* and all of them on

the subsequent 1983 album, *The Final Cut*, which he immodestly sub-
titled 'a requiem for the post-war dream by Roger Waters, performed
by Pink Floyd'. When he then announced he was leaving the group,
pronouncing them to be 'creatively a spent force', he seems to have
assumed that his departure would bring down the curtain on the
group he had begun as the Screaming Abdabs in a student flat in north
London in 1964. It was not to prove as simple as that. It rarely does.

Waters was forty-two when he announced he was walking away.
By the age of forty-two most people have responsibilities, even those
who thought they had avoided them by running away to join a band
when they were kids. In fact it was to prove a lot easier for the members to exit their marriages than it would be to leave the band. All
bands are begun on a whim. They only properly come to a complete
stop when the last lawyer fails to present his last bill on account of
his being dead. This was still a long way off.

The solo efforts that followed Waters' departure clearly appealed
to his supporters. They entered the chart. The problem was they
exited soon afterwards. There was none of the clacking of the celes-
tial abacus which had traditionally accompanied the release of a
proper Floyd record. Waters must have suspected he would not be
quite as bankable in his own right as he had been as a member of
the group, but even he must have been surprised by just how much
harder it was on his own. For a start, given a choice between putting
out a record by the bloke who wrote all the hits of Pink Floyd and
putting out a record by any old group that could call itself Pink Floyd,
it was clear the record company would choose the latter every time.
The same applied to promoters and the general public. The truth was
that after all these years the name Pink Floyd was far more famous
than the names of Roger Waters, David Gilmour and Nick Mason.
Furthermore the latter pair, who were as quiet as Waters was assert-
ive and as apparently self-effacing as the bass player was brimful of
himself, slowly and undramatically made it clear they were content

to continue – and, what's more, to continue as Pink Floyd. Waters would not be able to consign his old band to the archives. Pink Floyd was bigger and more immovable than any and all of them.

The individual members had by then settled into lifestyles that took account of their new affluence. Waters built his own studio, which was called the Billiard Room in honour of the piece of equipment that seemed almost as important as the recording equipment therein. Gilmour went one further, buying up a Victorian houseboat which he saw advertised in *Country Life* and converting it into a studio where he could record while watching the ducks and the rowers drift by. Mason would lay down his drums and then go off to pursue his real passion, which was vintage motor cars, occasionally selling one when a cash injection was required to underwrite a tour. Rick Wright, who was by then semi-detached, spent most of his time in Greece with his wife.

Waters, whose tongue was inclined to run away with him, increased the aggravation between him and his former brothers-in-arms by referring to the rest of the group as 'the Muffins' and claiming that Gilmour et al would not be able to make an album without him. This of course made Gilmour all the more determined to do precisely that. It was important that founding member Nick Mason remained on the strength, even though he was spending most of his time on motor sport and didn't actually play anything on the next album (in fact for four years he hadn't played the drums at all), and Rick Wright was brought back in on reduced terms, largely to stand up the idea that the group was definitely a going concern and to give the lie to Waters' claim that they would be a sham without him.

When, in 1988, Pink Floyd announced that they were going to go on tour, Waters threatened to take legal action against any North American promoter who dared to offer for sale tickets for this band which he claimed had no right to exist. Michael Cohl was the first to test his resolve, placing on sale sixty thousand tickets to a Toronto show which sold out within hours. Other promoters followed. The new Pink Floyd album, *A Momentary Lapse Of Reason*, which most critics agreed sounded like a David Gilmour solo record, had come out in September 1987. It was only kept from the number-one slot by Michael Jackson's *Bad*. This was a good deal better than Roger Waters' record *Radio K.A.O.S.*, which came out the same year and barely scraped the Top 50. Incumbency had triumphed. Possession was clearly nine tenths of the law. Pink Floyd had won. The big rock brands were far bigger than the people who had built them.

Ever since Live Aid, TV companies all over the world had salivated at the merest mention of the prospect of a massive live spectacular, something that would give them the opportunity to present very well-known works performed by comfortingly familiar faces in grand settings. In this they were encouraged by civic boosters, newly keen to put their cities on the map of a fast-flattening world where travel was becoming easier and European harmonization made the crossing of borders frictionless for entertainers. One Saturday night in the spring of 1986 I could be found blundering around in the darkness of a huge city park as the French musician Jean-Michel Jarre presented a sort of *son et lumière* using the entire landscape of downtown Houston, Texas, as its backdrop. This was attended by a crowd that was estimated by someone as numbering more than one and a half million souls. It was difficult to see who was served by events on such a scale. They invariably involved audiences who were either fatigued or bored. They always left a record-breaking amount of litter behind them. The TV pictures were never quite as sensational as they hoped they would be. Nonetheless there was demand from the broadcasters and so they came to pass.

In 1989 Pink Floyd climaxed their Italian tour with a free show in, of all the fragile jewels of a world before electricity, Venice. It was originally proposed that the band – the three-piece now tricked out with a dozen additional musicians – would perform in the ancient Piazza San Marco. Thankfully wiser counsel pointed out that the volume itself could do damage to the ancient stones. By then the idea to televise the show was in place and so there was nothing for it but to have Pink Floyd perform from a stage that was floated on a giant barge in the middle of the Grand Canal. There were those among the city fathers who thought it might not be a good idea to attract two hundred thousand people into a city struggling to cope with its usual fifty thousand. They were brushed aside by the promoters of Big Rock, now firmly in its imperial phase, newly drunk on scale and evidently not caring that porting a late twentieth-century rock show into a place that was in any way precious risked destroying the very thing that rendered the place precious in the first place. The only people who really wanted these gargantuan shows were boosters of tourism, TV schedulers and musicians, who like to be able to say they've been the first to put a new mark on the earth.

In the first years after he left Pink Floyd, Roger Waters had been asked whether he would ever perform *The Wall* again. After all, it was his work. It was his vision. He said he would only do so if the Berlin Wall came down. In 1989 it did. Serious historians attributed its crumbling to the inability of the Soviet Union to keep pace with the Americans' spending on arms. Sentimentalists traced it back as far as the previous year when Bruce Springsteen had played in front of three hundred thousand East Berliners and read aloud a little speech he had written out in phonetic German. The speech said that he hoped that rock and roll would help bring down all barriers. Then he played Bob Dylan's 'Chimes Of Freedom'. Neither he nor the thousands who cheered that day would have dreamed that within a year and a half of the concert the barrier to which they thought he referred, the Berlin Wall, which had been a seemingly immutable fact of life for the young people who had grown up looking at it and a powerful symbol for the rest of us who had seen it on Harry Palmer films, would be effectively down.

By 1990 TV had become hot for events bringing together music and world affairs because they appealed to the star-struck, rock-raised people who by then were running TV. Suddenly it seemed that nothing really happened unless it happened on TV. The Berlin Wall had been breached on live television in 1989. The timing of Nelson Mandela's release from prison in February 1990 had been arranged with the requirements of US prime time in mind. The crumbling of Europe's most famous actual wall seemed a golden opportunity for a performance of the story of Europe's most famous metaphorical one. Surely if you could organize a star-studded version of *The Wall* in front of the remains of the most famous wall in the western hemisphere then there would presumably be no reason why that would not amount to the biggest show on earth. And surely that would put Pink Floyd's Venice spectacular in its place.

The problem was that Roger Waters was many things but he wasn't really famous in his own right. Not as far as TV was concerned. At every stage of their rise Pink Floyd had been represented by visuals – cows, prisms, pigs – which didn't actually feature the members of Pink Floyd. Now Roger was reaping the whirlwind of that dogged pursuit of anonymity. It seemed that not even a majority of Pink Floyd fans knew his name so it was imperative that the performance of his masterwork should involve names they did recognize. At first he hoped he would be able to engage the likes of Rod Stewart and Eric Clapton as guest soloists, but as the day drew nearer it turned out they were all washing their hair. The British end of the business knew how bitter the dispute within Pink Floyd was and clearly preferred not to take sides. With just a few weeks to go, $10 million of costs already committed and with the performance site still being swept for mines left over from the Cold War, Waters was obliged to fly to Los Angeles and recruit American names like

Cyndi Lauper and the Hooters. These carried rather less cachet but were unlikely to say no.

The show, which was staged on 21 July 1990, did not turn out to be quite the game-changing spectacular hoped for. It was one of those events which, unlike Live Aid and Woodstock, tends to shrink rather than grow in the public memory. There were any number of luminaries on the stage – alongside Cyndi Lauper, the Scorpions, Jerry Hall, Van Morrison, Sinéad O'Connor and Joni Mitchell – together with the Marching Band of the Combined Soviet Forces, the Rundfunk Orchestra and Choir, the Red Army Chorus, extras who abseiled on to the stage, looming figures from the imaginings of Gerald Scarfe, Paddy Moloney and his tin whistle, James Galway with his flute, the actual Brandenburg Gate, a crowd of a quarter of a million, and a fake wall of polystyrene which collapsed on a command from designer Mark Fisher to reveal a remaining section of the Berlin Wall, but even all that somehow failed to capture the imagination. The resulting live album didn't generate anything like the payday for the charity that had been widely predicted. The charity was wound up a few years later. That was because – as Leonard Cheshire, the Second World War hero who had devoted his post-war life to charitable work, couldn't be expected to have known but Roger Waters may in the dark night of his anxiety have already suspected – it was just a bunch of names. Even if those names were as venerable as Van Morrison and Joni Mitchell or popular like the Scorpions, they weren't Pink Floyd. Even Roger Waters wasn't Pink Floyd. When asked about it in the days after the event, Waters pronounced himself pleased that people would now understand that *The Wall* was his and not anyone else's. What everyone else was saying behind their hands was that if it had been Pink Floyd it would have been a success.

In 1990 a meeting took place between Gilmour and Waters at which they decided which bits of the joint heritage each party would be permitted to keep on using. A lot of these things were the non-musical items such as the inflatable pig with which they had been associated since the mid-seventies. The pig had clearly been Roger Waters' idea and so it made sense that he should be able to use it in his live shows, at some of which he would unblushingly bill himself as 'the genius behind Pink Floyd'. The rump Pink Floyd themselves would in time regale their audiences with their own porcine dirigible. In order not to infringe upon their former bassist's rights they made sure their pig was equipped with testicles. An action of this kind will tend to support the view of those people who believe that although you can take the band out of the sixth-form common room, you can never entirely take the sixth-form common room out of the band. Middle age was never going to change that.

7

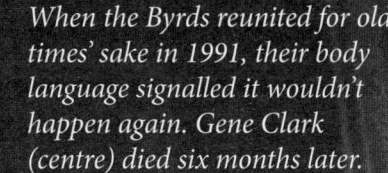

When the Byrds reunited for old times' sake in 1991, their body language signalled it wouldn't happen again. Gene Clark (centre) died six months later.

NO GOIN' BACK
FOR THE BYRDS

We picture rock stars the way we picture footballers, as blokes in their twenties and early thirties. At that age we don't expect them to do much thinking about the future, to set anything by or consider their retirement. At that age it's all about forward motion, from the big album to the inevitable solo projects. At that age they tend to be surrounded by people who are encouraging them in the view that they are the true talent. Therefore they should get a greater share of the spoils.

At some point in their forties, they wake up to the discovery that in some senses the future may be behind rather than in front of them. And that future is likely to involve some bridge-building with the people you previously thought you had left behind, and probably some recognition that the band you left behind is the thing that matters. And the aspect of the band that matters most is the name, because that's the thing that sells tickets.

It was ownership of the band's name which entitled Dave Gilmour and Nick Mason to go on tour playing *The Wall* and other songs which Roger Waters considered his personal property. First arrived at in the mid-sixties when somebody suggested combining the names of American folk singers Pink Anderson and Floyd Council, the name Pink Floyd grew to perfectly encapsulate the gnomic appeal of a group setting out to be as difficult to read as possible. As soon as the general public got to know the full name, those who considered themselves early adopters dropped the qualifying adjective, referring to their favourites as the Floyd. The same thing applied to the Dead, the Stones, Sabbath and Zeppelin.

The idea of groups of young men coming together to play music and then giving their newly formed group some kind of cryptic name that went on to assume a totemic significance was one of the foremost contributions rock music has made to Western culture, because once the name has been established nothing will shift people's attachment to it. It's one of the rules of rock that all the names bands consider calling themselves sound absurd in retrospect whereas the one they arrive at and then ride to fame on appears as unarguable as the name of a planet. If the Beatles had turned out to be just another group from Liverpool it would have been easy to blame it on their terrible, punning name. What else could they possibly have expected? Names not adopted always have the faint whiff of desperation about them. When the Byrds signed their record deal with Columbia in 1964 they were called the Jet Set. It's difficult to imagine them ever having a cult-like following had they continued to be called the Jet Set. They adopted the Byrds name in a hurry, to avoid being called the Beefeaters, which was the kind of name American groups were hastily adopting at the time in the wake of the British invasion. In the tradition of Beatles, Animals and Yardbirds, Byrds seemed agreeably zoological, its replacement of the 'i' with a 'y' lending it a Gothic note.

It was only latterly that their name was rendered as a logo. The big acts of the sixties, who were the first bands to become brands, didn't realize this until after it had happened and thus were very slow to cotton on to the need to protect their trademarks in the same way a beer brand would. The famous drop-T Beatles logo was an afterthought, hastily improvised by the owner of the drum shop where Ringo acquired his first Ludwig kit; it was never used on their original albums and it wasn't actually protected by law until thirty years later. The Yardbirds had their characteristic hand-drawn logo from very early on, but that was thanks to their friend Hamish Grimes. (Grimes was also the person who painted the legend 'Clapton is God' on a wall and then photographed it, thus seeding the myth that this was the work of Clapton's fans, a myth that is still current sixty years later.) The person who made logos compulsory in rock was Jac Holzman of Elektra Records who in the mid-sixties was the first to realize the value of luxurious, mysterious packaging, and made sure his bands the Doors and Love were all better known for their typography than their faces.

The three front men of the Byrds, Roger McGuinn, David Crosby and Gene Clark, had all been solo performers on the folk scene until they suddenly observed in 1964 that all the action was in groups. They went to see *A Hard Day's Night*. They went twice. The second time they took a pen and paper to note down the details of the electric instruments the Beatles played. The one member who actually played on the recording of their signature hit, Bob Dylan's 'Mr Tambourine Man', was the singer McGuinn. The other singer, Clark, left the group early on, claiming not to like the flying, which is often music business code for a nervous breakdown. A little further down the road the other guitarist, Crosby, left because the band weren't doing enough of his songs. Then drummer Michael Clarke, who had been recruited on account of his nice hair, left, leaving McGuinn to continue as the Byrds with a variety of hired hands. In 1972 he disbanded the group. He did this in order to re-form the Byrds with the original members. Their 1973 reunion album began with a song called 'Full Circle'. The air of finality would turn out to be misplaced.

When this project flopped, the world having moved on to the Eagles, the members went their separate ways again, going on to perform as solos or as members of bands. These met with varying levels of success, none of which overshadowed the legacy of the original group. When one by one these ventures ran out of steam the members began to face the hard economic fact that the further they strayed from the original heritage of the Byrds the harder it became to attract an audience. The world has a way of telling you what it values you for, but it often takes a while for this message to get through. The former members never seemed to take too much persuading to do the old songs as part of their shows or to invoke the name of the band they had walked away from. Gene Clark even had one album called *Firebyrd*. Roger McGuinn had another called *Thunderbyrd*. The more time went on the more relaxed they seemed to be about trading on their past.

When in 1991 McGuinn, the man who had been the voice and face of the Byrds' big hits, returned with a new album in his own right he was under new management. This new handler was his fourth wife, Camilla. She it was who had rescued him from the verge of bankruptcy. She had persuaded him that continuing to pay the wages of a full band was a one-way ticket to ruin. Another reason for a spouse becoming the manager, which happened in many cases, was you didn't have to pay them. If you didn't do tours and your records were dead three weeks after release there was no option unless you were prepared to cut your cloth the way the McGuinns had done. These days, Roger said in an interview, 'we' played a hundred gigs a year and shared the driving. The show was acoustic. He played 'Mr Tambourine Man', 'Chestnut Mare', 'Ballad Of Easy Rider', all the ones the fans wanted to hear. They even made a small profit.

In the early nineties there were definite signs that the Byrds' moment might be nigh once more. McGuinn had noted that hipper groups like Tom Petty and Green on Red were beginning to pay tribute to their influence in interviews. In Los Angeles in the 1980s there had already been a whole scene that gloried in the name the Paisley Underground which apparently set out to celebrate the music that had come out of the same place twenty years earlier. McGuinn's new record featured co-writes with what seemed like young admirers – Petty, Stan Ridgway and Elvis Costello. 'It's like James Dean,' he said. 'When you're not there people build up stories about you and you get bigger than life.' The burnishing of the story of the Byrds into myth was further boosted in the same year with the publication of a biography of Gram Parsons, a former Byrd whose dissipated good looks, drug-related death in 1973, botched cremation at Joshua Tree and posthumous legacy of death-foreshadowing songs had given him pride of place in the pantheon that indie rock, which was never less than obsessed with the appearance of things, seemed to be building for beautiful losers. Parsons died at the age of twenty-six, only a few months after he had sung the old gospel song 'Farther Along' at the funeral of fellow Byrd Clarence White, who was still under thirty. White's death had inspired the Parsons song 'In My Hour Of Darkness' with its line 'the music he had with him so very few possessed'. By the time this came out Parsons too was dead, which made him easier to reminisce about and also helped build the myth of the Byrds. Sometimes it seemed that the band's former members were workshopping a movie in which star-crossed Southern boys from American Gothic backgrounds came to Hollywood and proved simply too good and too thin to stay the course. It all helped build the brand.

Suddenly there was a market for some old. After a decade that seemed to have been dominated by shiny, happy pop music, it was hankering for some American dirt beneath its fingernails. In 1991 America seemed to be excited about two new groups in particular who both came clad in the raiment of 1971. Ola Hudson had been a costume designer to the glitterati of the seventies. That year she told *Rolling Stone* how she had raised her son Saul against a background of Led Zeppelin. In the light of this, the fact that Saul had grown up to be Slash of Guns N' Roses, a group that sought to ape the Viking swagger of the old Barbarians, staging deafening re-enactments of seventies warhorses such as Paul McCartney's 'Live And Let Die' and Bob Dylan's 'Knockin' On Heaven's Door', seemed entirely unsurprising. The other act that borrowed from the seventies was fronted by a pair of brothers who arrayed themselves in the chiffon scarves and rapscallion headgear of the Rod Stewart-fronted Faces. The Robinson brothers of the Black Crowes even went so far as to say, 'There's no new music ever, period. It's all an interpretation of music that's gone before', before going off to comb thrift stores in search of albums by Back Street Crawler.

At the same time in Britain, Primal Scream engaged former Stones and Traffic producer Jimmy Miller who put the maracas up front on their 'Movin' On Up', which itself was based on Stephen Stills' 'Love The One You're With', a hit from twenty years earlier. Even the big movie release of the year 1991 was Oliver Stone's film about the Doors. It appeared that very few people were talking about the future but a lot of people were talking about the past. This seemed to offer an escape from the sculpted cheeks and voluminous trousers of Vanilla Ice and MC Hammer, whose lease on the public imagination was about to expire. It was all adding up to a propitious moment for a Byrds comeback.

In January 1991 the five original members of the Byrds were called to New York to be invested into the Rock and Roll Hall of Fame. This seemed ideal timing. McGuinn, Crosby and bassist Chris Hillman had been going out as a three-piece and it had gone well enough for them to wonder how well it would go if they were to go out as the Byrds and whether if they were to do so the other two would insist on being included. Managers began looking into who had the rights to the original name. What they discovered was that the member who had been using their name at the time when the rest didn't seem all that bothered about it and therefore, in the eyes of a judge, had the greatest claim to it was the one person any fan could have told them had the least to do with the sound that had made them famous. This was Michael Clarke, the drummer, who had been a bongo-playing beach boy before being swept up in the group for anything but musical reasons. Clarke's manager even argued in court that if it hadn't been for his client's good looks the band might not have made it in the first place, which was probably making a slightly extravagant claim even for the owner of such a killer fringe. The five of them had an awkward evening at the Rock and Roll Hall of Fame. The fact that Michael Clarke and Gene Clark were placed on a separate table from the other three is testament to that awkwardness. When somebody took the step of inviting them to join the trio, Clarke got sufficiently stuck in to the free drink to have Crosby – that's David Crosby – suggesting he should be going to a meeting.

As it turned out there was to be no rehab. There was to be no money-spinning reunion tour. There was to be no reconciliation. When on 24 April Roger McGuinn played the Whiskey A Go Go on Sunset Boulevard the whole show was carried on radio stations across the country courtesy of one of those sponsorship deals paid for by a motor company. This being high profile and this being Hollywood, it seemed reasonable to assume that at some point in the evening somebody notable should be called up, apparently without planning, to lend a harmony, get in the gossip columns and make everybody's evening. Out there in the audience, keeping it all together, drinking Coke, staying sober and hoping it might be him, was Gene Clark, the man who had supplied the harmonies that had charmed the world back in 1964. Surely it would be only proper and fit to put the act back together on this particular evening, even if just for a few golden moments. It wasn't to be. 'I'd like to bring up Stevie Nicks to help me on this one,' said Roger as the crowd and the radio and the sponsors went wild and Clark presumably composed his features into a shape that provided cover for such an agonizing slight.

A month later Gene Clark died at the age of forty-six. The cause was a bleeding ulcer exacerbated by years of drug and alcohol abuse.

He was laid out in the casket in an outfit he had previously worn on an album cover. The body was on view, after the American fashion. The air crackled with grief and ego. One of the mourners was his old drinking buddy David Carradine, the actor who became world-famous through the TV series *Kung Fu*. Overcome with booze and chemicals, Carradine horrified the mourners by grasping Clark's body by the lapels of his old jean jacket and trying to force him upright while making allegations about a historic sexual encounter. These allegations would have been libellous had the person they were addressed to not been dead and the onlookers too horrified to properly recollect them.

The Byrds never did get back together.

8

In the MTV Unplugged
format, long-established
artists performed from a
sitting position, pretended
to be meek and mild, and,
in cases like Eric Clapton's,
enjoyed the biggest hits of
their careers.

ERIC CLAPTON'S TRAGIC HIT

The greatest net beneficiary of the video age of pop, which began in 1981 with the launch of MTV in the United States, making enormous stars of Michael Jackson, Madonna, Duran Duran, U2, the Police and others, was not so much the music industry as the industry that rented out the fancy dress in which the music industry felt compelled to present its hit artists during that era. For ten long years those who had formerly been seen to toil at the controls of the heavy machinery of rock were suddenly transformed into pirates, cowboys, astronauts and dandies, anything it seemed but musicians pursuing their traditional craft of strumming and striking.

The fancy dress could not go on for ever. Once pop music has travelled sufficiently far in one direction it has little choice but to travel an equal distance in the opposite. Thus it was that after the dressing-up came the dressing-down. Upon the heels of those ten years of frantic choreography there came an era of performing while sitting down, with all the apparent introspection that such sitting-down implies. Following a decade during which musicians had brandished their untethered instruments on mountainsides, from the decks of yachts at sea, in the furthest reaches of the desert, on the battlements of medieval castles, in scrapyards full of abandoned material from the Cold War, in a thousand places where there was clearly no supply of electricity and they plainly had no business being, there was nothing to do but to come indoors, shrug off the raiment of let's pretend and submit to a format that would apparently prove whether they truly had the right stuff.

The invention of the format, which had been launched in 1989 under the name *Unplugged*, is claimed by more than one MTV producer. The origination myth remains the same no matter who tells it. The inspiration always came from the experience of seeing an arena act best known for energy-intensive rabble-rousing suddenly sitting down and presenting themselves like a latter-day skiffle group, as if to say this was how they were most comfortable, as if to communicate the message that this was who they actually were. These interludes had been inspired, whether they knew it or not, by the section in the 1968 Elvis Presley *Comeback Special* where El and his old buddies sat in a circle with acoustic guitars and percussion instruments and reconnected with the music that got them started years before by vamping on the old tunes.

All television is an illusion. The *Unplugged* illusion was that the audience were being permitted a glimpse behind the scenes rather than just another highly rehearsed performance. Furthermore, all TV is best understood with the sound turned right down. Although the core promise of *Unplugged* was that since the musicians were no longer playing through amplifiers you ought to be able to experience them at their purest, the fact is that you could equally divine what it was saying about music from the way the artists perched on their stools, the way they looked at each other through their fringes, the manner in which they moved haltingly from one song to another and the nervous glances they appeared to exchange when one of them was about to attempt some high-wire feat of musicianship. The apparent spontaneity was part of the charm. Temporarily deprived of electricity's power to subdue their audiences and often performing from a studio floor which was below their audience's eyeline, they could even appear attractively frail. In its way *Unplugged* was no less spectacular than Roger Waters doing *The Wall*, with this particular spectacle announcing that live music was work of rare delicacy, like threading a needle or performing keyhole surgery. The very act of performing it in the *Unplugged* fashion advertised something that had been lost in the thud and blunder of live performance or the mad razzle-dazzle of video. That something was the apparent sensitivity and sincerity of the musicians and the quavering purity of the songs.

Unplugged glorified the song rather than the show, but it was quickly adapted to the demands of the egos of the performers. It began, like most music TV formats, with grand ideas of challenging superstar acts to vie with each other on a level playing field. Come along and join in. It quickly transpired that if you wanted the big names you had to rewrite the rules to their satisfaction. Early on, the producers booked Joe Walsh and friends in the hope that a few other Eagles might show up among the latter. Not only did they not turn up but they found that chief Eagle, Don Henley, would not allow them to broadcast Walsh's version of his own 'Desperado' and would indeed hold that song back until he was booked to star in his own *Unplugged* in his own right. This was a first taste of the realpolitik of dealing with middle-aged rock stars who'd been round the block more than once and had their own reasons for including or not including the guys who were apparently their dear old mates.

Unplugged gave MTV a perfect way to showcase Boomer acts that were increasingly uncomfortable with the teeth-and-tits demands of the pop video. They were keen on the exposure but cautious about the scrutiny that came with it. In fact the bigger the names the less relaxed they were about taking any risks with their only shot at the format. The big names all exacted a price for their cooperation. Not for them the simple business of turning up at MTV's studios and turning out an unpretentious performance. Mariah Carey didn't just show up with her hairdresser and make-up artist, she also brought not one but two of her own lighting men. Rod Stewart had twelve musicians and a string section. Bob Dylan insisted he be recorded on two consecutive nights to make sure that they got a usable forty minutes out of it. Paul McCartney commanded that they come all the way from the United States to film him playing in a barn on his Sussex estate. Neil Young walked out halfway through the taping of his. Jimmy Page and Robert Plant didn't invite John Paul Jones, giving theirs the title 'Unledded' in case there should be any doubt that theirs was not a Led Zeppelin reunion. Jones didn't even know the show had happened until it had been completed. Bruce Springsteen ditched the whole *Unplugged* concept and played with a full electric band. Nirvana did hardly any of their own songs, opting instead for favourites by David Bowie, the Meat Puppets and Lead Belly.

In many cases the stand-out song was a standard such as Don Henley's performance of 'Come Rain Or Come Shine', or a tune associated with someone else such as Mariah Carey's take on 'I'll Be There', or Nirvana doing 'The Man Who Sold The World', performances which could be interpreted autobiographically if desired. Neil Young took advantage of his *Unplugged* recording to dust off 'The Needle And The Damage Done', a song from 1972 which had been inspired by the drug-related deaths of two people close to him. A close-up of the craggy features of a middle-aged man singing of bitterness and regret seemed to sum up *Unplugged*'s voracious appetite for tragedy.

On 20 March 1991 Eric Clapton was in New York. Just coming up to his forty-fifth birthday at the time, he was a figure whose domestic set-up had long been famously complicated. His marriage to Pattie Boyd had foundered on the twin rocks of his drinking and philandering and the couple's unhappy experiences with attempting to conceive. His fame and wealth made him attractive to young women across many continents, and his association with the fashion business provided him with an opportunity to meet many of the tallest and most beauteous of them. Lory Del Santo, who was one such, had been introduced to him in Milan by an Italian promoter. She claimed not to have heard of him. This seems unlikely: even in the days before Wikipedia, go-getting girls like Del Santo usually had enough general knowledge to ensure that they didn't end up on blind dates with men who were neither famous nor wealthy.

In 1986 she had a son by Clapton. He later described attending the birth as 'the first real thing that had ever happened to me'. However, the couple never lived together in any settled sense and by 1991 she was living in New York with a new partner. On the date in question Clapton went to pick up four-year-old Conor and Del Santo to take them out for the day. Before he got there the boy had fallen through a window which had been left open for cleaning. The apartment was on the fifty-third floor. Clapton, who by his own admission closes himself off when tragedy strikes, was the only one who could identify the body.

When I interviewed him later that year I was told, as is the form on these occasions, not to bring up the subject. Equally inevitably, he brought it up himself. This was partly the natural reaction of a grieving parent, who knows there is no way of avoiding a subject like this, but also the reflexes of an old pro, who knows that even the most terrible events are grist to the interview mill. He talked about how he had responded to the emptiness he felt inside by going on a millionaire's shopping spree. He had bought a house in Chelsea because he could no longer bear to be in the country house where he had lived with Pattie. At the same time he was supervising the building of a villa in Antigua. It was when, in the middle of this, he put in an offer on another country house, this time in Oxfordshire, that his manager put a stop to it after a cathartic two-hour fight in his office.

In the midst of this he was helping prepare a live album based on his annual multiple-night stand at the Royal Albert Hall while also composing music for the soundtrack of the Hollywood thriller *Rush*. He told me that he had been toying with some pieces of music inspired by his memories of his son but he thought the music would be unlikely to see the light of day commercially.

He was working on this material with Will Jennings, a Texan who specializes in providing noble-sounding lyrics for film producers looking for a big cathartic moment, and big-name musicians to whom words of any kind do not readily occur. Jennings wrote the words of Whitney Houston's 'Didn't We Almost Have It All' and also supplied the sentiments that swelled 'Up Where We Belong', to the strains of which Richard Gere carried off Debra Winger at the end of *An Officer and a Gentleman*. Because Jennings had written the lyrics for a number of Steve Winwood hits, many of which seemed to wish to associate themselves with the idea of slipping the surly bonds of earth, Clapton called him in to help when he had to write songs for the movie soundtrack. Jennings had effectively moved in with Winwood when the singer was rattling around a house in the country from which his wife had removed all their possessions. He seemed to slip naturally into the role of confessor to members of the rock gentry, a bunch of men who had grown up at the end of the Second World War before the invention of men having feelings.

While those sessions were taking place, Clapton presented Jennings with the first verse of a song addressed to the son who had died. These lyrics mused on whether he and his son would recognize each other were they to meet in heaven. Far from feeling this was too personal an undertaking to involve anyone else in, he insisted that the other man take 'Tears In Heaven' away and finish it. Jennings was so conscious of the sensitivity of the subject matter that he never considered this song ever being a commercial proposition. It was stuck away as the last track on the soundtrack album *Rush*, which came out at the beginning of 1992.

In the same year Clapton was returning to public performance with his own *Unplugged*, which was recorded on 25 August. By now this TV format was such a recognized vehicle for superstars seeking a refit that it was recorded close to Clapton's home in England, and it was such a reliable source of marketable live recordings that the audio was overseen by Clapton's producer Russ Titelman. Clapton correctly thought the resulting recording was underwhelming and wanted to restrict its circulation. His manager and the record company, who could see the appeal of Clapton performing a song associated with such an appalling tragedy, and at a volume which meant it could be played in coffee shops, thought otherwise. They were right.

His *Unplugged* turned out to be the biggest-selling album of Clapton's career, moving over twenty-six million CDs worldwide. The reason for that was 'Tears In Heaven', which became Clapton's biggest-selling single in the United States and for many people the best-known recording in Clapton's career. If anybody wants to know what it cost him, says Clapton in his autobiography, they should visit the grave of his son.

Unique among pop musicians in finding his true voice in middle age, the Brentford-based craftsman made a series of quietly brilliant albums about the loneliness of the long-serving rock star.

9

NICK LOWE'S
INDIAN
SUMMER

The term 'one-hit wonder' is frequently used as a jibe. This ought not to be the case, particularly when the people using it, like the overwhelming majority of professional musicians, have never had the experience of a hit of any kind. Even those who have had the rare privilege of having a few hits realize that because the lion's share of their income derives from one song they are all one-hit wonders. These special songs tend to go on paying the bills long after they drop out of every chart in the world. The greater part of the money these artists receive every year from the collection agencies that calculate the cash that comes from being played on the radio, in elevators, at the hairdresser's and, since the dawn of digital dissemination, down numberless invisible filaments all over the known universe has been generated by just one piece of work that they did long ago.

I once asked Sting's publisher if this one-song theory held true. He allowed it probably did. He said he could check into a hotel anywhere in the world, turn on the radio and within a couple of hours he would hear a Sting song 'and it will be "Every Breath You Take"'. Gary Kemp wrote a number of hits for Spandau Ballet but says by far the biggest is 'True'. Hugh Cornwell of the Stranglers had no hesitation in saying the one song in his case was 'Golden Brown'. These are the kind of songs that seem to make their way in the world without the help of their creators. They're not always hits the first time round. Song publishing is a long, long game, as many young songwriters have had to wait for their old age to discover.

As rock entered its fifth decade a tiny handful of these songs came to have their day in the sun, often years after they were first written, recorded, released, deleted and given up for dead. Joe Cocker's 'Woman To Woman', for instance, which had done nothing when it came out in 1972, had an entirely new lease of life in the eighties and nineties as hip hop producers gleefully stripped it for parts, using it on massive hits like Tupac Shakur's 'California Love'. Kimberley Rew's 'Walking On Sunshine' was still being reached for by film editors seeking to announce the arrival of summer long after it had limped out of the lower reaches. In the end the drummer of Katrina and the Waves actually retired from playing in order to devote all his time to managing that one song. It matters not how long that massive hit takes to arrive so long as it does. It can be a matter of decades.

Nick Lowe had written '(What's So Funny 'Bout) Peace, Love and Understanding' in 1974 for his pub rock band Brinsley Schwarz, a group that was a byword for whatever is the polar opposite of commercial success. At the time approximately five people heard it. Brinsley Schwarz split up not long afterwards and Lowe went on to become the house producer at Stiff Records, which was starting as an independent at the time of punk. They put him to work producing the Damned, who used to call him 'grandad' in honour of the fact that he was twenty-six. This was one of those times in the history of popular music when people's age was wielded as an accusation. When Elvis Costello took to including the song in his live show at the end of the seventies it was widely assumed he was being sarcastic. Even after he had finished with it the song remained a charming obscurity, known and loved among the cognoscenti but not much further than that.

However, as Bob Seger sang, rock and roll never forgets. In 1992, almost twenty years since it had been first recorded, it was rescued from the anonymity to which it seemed to have been consigned by the exquisitely manicured and wholly unlikely hand of Arista boss Clive Davis. Davis was in the midst of making Whitney Houston a movie star with *The Bodyguard* and was overseeing the accompanying soundtrack album. Once the main duties of promotion had been discharged he still had room on the second side for a bunch of up-and-comers from his own label. One of them was American musician Curtis Stigers, who offered his cover version of Nick Lowe's song. Had he known that *The Bodyguard* was going to turn out to be the biggest-selling soundtrack album of all time he might have chosen one of his own compositions instead. As it turned out, the inclusion of his version of Lowe's song ended up earning for Lowe the biggest royalty cheque of his professional career, all as a consequence of a set of actions entirely beyond his control and the magical power of a market for physical product that in the early nineties seemed to be growing exponentially. At the time CDs were being sold almost as fast as they could be produced and at higher prices than recorded music had ever previously commanded. During 1993 *The Bodyguard* soundtrack sold a million actual physical copies – in one week alone.

How much that cheque was for we will never know. Rock stars are traditionally indiscreet about every aspect of their careers apart from the fiduciary. It was whispered in the music business that this stroke of good fortune had made Nick Lowe a wealthy man. That's a description which has no absolute definition, particularly in the context of musicians, who have the most irregular flow of income imaginable. When this was raised in subsequent years he pointed out that a great deal of it had gone on subsidizing his own band for an American tour, since by this time, when *Bodyguard*-type sales were unknown and record companies were no longer handing out money for tour support – money which in any case was entirely recoupable from royalties – it was increasingly the case that if artists wanted to go out with the band of their choice they had to pay out of their own pocket and take the risk of not getting it back at the box office.

Lowe was in his mid-forties but had yet to do anything that seemed like 'settling down'. He had previously been married to Carlene Carter, the stepdaughter of Johnny Cash, with whom he shared a somewhat abnormal domestic set-up in which both parties were in truth married to their individual careers. By 1994 he had come out of a long relationship with the TV presenter Tracey MacLeod, at which point he released an album called *The Impossible Bird*. This turned out to be the first of a series of critically applauded records in which he ruefully explored the life of a middle-aged man, another one of those figures who, as Bruce Springsteen pointed out, had had their adolescence prolonged and adulthood endlessly postponed by rock and roll.

Mike Yarwood used to be a popular British television entertainer. Most of his TV shows were devoted to impressions of politicians and film stars. Each would finish with him singing a favourite tune which he would introduce by smiling sheepishly and saying, 'And this is me.' Whenever I encounter any of the records Nick Lowe put out in the second half of his career after the punctuation mark provided by his Whitney Houston windfall, I can't help thinking of Yarwood's words: here was the former man of a thousand voices finally settling on one; here was a man who had previously prided himself on an ability to flit from mood to mood without sounding overly committed to any one seeming to be suddenly forced to survey the empty fridge of a man who had arrived in middle age without the compensations of family and was therefore moved to sing a different kind of blues. There were glimmers in these songs of truths most songwriters prefer to conceal. They revealed that his career possibly hadn't gone quite as well as it might: how these days he reached into the laundry for the cleanest dirty shirt and on bad ones he would wake up fully clothed with the front door open wide; how as he picked through the detritus of his superannuated bachelor life, surveying the untouched takeaways and the garage flowers, he faced the realization that there was nowhere to run from what lack of love had done.

Seasoned Lowe watchers liked to refer to these albums as his Brentford Trilogy in honour of the unglamorous London suburb where they were conceived. Everything about them seemed like an exercise of self-deprecation in the English style. In order to work the songs out he would spill them into the empty air while pacing around the function room of a local pub. When the time came to record them he would repair to a tiny studio in Camden Town. Because this had formerly been a dairy, he and his engineer Neil Brockbank christened it Gold Top Studios in honour of the famous Gold Star Studios where Phil Spector had made his masterpieces. He didn't do anything to discourage people from associating the songs he was singing with the life he had led. Whether they were true to Nick Lowe's real life we could not possibly know, nor would we have any right to know. What was most important was that they sounded true. They are also the greatest mid-life crisis records in rock and roll. What made them different from the middle-aged records that everybody else would go on to write was that they accepted the great learning of middle age, the learning which seems to evade so many of his contemporaries, and that is that by this point you really have nobody to blame but yourself. To one of the best of these albums Lowe gave the most piercingly honest name a fifty-eight-year-old rock star could ever give any album. He called it *At My Age*.

Even before becoming prime minister in 1997, Tony Blair gained a reputation as the first public figure of his generation to be able to speak rock.

10

THE ROCK GENERATION TAKES POWER

n May 1994 John Smith, the leader of Britain's Labour Party, died suddenly at the age of fifty-five. That meant the party, which had been in opposition since Margaret Thatcher's election in 1979, was forced to elect a successor many years earlier than expected. As a result they ended up with a leader who came from a younger generation. The winner of that election, Tony Blair, was born in 1953, some fifteen years later than his predecessor. He was therefore as different a person from Smith as Baby Boomer Bill Clinton was from the previous occupant of the White House, Second World War veteran George Bush.

As far as the political elites were concerned, this was a changing of the guard. Picture desks, which formerly went scrambling for images of old army buddies of the newly anointed, were now looking for shots of the new leaders in their rock festival days, wearing flares and, with a bit of luck, rolling joints. One of the things that got them excited about Blair was that it was known that while at university he had briefly been the leader of a group called Ugly Rumours which had played a few gigs in and around Oxford. This was in the era when everyone was under the spell of the Rolling Stones' *Sticky Fingers*, and it was said that his performance of their 'Live With Me' was something of a showstopper. According to those who were there, his qualifications for this role were less musical than theatrical. Even at an early age he was possessed of a quality invaluable to both a lead singer and a parliamentary performer – an invulnerability to embarrassment.

Because the editor of the music magazine Q, Mark Ellen, had also been a member of the same band at Oxford, it was natural that he should extend an invitation to the new leader of Her Majesty's Opposition to say a few words to the rock stars and music business bigwigs gathered at the magazine's annual awards lunch. Past interactions between famous British politicians and famous British rock stars had been sporadic and unconvincing. Harold Wilson knew little about the Beatles except that they were popular and Liverpudlian and therefore having his picture taken with them might benefit him in a small way at the next election (he represented the constituents of Huyton, just outside the city of Liverpool). When Jeremy Thorpe capered with Jimi Hendrix and a Gibson Flying V he was clearly entirely unfamiliar with both. Margaret Thatcher's tone-deafness when it came to all matters of popular culture was legend among her handlers. She had no earthly idea why she was being asked to be photographed negotiating a particular zebra crossing in St John's Wood, and when she was on *Desert Island Discs* she only sounded excited when namechecking '(How Much Is) That Doggie In The Window'. John Major, the prime minister that the former singer of Ugly Rumours faced across the dispatch box, remembered listening to Nat 'King' Cole at Young Conservative dances, but he was never at ease with pop.

Blair, on the other hand, was not simply at home with pop. He understood the value of being able to talk about it and could also, as was immediately apparent when he took the stage at that lunch, read a room. The meat of his remarks, which praised the unique creative contribution of Britain's rock musicians to the balance of payments and the profile of the nation, may have been the standard boilerplate that politicians adopt when blowing smoke up the fundament of any group they wish to get on side, but what made them convincing was Blair's casual mention of the striking hairstyle of Leslie West of Mountain and his reference to their *Nantucket Sleigh-ride*. This impressed the room because it had clearly come from experience rather than the pen of a speechwriter.

Blair went on to remark that the records of his generation's heroes, the Beatles, the Stones and the Kinks, would live for ever but he thought the same could be said of the records of U2, the Smiths and Morrissey. This was fast becoming the party line of Britpop, that the new groups riding high on the charts in 1994, turning up on *TFI Friday*, talking themselves up with Chris Evans and in the pages of the lads' magazine *Loaded*, tumbling out of cabs and into the Met Bar and getting their pictures taken by the same photographers who had been responsible for the imagery of Swinging London thirty years earlier, were tapping into the same fount of national genius as the old ones. This desire on the part of new bands to belong to an old tradition and the equal and complementary desire of the old bands to be seen as still vital was the secret sauce of Britpop. Suddenly the names of the sixties seemed *au courant* all over again.

The winners of the best new act at the awards that year were Oasis. Oasis were interesting in that they were a genuine popular phenomenon, probably the biggest British rock band since the Sex Pistols. But there was an interesting difference with the Pistols, who had ruthlessly suppressed their own pasts so that nobody should suspect they had ever been fans of Van der Graaf Generator or Magma. Oasis, on the other hand, seemed to talk so much about their reverence for the past that you suspected they were exaggerating for effect. Their first album took so long to complete because they were intent on its sounding as dry as the Faces' seventies recordings and would look at the picture of the band lined up on the football pitch on the gatefold of Rod Stewart's *Never A Dull Moment* and dream of looking like that. The cover of their album *Definitely Maybe* featured the members of the band among their souvenirs, including old pictures of footballers from the seventies, and had been set out to emulate the back-cover photograph of the 1966 compilation *A Collection of Beatles Oldies*. It looked like everything old was about to be new again.

In every interview he gave, the band's leader, Noel Gallagher, enthused about the Beatles in a way nobody had done in years. When they made their first Glastonbury appearance that year they encored with 'I Am The Walrus', the ideal Beatles song for them in that it had a plodding tempo they could master and lyrics that didn't make any sense at all. Noel was touchingly open about how he had based some of his songs on theirs. Often it was difficult actually to detect the debt they owed to the Beatles, but it was there in their look, in the boyish fringes, the blacked-out Lennon specs, the chippy Northernness, the sense of cuteness on the edge of corruption. Oasis didn't sound like the Beatles at all but they did, when glimpsed in a certain light, look like them, and in this new era of cosplay rock, that, in the end, was a lot more important.

Blair's bullet points before the music business attendees that day were all points of view with which an audience of record company people is ever keen to associate itself. Equally obvious was how starstruck he was to be in the same room as Bono, Ray Davies and the members of Oasis. They were equally flattered by the fact that a senior politician actually knew who they were without having to be told. In the event, and in the years following Blair's election in 1997, both politician and pop stars rose on the thermals of the other's esteem. The record business people were thrilled to have Downing Street occupied by somebody who could tell the difference between the Everly Brothers and the Allman Brothers. The politicians were just delighted to be photographed with people who could get them on the front page.

It was all so different from the old regime. One of John Major's last acts in Downing Street was handing out the first rock knighthood to Cliff Richard. This seemed a profoundly John Major thing to do. His successor was probably glad he had done the job so that he didn't have to. Following Blair's accession to high office the gongs for rock luminaries came thick and fast, with George Martin, Paul McCartney and Elton John all being knighted and lesser honours being doled out to anyone whose elevation would earn favourable coverage in newspapers and TV programmes, organs of the media which were now under the control of people who had been shaped by pop and were therefore only too keen to see their own teenage heroes raised to this pop-cultural peerage.

It was Tony Blair's good fortune to arrive at the same time as Britpop, a musical movement that had national continuity at its core. His age meant he was young enough to appreciate Blur and Pulp while old enough to be able to remember the glory days of the Rolling Stones and the Kinks. During the first years of his government it suited him, the leading lights of the British music business and the British media to pretend that the rest of the world was every bit as fixated as they were on the doings of Blur and Oasis. The truth is it never was. Cool Britannia was largely for consumption on the home front. The picture of Liam Gallagher and Patsy Kensit under the Union Jack duvet was the dominant image only on the cover of the UK version of *Vanity Fair*. Everywhere else it was a small drop-in.

Nevertheless the big noises of Britpop were high on their own supply and talking up the chances of another British invasion of the States. Liam Gallagher had told America: 'I think we'll be the most important band in the fucking world. If time is on our side and no one dies then we'll be the new Beatles.'

As it turned out, there was no call for any such thing.

11

Former Beatles roadie Neil Aspinall (left) saw his Beatles' Anthology project arrive just in time to be hailed by a new generation of superfans like Noel Gallagher of Oasis.

THE ONLY ACT BIGGER THAN THE BEATLES

n 1995 EMI, the record company whose products once came emblazoned with the boast 'the Greatest Recording Organisation in the World', did what all the other British record companies were doing at the time and abandoned their headquarters in London's West End for a move to the west of the city. EMI was the only one of those record companies that felt it was important they take part of the fabric of that old building with them to their new HQ. That part was the stairwell over which the young Beatles had stuck their heads for Angus McBean's camera in 1962, thus accidentally creating an image sufficiently memorable for them to be called upon to restage it in the late sixties.

Just before the staircase was ripped out to be taken across town and reinstalled as part of a display in the company's new offices, the four members of Blur took up their positions in the same place, looking as flushed with delight and embarrassment to be doing so as any bunch of tourists marching over the zebra crossing at Abbey Road. It was a classic Britpop homage. Being members of a new generation, Blur couldn't help appreciating the lustre of the Beatles' legacy and noting the Fabprints which were all around them. The same had not applied to earlier generations. I went into the old EMI offices many times in the late eighties and it never occurred to me to look up in reception and see exactly where that iconic photo had been taken. In the eighties it seemed we had been looking forward.

This all seemed to change with Britpop. Suddenly everything was heritage.

Neil Aspinall could not have been expected to know this when in the seventies he began the groundwork for what was supposed to be the official filmed account of the career of the Beatles. Aspinall had been on the Beatles payroll since 1961 and didn't leave their employ until 2007. A school friend of Paul McCartney, he had originally been one of the two roadies who were with the Beatles every step of the way during Beatlemania and beyond. When Brian Epstein died in 1967, Neil was given the job of running their company, Apple Corps. He survived throughout that organization's storm-tossed years by keeping his head down when the new manager, Allen Klein, was around and keeping the considerable number of things he knew about the four members of the group close to his chest.

Turning up every day to the Apple offices during those long years when the world seemed to have forgotten the Beatles, Aspinall was playing the longest game in town, which was not something to which pop music was accustomed. Ten days before his murder in 1980, John Lennon had given a deposition to aid Aspinall in Apple's legal action against the producers of the unsanctioned Broadway show *Beatlemania*, which had run from 1977 to 1979. In the course of this John revealed that the four members had been planning a retrospective documentary to be called *The Long And Winding Road*. In the same evidence Lennon also mentioned that he and McCartney had indeed been watching *Saturday Night Live* on the evening in 1976 when producer Lorne Michaels broadcast an appeal to the Beatles to re-form on his show for the same nominal sum all the other acts were paid. If George and Ringo had been in New York at the time, he said, they might well have taken him up on it.

By 1996 Neil Aspinall was presumably deeply relieved that none of the reunions that had been hinted at had ever come to anything – relieved because over the years he had been stealthily acquiring anything involving the Beatles in order that it might be used by the Beatles and nobody else in the exploitation of their legacy. Aspinall made sure that the copyrights of the classic images of the group were bought up, often by third parties secretly working on his behalf. All the clips of the Beatles performing had been withdrawn from circulation; TV producers looking to screen old films would be told they were unavailable. This deliberate stoking of demand by keeping something away from the public had been pioneered by Disney in the movie business: they would release their big hits once every ten years and then return them to what they called 'the Disney Vault'. Keeping the crown jewels off the market in this manner would ensure that they remained fresh for new generations. It also meant you could charge more for them when they returned in a new form. The people at Apple had noted well how Bob Dylan had launched his so-called *Bootleg Series* in 1991 and was now charging more for material that had apparently not been considered good enough for release at the time it was made than he was for his latest album.

To get to the point where they might benefit from these promising new economics, Aspinall had to keep his illustrious employers on side, which never got any easier. Paul McCartney had always been the foremost Fab when it came to promoting their legacy, but by the mid-nineties the member who was suddenly most keen on a payday was the one who had historically been most ambivalent about exploiting their past. That was because George Harrison had lost a great deal of his personal fortune subsidizing Handmade Films, most recently and expensively with *Shanghai Surprise* with Madonna and Sean Penn. By the mid-nineties even CD sales were beginning to flatten. The halcyon days of bands like Fleetwood Mac living large on the royalties from albums continuing to turn over were gone. It turned out that even the man who had written 'Something' could do with a serious infusion of cash. This kind of big payment would only come from signing a new deal with a record company in order to put out a nominally new record of old material; and that meant effectively relaunching his old group.

Something was stirring. The economics of pop had once been skewed in favour of novelty. Anything old tended to be knocked out cheap. In the seventies EMI had put out a Beatles compilation called *Rock 'N' Roll Music*, which drew sharp criticisms from the former members of the band, who had clearly not been consulted at all. 'It made us look cheap and we were never cheap' was how Ringo put it. A decade later EMI's marketing department was working on a scheme whereby lucky consumers could obtain an actual cassette featuring a rare mix of 'Love Me Do' in exchange for £2.49 and four ring-pulls from cans of Heineken. By the nineties this had begun to change. The Dylan campaign proved that if you were selling rare material by an act that was *sui generis*, there seemed no limit to how much you could charge for it, particularly if you packaged it shrewdly enough. The people buying weren't just ageing Boomers, they were younger people who just wanted to experience the joy of buying a Beatles record, and the more often they could do it the better they seemed to feel about it.

The turning point for the emergence of this new retro-market was Bob Dylan's *Biograph*, a boxed set which came out in 1985 and sprinkled a few previously unreleased recordings among the familiar classics, thus ensuring that light consumers would want to buy it and heavy consumers would have to buy it. It was the success of *Biograph* in restoring the lustre to a brand that had been rusting at the time which encouraged other giants to plan their own reissue programmes. The most significant thing about *Biograph* was the fact that nobody considered it too expensive. The price helped underscore the value of what was in the package. In the words of that ad for premium lager, its expense was what made it reassuring. There was no evidence for believing that it would have got more take-up had it cost less money. The ads listed all the key features – the digital remastering (a process highly valued by people who didn't know what exactly it was), the songs that had never been released before, the booklet in which, it was said, the artist shared insights into the records – as though providing the buyer with the proof that this was a sound investment rather than a rush of blood to the head of a man coming to terms with the fact that he was not the artist he once was.

This was taken to a new level with the Beatles' *Anthology*, which was released in 1995 as three separate two-CD sets timed to coincide with the different phases of the accompanying TV documentary series. The irony is that when George Martin had checked in the vaults just a few years before he had reported there was nothing by the Beatles of interest that could possibly be released. In making that judgement he was clearly thinking about the market for recorded music as he had known it in the seventies and eighties, decades which valued finish above all things. It's also possible he was thinking about the original Beatles fans when he should have been thinking about the new ones, the many who had come to them via ELO and Wings. These were the people who had been harbouring so much love for the Beatles in their breasts that they ached to express it in monetary terms. These people didn't want Greatest Hits. They wanted anything but. They wanted not-hits. These people wanted everything they hadn't previously been able to get their hands on. Which is what *Anthology* provided: alternate takes, false starts, unfinished backing tracks, studio chat, a journey into a distant past, a magical intimation that, although the accident of their birth might have meant them missing out on the purplest patch in the history of pop, now, thanks to the new technology's ability to wipe the grime of ages from the murkiest of old recordings, they could taste an entirely new sensation. For such bright-eyed disciples the chance to hear a demo of 'No Reply' or Take One of 'Strawberry Fields Forever' was the pop music equivalent of peering over the

shoulder of Howard Carter as he held up the candle which illumin-
ated the first glimpse into the tomb of Tutankhamun.

It took a lot of flattery and negotiation to bring *Anthology* to
fruition. The title couldn't possibly remain *The Long And Winding
Road* because that was clearly a Paul song. George's mate Jeff Lynne
had to be brought in to oversee the singles, which were based on
demos John had done years after the Beatles, primarily so that Paul
couldn't put his stamp on them. 'Free As A Bird', the first of these,
went to number two on the back of wall-to-wall radio play which its
quality really didn't justify. The TV series started off with strong rat-
ings in November and then faded away but by then they had banked
the $20 million they had been paid by a US network. The albums of
off-cuts and remnants turned out to be EMI's biggest sellers of the
year. Then there were the DVDs. If devoted fans had bought everything that was available that year they would have spent nearly £100,
which was significantly more than even the most passionate Beatles
fan would have spent in the whole of the sixties.

When the Beatles had received their first modest payout following the middling success of 'Love Me Do' in 1962, John and Paul
were already earning six times as much for writing that very rudimentary song as all four of them would get for recording it. The
same multiple would go on to apply throughout their careers. The
only thing that would change over the years was the size of the sums
being multiplied. Pete Best, who had been fired by the Beatles and
replaced by Ringo Starr in 1962, said he made not far short of a million pounds for his participation as a mere player on just seven
tracks on just one of the six CDs which made up the full *Anthology*
series. What the Beatles who played on all the tracks and wrote the
overwhelming majority of them made must have been many times
that. For George Harrison, who was said to have lost $20 million on
his adventures in the screen trade, it would never be quite enough.

When the dust raised by Cool Britannia had settled, the one clear winner appeared to be the Beatles. This seemed to be underscored by the 1994 publication of *Revolution in the Head*, a book by Ian MacDonald, which examined every one of the Beatles' recordings in a way that pop music had never been examined before. It concluded that they were operating on a plane way above anybody who came before or followed them. In its wake came many attempts to examine other people's careers through a similar lens, which only went to prove that you couldn't. Almost thirty years after they had ceased operating as a band they were now regarded as the alpha and omega of the whole game; their popularity was without parallel, all the critics seemed agreed they were the *ne plus ultra* of pop, nobody in pop music had ever matched the velocity of their changes, in terms of the new overarching currency of the time they were the acme of cool. The band might have broken up but it seemed they would live on.

There was no longer any point waiting for another act to be bigger than the Beatles. It appeared that the only act that would be bigger than the Beatles was the Beatles. Now, thanks to the million and one ways in which modern technology was making it possible for us to play with the past, it seemed they could be ours to toy with for just as long as we wished.

The Sex Pistols' 1996 reunion was billed as the Filthy Lucre tour. They were not alone in ignoring their past differences to seize a once-in-a-lifetime chance to top up their pensions.

12

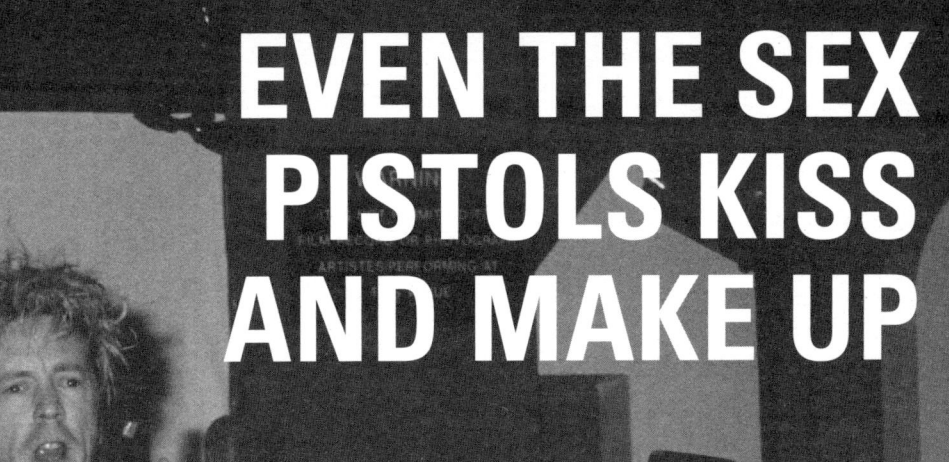

EVEN THE SEX PISTOLS KISS AND MAKE UP

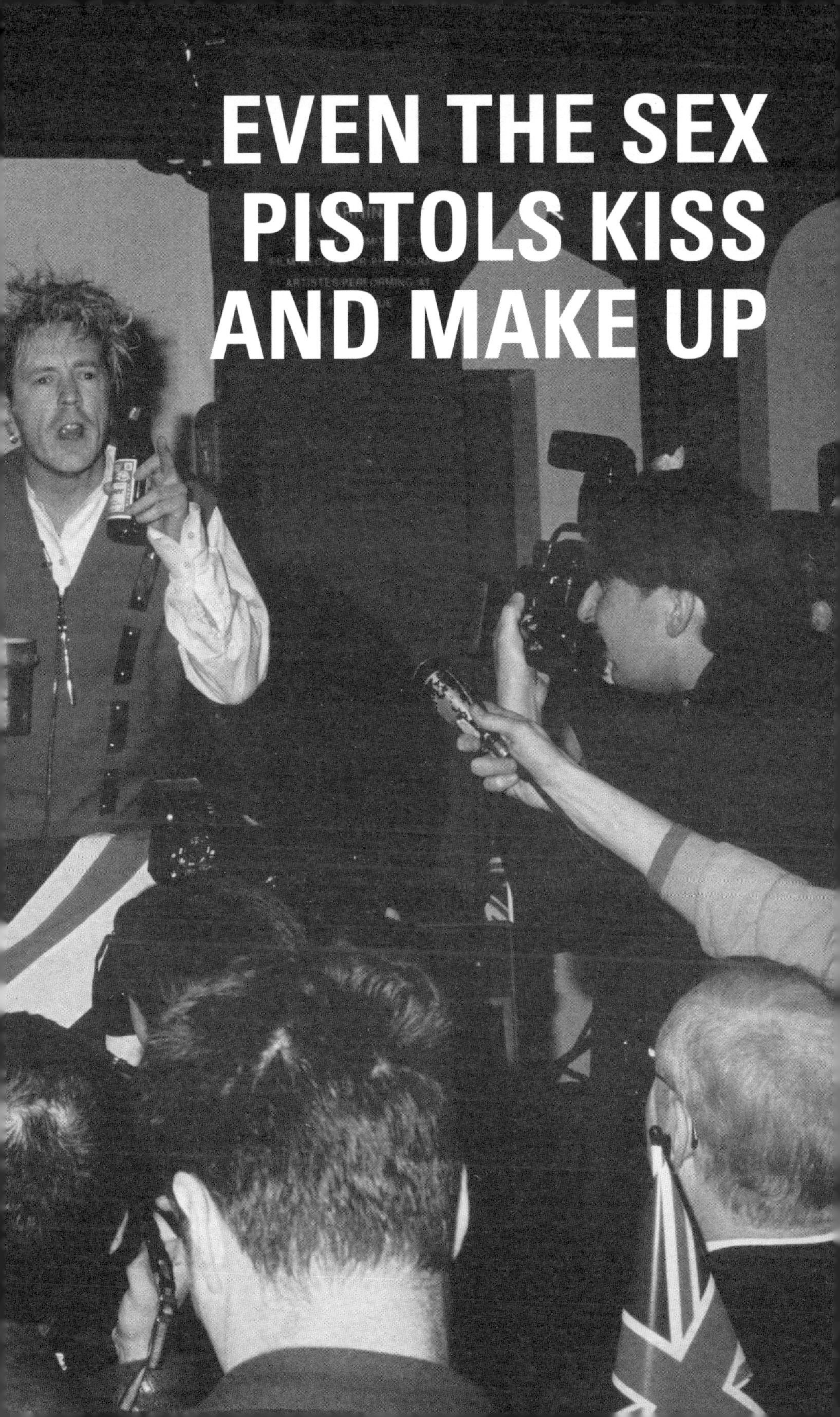

I n November 1996, Crowded House staged a free show called Farewell to the World in front of over a hundred thousand people in the magnificent surroundings of Sydney Harbour. The show marked the finale of a career that had lasted just over ten years, which at the time seemed quite long enough. It attracted devotees from all over the world. Crowded House fans were members of a generation for whom intercontinental travel was a habit, and the world was flatter and easier to navigate than at any stage in the lives of the people there.

It was a family occasion on a grand scale. People had come along to be there and also, as was increasingly the case since Live Aid, to have been there. The hardcore fans were close to the stage, where they watched in a different way, as hardcore fans always do. They watched faces, not fingers, scrutinizing the way the others looked at drummer Paul Hester, who had always been a loose cannon, and searching for clues as to how the others felt when Neil Finn's brother Tim came on stage. Even after ten years, there was a lot of baggage, as there is in any family.

They finished with 'Don't Dream It's Over', one of those songs which was built for the shedding of tears, and then, as fireworks were detonated from the top of the Sydney Harbour Bridge to the tune of the Disney song 'When You Wish Upon A Star', they waved goodbye to a crowd that was bigger than any they had played to in the past, walked off stage and fell into each other's arms backstage like a sporting team that had just been through an experience most of us can barely imagine. I happened to be standing nearby, listening to the crowd and the fireworks, and thinking such an experience must be very difficult to turn one's back on for good. Moments like these force a band to realize that this bond they have with the audience is the most important thing they've got and they are beholden to think carefully about how they choose to use it or not.

There aren't many moves a band can make. As Robert Forster of the Go-Betweens pointed out in his book *The 10 Rules of Rock and Roll*, after the third number a band has shown you pretty much all it's going to show you. Rock shows aren't strong on new information. There are no plot twists, no cliffhangers. After a certain amount of time, the most revealing story is the larger one told on a bigger canvas and with a wider time scheme. It's the story of the band itself. In its lifetime there are only two big moves a band can make: one is breaking up, the other is getting back together.

1996 saw the standard exits and re-entrances. The Ramones called it a day after twenty-plus years. During that time they had scrapped about everything from their differing political stances to who slept with whose girlfriend, while managing to keep their unswerving loyalty to the band's *esprit de corps*. They might squabble about everything else but nobody argued with band policy where it pertained to truly important matters like songs or haircuts. The Ramones' twenty years at the top were a walking repudiation of the notion that fans wished their favourites to change with the times. What they craved most from their favourites was reassurance. In fact they would have resented it deeply had the band changed in any way.

In the same year the Ramones were disbanding, the Monkees were getting back together again to play a thirtieth anniversary tour. This featured Davy Jones, Micky Dolenz and Peter Tork but not Michael Nesmith. The latter didn't feel the need to work quite as much as the others owing to his mother having invented liquid correction paper for typists and as a consequence being in a position to bequeath her son independent means. Between their first break-up in 1969 and the time of writing, the Monkees have toured eighteen times. So persistent have the tensions in the group remained that they have never once fielded more than three members at a time.

Some groups split up and re-formed so often it was difficult to keep track. In 1996 the reliably preposterous Kiss, who had unmasked themselves in 1983 in a bid to keep the magic alive, decided that the best policy this time round was to re-form with the original members and actually put the masks back on. This felt rather like an elderly striptease artist attempting to enthuse an audience by getting dressed all over again. Other farewells were difficult to put a brave face on, as in Love's withdrawal from live work in 1996 owing to Arthur Lee's jailing on firearms offences.

Eventually, it seemed, everybody's phone rang, and most people who were available answered in the affirmative. This even applied to those who never liked to think they were in the same game. In 1996 even the Sex Pistols announced they were coming back. 'We've found a common cause,' said John Lydon, who had obviously been polishing his barbs, 'and that's your money.'

Increasingly it seemed a successful reunion was all about picking your time, which depended on an understanding of where the audience were in their lives. Nick Duerden, who wrote *Exit Stage Left*, a book about how pop stars deal with the afterlife of stardom, when the phone doesn't ring quite so often and the car is not always purring outside, argues that most of the Third Age musicians he spoke to agreed that nobody actually likes a pop star in mid-life.

When they're still hanging around after their moment has passed, plugging the new single that nobody is interested in, they're an embarrassment to everyone but themselves; like a former boyfriend who still comes round to visit his ex's parents, they're an unwelcome reminder of the yesterday the audience devoutly wish to outgrow. Martin Fry of ABC remembers those as the years when he used to do gigs on his own, with the help of a boom box and a backing track, because there was simply no market for anything bigger. In recent years he has been able to appear at big venues with a full band and in some cases an actual orchestra, which doesn't come cheap. He's been able to do this because he and his fans have finally got past the difficulties of middle age. The teenagers who originally bought 'All Of My Heart' back in 1982 have emerged from the long tunnel of the years when they were too exhausted by bringing up children even to think about going out and are once again in the market for having their youth celebrated to the music of Martin Fry and ABC.

Once a pop star has pushed through the middle years we can categorize them as 'a survivor'. We invariably take this as good news because if they're a survivor that must mean we are as well. Nobody wanted to know about David Bowie when he was having his Tin Machine mid-life crisis in his early forties but by the time he was into his sixties he could do no wrong again. (During that time he was so determined to be just one of the band that interviewers were warned not to direct questions to him. Some bright spark got round the problem by opening with the question 'Which one of you is the singer?') You could say much the same of Leonard Cohen and Bob Dylan. They had to get through their mid-life crisis years in the eighties in order to enter the broad sunlit uplands of their sixties, beyond which they stood a good chance of being reborn as 'a legend'.

Something of the kind happened to Crowded House. In November 2016, twenty years after their Farewell to the World, they returned to Sydney Opera House to mark the anniversary of their first goodbye. This time they were short one member, original drummer, Paul

Hester, who couldn't live with the band and couldn't live without it and had died by his own hand in 2005. Neil Finn may have been thinking about him and the blessings of being a member of a band that people still wanted to hear thirty years on when he said from the stage, 'What a glorious night to be alive on the planet.'

The extent to which pop
music had burrowed its way
into the establishment by
the time of the state funeral
of Diana, Princess of Wales,
in 1997 was dramatically
underlined by the choice of
the erstwhile Reg Dwight to
sing her to her rest.

13

ELTON IN THE ABBEY

I n the first days of September 1997, in the week between the death of the Princess of Wales in a Paris underpass on the Saturday night and her state funeral at Westminster Abbey the following Saturday, in the week when Radio One took to playing nothing but instrumentals, in the week when it seemed that all of show business had been told to remain at home and await further instructions, the fifty-year-old Elton John received a phone call from Richard Branson at his Windsor home.

Elton was not surprised to discover that Branson had manoeuvred himself into a position where he was advising on the upcoming event or that he was ringing Elton with a request. The way it was conveyed to him was that some of the tens of thousands of mourners who had queued in central London to sign the book of condolences were spontaneously adding quotations from 'Candle In The Wind', Elton John and Bernie Taupin's 1973 song about the passing of Marilyn Monroe. Therefore, it had been reasoned, it would be fitting for Elton to perform an adapted version at the funeral in Westminster Abbey.

The fact that the person presenting this line to Elton was someone with no small experience of getting rock superstars to believe that in saying yes they would be answering the call of the nation rather than the demands of their own ego goes some way to explain the alacrity with which Elton gave his assent. The fact that somebody in the royal household was alive enough to the need to make sure this solemn national event also had some stardust about it speaks volumes for the way that, in the waning days of the twentieth century, pop music was beginning to replace sacred music at the national festivals of hatch, match and dispatch.

There was now a sort of equivalence between the royal family and rock royalty such as their Windsor neighbour Elton John. They both did a lot for good causes, both were from time to time seen in ludicrous outfits and both had been part of the national life for so long that most members of the public would have had the greatest difficulty explaining how they got there. Neither group was expected to have a private life which could in any way be at odds with their public role. By now it was clear that both were in their roles for life and both were deeply conscious of the fact that they served at the pleasure of the public. Both had learned over the years that the public will tolerate change but only gradually.

Music is not something the British royal family have traditionally had much enthusiasm for, although they were shrewd enough readers of the national mood to know when an association with music and musicians could do them some good. The reason the Beatles were booked on *The Ed Sullivan Show* in the United States in 1964 was because they were identified as being the only one of the new wave of shaggy-haired beat groups to have received royal approval in the shape of an invitation to appear at the Royal Command Performance. When the following year they were awarded their MBEs, the Queen was sufficiently savvy to understand that it was worth losing the approval of a few crusty members of the older generation if it meant getting a few of the younger generation on side.

Nonetheless her own children grew up seemingly untouched by the fashions and passions of the youth of their generation, preferring the company of horses and military types to models and rock stars. When the Queen's second son, Andrew, was twenty-one, in 1981, somebody at the Palace thought it would be a bright idea to invite Elton John to the party. In his autobiography, Elton paints a recognizable picture of the Queen shuffling around the dance floor with her handbag while Bill Haley's 'Rock Around The Clock' played through the world's quietest disco, the sovereign maintaining a firm grip on the royal reticule throughout. When called upon to associate with pop people, the royal family did so with the same grim sense of duty they brought to the honouring of officers in local government. Nevertheless they were happy to use and be used. Bob Geldof had known how important it was to make sure that Charles and, more to the point, Diana should be the guests of honour at Live Aid. That appearance alone moved the royal family back into the mainstream of British life.

The other aspect of the offer Branson was making to Elton when he phoned him that week, a feature which would have been immediately apparent to anybody else in the music business, was that what he was being offered was not merely a great honour but also the most irresistible plug spot that had ever been laid at the feet of the former pub pianist called Reg. This was going to be one of the largest TV audiences that had ever been gathered. For the duration of his performance he would be the cynosure of the largest number of eyeballs and ears assembled in the history of creation. His peers, he knew, would be quietly furious that they hadn't got the call. Of course he was going to do it.

It wouldn't be Elton's first funeral that summer. Just six weeks earlier he had performed with Sting at the rites for his friend the fashion designer Gianni Versace in Milan. At any gathering of show folk, no matter how grievously they may be mourning the passing of the person in the casket, a significant number of the congregation will be thinking if only they had been asked to do the reading or sing the big hymn rather than one of their rivals the show would have been improved. Elton was at least a genuine friend of both Versace and the late Princess, in her case founded on their shared enthusiasm for AIDS research and white-hot gossip. Now the call had come for him to do something. Elton snapped into action.

Bernie Taupin was contacted and told he had to provide the adapted lyrics. It wasn't long before the fax machine chattered into life and out came the words, which were newly addressed not to Norma Jean but to 'England's Rose'. Elton's only stipulation for the performance was that he should be provided with a teleprompter in case he forgot the words or, as would be entirely likely with a song he had sung thousands of times before, entered a performer's trance, slipped into the original words and woke up singing about the deceased being found in the nude. The request was granted.

One observer who was in the Abbey that day said she didn't know how he did it and remarked that he appeared to be shaking. This would be to underestimate the toughness of the really big rock star names who love nothing more than to be asked to take the biggest stage and do their stuff. This was the same Elton John who had gone from a very taxing day of giving evidence in the High Court during his action against his former manager directly to the airport to fly to a foreign country in order to perform in front of tens of thousands. People like Elton are born performers. It is what they do. These are the people who go into immediate action whenever a fridge door opens. How much more animated do they become when they are called upon to perform in front of multiples of millions? In his autobiography he was candid enough to say that he had to forget whatever emotions he might be feeling. 'I'm a performer. This is what I do. Get on with it.'

It was impossible to fault the professionalism with which he delivered the song. Not everybody watching appreciated it. A friend's father, a Second World War veteran who was more accustomed to state occasions that were reassuringly starchy and whose idea of appropriate music might have been 'I Vow To Thee My Country', reported to his son that he felt the music had been beautifully done 'before this awful fat man came on'.

But by 1997 it was the veteran and his ilk who were out of step. The nation increasingly looked to pop to express everything. Forget the sacred music and the Italian opera. It was this old pop warhorse, this staple of Magic FM, who carried the day. It was only because Elton worked entirely from lyrics dreamed up by Bernie Taupin, a man who had at least some of the reflexes of a good hack on a daily newspaper, that the song had come about in the first place. It was only because Taupin remained above all the dispassionate pro secretly tickled by the idea of being asked to do a rewrite on the hoof that it was revised as quickly as it had been. It was the hit of the day. The service was relayed to millions who were following the funeral in the streets outside and it was Elton's song they hummed along with rather than the devotional material.

For most people of middle age or over, the reaction of the British public on that funeral day provided a slightly uncomfortable encounter with a nation which in some respects they no longer recognized. Even Baby Boomers who had grown up with parents who lived through the Blitz but still rarely gave way to tears were brought up short by the sight of thousands of people who had never endured a global conflict flinging flowers in the path of a car going down the Finchley Road, their faces distorted in a rictus of grief for somebody they had never known. *The Times* in its report the day after the funeral noted that the crowds in the street broke into applause in response to Charles Spencer's line about his sister 'needing no title' to command people's hearts, ignoring the small matter that they were mourning her because she had been a celebrity, albeit one of rare beauty and grace, and she had attained that celebrity by marrying a king-in-waiting.

Elton, who cannot abide to be idle, went straight from the Abbey to the recording studio, where he put down the vocal for the single release, which would be coming out in aid of charity. When it appeared in the shops the following week people flocked in their millions to buy it, making it the biggest-selling single since records began and compelling *Top of the Pops* to climax each week with footage, of all things, of a funeral. After a few weeks even Elton thought they might have gone a bit far and that people were beginning to rather enjoy wallowing in high-minded grief. He refused to talk about his friendship with her on American TV for fear that he be seen as cashing in.

Elton playing the royal funeral provided confirmation, if it were required, that rock stars were now not merely parts of the establishment, they were also wooed by the establishment because they were seen as a way to the nation's heart. Ever since Queen Victoria lost her grip following the death of her beloved Albert, the House of Windsor has looked for signs they might be losing their claim on the nation's affections. Making a fuss over its pop stars seemed a harmless way of securing them. It's unlikely anyone actually planned it this way but the choice of a trite pop song to usher Diana into the hereafter probably did more to underline the idea that she was 'one of us' than all the calculated blandishments of politicians and courtiers.

It also did Elton's public standing no harm. On 7 September, the day after the funeral, Watford Football Club were at home at their Vicarage Road ground where they were entertaining Wycombe Wanderers in a First Division fixture. Elton had recently resumed the chairmanship of the team he had supported since he was a boy. As he entered the directors' box to take his seat before the match the entire crowd applauded, which is far from standard behaviour where football club chairmen are concerned. At the same time the stadium PA began to play the new 'Candle In The Wind'. In the background you could still hear the crowd chanting 'El-ton! El-ton! El-ton!'

14

Far from having just been born, the 1998 Madonna hit 'Ray Of Light' was, like so much modern pop, built using parts from somebody else's old album track and put together by committee.

MADONNA MAKES NEW HITS FROM OLD FLOPS

*R*ay Of Light was the first album Madonna released after giving birth to her first child in 1996, and the former Material Girl was keen that it reflected her new-found interest in spirituality and the fundamentals of life. Initially she wanted it to be called *Mantra* and spent several hours in the studio with high-priced fashion photographer Mario Testino until they could come up with a cover image in which she appeared sufficiently reborn. In one respect the resulting album was anything but natural. There were hardly any musicians on it. It was produced by the British electronic star William Orbit, who preferred to work with machines.

This was the beginning of a major sea-change in the way pop music of the future would be made. The rise of electronic dance music with its appetite for trance-like repetition made the old form of narrative songwriting redundant. Samples and sequencers put the control of the musical sounds entirely in the hands of the producer. The compatibility of compact discs with affordable computers meant that any sound which could be ripped from a record could turn up on another record. When he was first hired for the project, Orbit sent Madonna recordings of fragments upon which he thought it might be possible for her to write her songs. Among those fragments was one that had been recorded and released over twenty-five years earlier in a world where neither Madonna nor digital technology were remotely conceivable, and it had languished unnoticed ever since.

Most of the musicians featured in this book were born either during the Second World War or in the years immediately following it. The bulk of them left school at fifteen. They began their working lives early. As soon as it could possibly be arranged they climbed into the back of a van and set off to make their living as a rock musician. They had little idea what being a lifetime rock musician entailed because when they did so there were few examples of people who had spun it out that long. All they hoped to do was get away from a normal life that didn't seem to offer a great deal in the way of excitement. They didn't have a career plan. They didn't think any further ahead than the next gig. They didn't dream of any further reward than the company of a warm stranger at the end of the evening.

Dave Atkins was one such member of this massive army of would-be rock stars. Born in 1943, he was brought up in one room above a fish shop in Clacton. When his parents bought him his first guitar the outlay of £20 represented a month's income for their entire family. He formed the Blue Star Skiffle Group, then plugged in with the Vampires before becoming the singer of the Tremors, who were the closest competition for Southend's other group, the Paramounts, who went on to become Procol Harum. It was then that he decided to take the stage name Dave Curtiss; he adopted the double letter because he felt it lent the name a certain elan.

The Tremors secured a residency at Butlin's in Clacton where they earned £20 a week. Even good money like that was not the most attractive element of the arrangement. The cherry on the top of this particular cake came at the close of every week when several thousand holidaymakers and their daughters checked out and several thousand new ones replaced them. Many of them were young women happy to throw themselves at anyone who had mastered Bert Weedon's *Play in a Day*. Given this happy state of affairs, Butlin's had little trouble recruiting young musicians. As Ronnie Hawkins had said to Robbie Robertson in faraway Canada at around the same time, 'You might not get rich but you will get more pussy than Frank Sinatra.'

The Tremors played Butlin's in the summer; in the winter they went to Hamburg where they would play until their fingers bled. They made a few records for Philips, which went nowhere, but they didn't care. Whatever this job was it was clearly better than the fish shop. They didn't have a plan. They didn't seem to need one. When an agent asked them to play a residency in Senegal they said, why not? Nine months later they were still there, earning good money but with nothing to spend it on. When they came back everybody was wearing chiffon scarves; it turned out the nine months during which they had been missing had clearly included the Summer of Love. Back in Britain, Dave then missed out on joining Jon Lord and Ritchie Blackmore in a new band called Deep Purple. Then he was in a trio with Steve Howe before Steve was lured away to be the guitarist in a band called Yes. At that stage things didn't look good for Dave. All the boats appeared to have left without him.

Clutching the straw represented by the unlikely success of song-writing duo Elton John and Bernie Taupin, who had been no-hopers themselves the year before, he got together with Clive Maldoon in Chelsea and the pair of them began writing songs. This was 1971, probably the last year that hopeful musicians could afford to live in Chelsea. One night Clive had a dream. Out of that dream came a song. Clive just blurted out the words and Dave put some chords behind them. They had to write it down before it vanished from their memory because in those days nobody could afford a tape recorder.

Then they had a break. Their mates in Deep Purple, by then estab-lished as a big name, needed four albums with which to launch their Purple label and so the first album by Curtiss Maldoon was recorded and released in October 1971. 'Sepheryn', the song which had come to Clive in his dream, was included on the album even though Dave wasn't entirely sure it was good enough. It didn't matter because the album got lost in the shuffle. That seemed to be it. The world apparently didn't require the services of Dave Curtiss and Clive Maldoon. Dave took the hint. He went off and did the kind of jobs musicians do when nothing is happening for them in music. Clive didn't take the hint. Even in the face of widespread indifference he kept going.

In 1976 Clive choked while taking downers and died. Dave took this as a sign and sobered up. He had no wife or children so his needs were relatively easy to meet. He ran a courier firm. He cooked. He got by. He figured as long as he had food in the fridge and a car to drive he didn't need anything else. Since music appeared to be done with him he appeared to have done with it. This remained the situation for the next twenty years, during which time Dave all but forgot that he had ever been in bands and nothing in the outside world seemed to wish to remind him.

Then, as the line goes in *The Godfather*, just when he thought he was out they pulled him back in. In 1997 the phone rang in his housing association flat in Acton. The caller was Keith West, a singer he had known back in the day who had once had a hit called 'Excerpt From A Teenage Opera' (also known as 'Grocer Jack'), whom he hadn't heard from in years. West asked him whether he knew that one of Curtiss Maldoon's songs had been recorded. By Madonna.

It wouldn't have been entirely accurate to describe Madonna's 'Ray Of Light', which was number two in the British charts at the time Dave belatedly made its acquaintance, as a cover of 'Sepheryn', the song that had occurred to the late Clive Maldoon in a dream. It was clear, however, that the engine of Madonna's hit was the same hook which they had written and recorded twenty-six years earlier. 'I feel', it went, 'like I've just been born.' It was clearly Dave and Clive's song from 1971.

The manner in which this hokey little prog ditty from the days of pounds, shillings and pence had come to form part of Madonna's hyper-modern dance record illustrated the way in which the record business of the late nineties was starting to make new battleships from the pots and pans of the past, thereby opening up the possibility that a song written in one era could lay dormant for decades, only to detonate many years later. This is what had happened in this case. One of the people William Orbit worked with was a British singer called Christine Leach. She happened to be the niece of the late Clive Maldoon and had covered 'Sepheryn' on a demo produced by Orbit. He had then included it among the fragments that he sent to Madonna. It was only when she turned out to like it and felt she could put her own personal spin on the lyrics that he found out that Leach had not originated it. When the album came out in February 1998 the authorship was credited to Madonna, the producer, the two men who originated it and Leach. Being the person with her name above the title, Madonna took 30 per cent of the publishing on the 'add a word, take a third' principle whereby the biggest name always takes the biggest slice.

While to all intents and purposes the people making the dance music that was popular in 1997 might have been working in different universes from Dadrock bands like Oasis, the sharpest ears in hip hop were increasingly combing old rock records from the seventies for samples which had that nutty something they couldn't produce themselves. The further that contemporary music making disappeared 'into the box', as computerized record production was termed, the more readily they reached for the snap and crackle of an old 45. Chris Stainton, who had played keyboards for Joe Cocker throughout the sixties and seventies, provided one instance. The biggest payday of his career has already been namechecked in these pages: the riff he originated for 'Woman To Woman', which was unearthed in the nineties and then sampled in twenty different hip hop cuts, culminating in Tupac Shakur's 'California Love', a massive hit all over the world in 1995. For Stainton it was the most money he'd ever made out of anything in a career that was more than thirty years long.

This sampling activity and the 'crate diggers' who prided themselves on being able to unearth tiny fragments from forgotten sides paid unexpected tribute to music which in many cases had either languished in complete obscurity or been familiar only to deep-end fans of the bands. The Rolling Stones, who couldn't buy a hit of their own after the 1980s, were still the greatest beneficiary of the Verve's globe-girdling smash 'Bitter Sweet Symphony' from 1997 because it had sampled a violin part which had featured on an Andrew Oldham Orchestra reworking of the Rolling Stones' 'The Last Time'. Make no mistake. That violin part was not simply part of the record's furniture, it was the hook, just as Led Zeppelin's 1975 album track 'Kashmir' was what powered Puff Daddy's 1998 hit 'Come With Me', just as Public Enemy's 1996 'He Got Game' wouldn't have been a hit had it not been based on the chassis of Buffalo Springfield's 1966 track 'For What It's Worth', just as Cypress Hill took Black Sabbath's 1970 recording of 'The Wizard' for 'I Ain't Goin' Out Like That' in 1993, and just as the hero of Kanye West's 2010 smash 'Power' was the part borrowed from King Crimson's 1969 release '21st Century Schizoid Man'.

This gave a whole new lease of life to records which should by rights have never been heard of again. As more and more hit records of the nineties were built using spare parts from records made in earlier decades, thanks to this sanctioned stealing the original records and the bands that made them became known to a new generation. It didn't just happen with records that had been hits first time around. Phil Manzanera has been guitarist with Roxy Music since 1972 and co-wrote some of their hits but the biggest payday he had in the course of his entire career was from the use of an instrumental he had put out on a flop solo album in 1978 which turned up again in Kanye West and Jay Z's 'No Church In The Wild' in 2011.

Madonna's 'Ray Of Light', as it was subsequently called, was a good-sized hit all over the world and it was a hit at a time when people still went out and bought records. Dave Atkins, who had previously had no need to keep in touch with the organizations that keep tabs on who gets paid what for their part in a hit, heard that Radio Two were trying to find him. When he emerged and got in touch with his old publisher he discovered that he had ended up with 15 per cent of Madonna's 1997 smash and that since the principal sum was so significant, this apportionment was most certainly worth having. At the time we spoke in 2011 Dave was looking at anything up to a million pounds for his share of the belated windfall from this song that he hadn't thought about for a quarter of a century. What was he going to do with the money? He was planning to use it to build a spiritual community in Bulgaria. The newly spiritual Madonna would no doubt have been pleased.

The advent of the digital revolution in music, signalled by the file-sharing service Napster, reduced the amount artists could make from recorded music while also ensuring that in future no old act would be forgotten.

ETERNAL LIFE ON THE INTERNET

I t began with Kate Moss and a computer. In 1993, two American high-school students decided to combine their adoration of the former with their addiction to the latter, convening after hours in the school laboratory to scan photos of the nineteen-year-old British model snipped from the many colour magazines that were selling hundreds of thousands of copies at the time and painstakingly upload them to this fledgling wonder which was beginning to be known to a select few as the internet. At this time the only people who could get on the information superhighway were nerds who understood something of code.

Apart from Kate Moss, Rob and Jeff's other passion was music. They began to read about a new form of audio compression that would enable them to reduce music files to a tenth of their usual size. This would render them small enough to make the idea of sending an actual recorded song down a phone line realistic. At the time this was a head-spinning prospect for the would-be rock star, who had long considered that the only thing standing between him and a vast audience was the difficulty of getting people actually to hear his efforts. As soon as Jeff got his hands on this technology the first thing he did was painstakingly convert a demo by his own band, the Ugly Mugs, and upload it to the newsgroup that specialized in 'alt music'. Having done so he stood back to see what happened.

Would there be anybody out there? He didn't have to wait long. The first response he got was from Turkey. The second from Russia. We like Ugly Mugs. Please send more Ugly Mugs. Tell us about Ugly Mugs. This was heady stuff. Here was the world of music apparently expanding and flattening before his very eyes.

To people such as Rob and Jeff, outliers of the first generation of digital natives, the future for up-and-coming rock bands appeared plain. Thanks to this new means of distribution there would no longer be any need for the star-making machinery of the record companies. The Ugly Mugs of the future would not need power brokers or gatekeepers. Under this new dispensation they could go directly to the fans. In a fit of altruism and curiosity, Rob and Jeff promptly set up the Internet Underground Music Archive – IUMA (eye-YOU-mah) for short.

They had but a hazy idea of how massive a task they might be taking on. From all over the world unknown hopefuls deluged them with tapes, which Rob and Jeff then dutifully uploaded. IUMA began to get some attention. It was written about in their local paper with the same sense of wonder that would attend a couple of local kids stumbling upon a cure for a major disease. Quite soon they had the big record companies beating on their door. This was still clearly the land of the blind and Rob and Jeff were one-eyed men. They were invited to conferences where well-funded grown-ups were happy to defer to their expertise in what everybody was confident would be huge. They were invited on to panels with people who had proper businesses with proper revenues and a surprisingly complacent view of the future. Jeff remembers being on one with the owner of the Tower Records chain who looked down on him and predicted 'only one of us will be here in ten years'. He would turn out to be incorrect about that. In ten years neither of them would be there. By then the revolution everyone had been so sunnily predicting for so long had happened. It came gradually at first and then with terrifying suddenness.

For that we have to thank Shawn Fanning. In June 1999 he was an eighteen-year-old student who had launched a new platform called Napster which allowed his fellow college kids to gain access to the tunes on each other's hard drives. Within a year it had twenty million registered users sitting up late at night in their dorm rooms indulging in the thrill of being able to download Metallica B-sides from the computers of other students in faraway Russia or Korea, all connected by a technology known as peer-to-peer exchange, which for a while allowed Napster's lawyers to claim they were no more encouraging people to trade illegally than the farmer who rents out his field for a Sunday-morning car boot sale.

The revolution which began with Napster upset every last certainty on which the music business had depended. It changed everything, but hardly ever in the way anybody had predicted. In 1999 David Bowie gave an interview to the BBC's Jeremy Paxman in which he asserted his view that the internet was now as exciting as pop music had formerly been; he stated this in the face of the traditional newsman's concern that society would collapse since people would no longer be able to check the news. At the time neither Paxman nor Bowie really knew what they were dealing with. Bowie was right about the fact that we were on the verge of a major change but nobody really knew how. The predictions of musicians were as off-beam as anyone else's. In 2000, those old hippies Graham Nash and David Crosby hailed the new means of communication as a forum in which people would be represented by their own words and not their identities. Pete Townshend promised that he would communicate directly with fans via email or in chat rooms 'like my friend David Bowie'. Terence Trent D'Arby used a 1998 announcement on his website to claim to be 'a holographic representation in the third dimension of what was requested by your souls that one of your favourite artists be'.

Within a short few years either side of the millennium the balance of power would, thanks to the internet, shift from the acts and their traditional 'owners', the record companies, to the fan communities. This would prove to be every bit as beneficial for the older generation as it was for the young. In the early days of Usenet, before the internet had adopted the language that allowed the rest of the world to join in, there were already 150 music newsgroups, most of them devoted to big names like the Beatles, Pink Floyd and Kate Bush. Just as significant was the one devoted to Peter Hammill, who was best known for having led a group called Van der Graaf Generator in the early seventies, a group which at the time would have been thought of as slipping into almost total obscurity. On the internet the playing field was flat.

Soon there would be no such thing as obscurity. At the time I had a colleague who would enthuse about a Belgian band called Universe Zero. They were so obscure that even John Peel wouldn't play them and so unfashionable that none of the music papers would write anything about them. In the mid-nineties, if you couldn't get played on either daytime radio or by John Peel you effectively didn't exist. The only reason my friend knew that Universe Zero existed at all was because he subscribed to a newsgroup on Usenet called alt.music.progressive and he had found that if he spent long enough on there, there was a chance he might eventually find himself corresponding with somebody who had also heard of them and might even be able to tell him whether they were still in existence.

The internet changed everything in the music economy. As the years went by musicians – particularly older musicians; particularly older musicians like David Crosby – were never slow to complain about the downsides. What they never fully appreciated was what we might call the Universe Zero effect, thanks to which devoted enthusiasts of acts far beyond the mainstream no longer had to wait for limited channels of communication to get around to featuring their favourites. Thanks to the computer in their home they could now go behind the counter and help themselves. Behind that counter there would be sufficient material for them to devote their every waking moment to. Thanks to the internet you could travel to the past for as long as you wanted. Thanks to the technology everybody had in their homes, the bands of the seventies continued to exist and engage with a new public long after their time was apparently over. In the day of physical product the new necessarily displaced the old. Once everything became noughts and ones the inventory knew no limit.

In 1995, an American student called Charlie Savage developed an interest in Pink Floyd and began spending time on Usenet reading about them. It was here that he first saw mention of the theory that if you started playing their album *The Dark Side Of The Moon* at the same time as you pressed play on a VHS of the 1939 film *The Wizard of Oz* there would appear to be all manner of spooky synchronicities between the two. Having tried it and found the results amusing, he wrote up the story for a local newspaper as part of his journalism course. It didn't go any further until he taught himself some HTML, posted the piece on his own rudimentary web page and then linked to it on Usenet. Two years later MTV were doing items about a phenomenon that was then known as 'Dark Side of the Rainbow' and it had spread as far as the *Washington Post* and then made its way across the ocean to Britain. It seemed to minister to a need to sit around and muse about rock records, and the older they were, the better.

Before the internet we assumed that the world of music was like the flat Earth proposed by early navigators. The space was finite. If you went too far you dropped off the edges and were never heard of again. The internet taught us that this needn't be the case. Thanks to the internet, everybody was out there for ever. If you went looking for even the most marginal act plucked from the very edges of your experience you would find that it still in some way existed, even if it was only in order to keep its website going, a site that sent out the same insistent message.

We're still here.

16

When Bill Clinton welcomed Joni Mitchell to the White House in 1998, they were both about to have their private lives fired into the public domain.

SOCIAL MEDIA PUTS AN END TO ROCK STAR MYSTIQUE

I f you wanted to spend time on the internet in 1997 you needed a good reason. Google was still a year away from being launched and you were probably using a dial-up modem. It would be another seven years before the launch of Facebook would make avoiding contact with strangers more difficult than achieving it. Nobody realized it at the time, but we were living through the last days of private life as it had been understood. Its disappearance would have far-reaching implications for rock stars, a tribe who in the twentieth century had been able to give their own account of their past life and have it widely accepted.

One of the first spheres of human activity to be roiled by the wide-spread availability of this technology was adoption. In that year Joni Mitchell's manager was contacted by someone claiming to be the long-lost daughter of the fifty-four-year-old musician. Among the managers of male performers, particularly those who became famous before birth control was widely available, such calls were something of an occupational hazard. Sometimes they led to legal proceedings and blood tests, at other times to a quick pay-off, and in a small number of cases, such as those concerning Rod Stewart and Mick Jagger, to a lifelong relationship with a child who had been born on what was once known as the wrong side of the blanket.

This was an unusual case because the rock star parent at issue here was female. Since it also concerned one of those artists who had been so well known for using the crooked timber of her real life as a jumping-off point for songs so direct and confessional that she included the line 'songs are like tattoos' in one of them, it was even more difficult to take. Hadn't those artists who came out of the coffee houses of the mid-sixties entered into a kind of compact with their followers, where they would have no secrets? Those devoted disciples, who had followed Mitchell's career for thirty years and measured their lives against hers, might feel slightly let down by the fact that there was a whole area of her past life she had chosen not to share with them.

The person who was seeking to be put in touch with the woman who had given birth to her in a charity hospital in Toronto in 1965, a year when most of Mitchell's contemporaries were wrapped up in folk-rock and mini-skirts, was familiar with the record *Blue* but had no clue that one of its songs, 'Little Green', was all about her, the baby who had been given up for adoption. This was a time when the father lit out for California and the young mother, who had already grievously disappointed her parents by saying she was going to the big city to be a folk singer, was left alone and bewildered with nothing to fall back on but her talent and a drive you don't find every day. The month after the baby was born she had set off to America where she married folk singer Chuck Mitchell. She had made her own wedding dress.

Within four years of giving up the child for adoption Joni Mitchell was world-famous, her songs covered by Judy Collins and Buffy Sainte-Marie. She couldn't get to Woodstock because the highways were blocked but she wrote the song that became its anthem. Among her romantic partners were Graham Nash, Leonard Cohen and James Taylor, the very people most likely to write up the experience as a song, a compliment she was happy to repay. In those days nobody sat around brooding over their scars. If an unfortunate experience occurred they wrote a song about it and moved on to the next. A certain flippant toughness went with the territory. When in 1971 *Rolling Stone* dubbed her 'old lady of the year' it was more likely to be regarded as a hipster compliment than an insult. Few guessed what she'd left behind in Canada.

The seventies was Joni Mitchell's decade. Once they were over she entered a difficult middle age. Like actresses who traditionally peak at thirty when they're playing the love interest, female singer-songwriters can find themselves relegated from fantasy girlfriend to spiky eccentric without even experiencing the faint compensation of a young-mum stage. In interviews she claimed the record business was a cesspool, overlooking the fact it was still very keen to work with her even though by then she hadn't written a hit in years. The lyrics of her records couldn't help but make her sound like the neighbourhood lady who didn't altogether approve of the way the world was going. She dismayed her long-term fans by giving them the one thing nobody ever asked for, which was a record dedicated to an elderly jazz musician. Like so many musicians looking at a low chart placing, she was more comfortable attributing her lack of commercial success to a conspiracy between radio programmers, greedy record executives and conniving politicians than she was accepting the more likely explanation, that the people who used to love her had decided to live without her company for a while.

This is the dilemma of the long-distance rock star. Long careers can only be sustained by fans prepared to go a similar distance. Their stamina is particularly tested by solo troubadours who need to remind the world of their existence by releasing a bunch of new songs about their lives every year or so and turning up in the arts pages of the newspapers and on the same old review shows to remind their fans of the obligation they faced to keep them in the style to which they had grown accustomed. By the time the twenty-first century was coming into view the likes of Joni Mitchell and Bob Dylan had released more albums than the likes of Charles Dickens and Henry James, famously no slouches, had published novels. How many Joni Mitchell records did a person need?

The phone call from Canada arrived when she was in this phase. It came from a thirty-two-year-old, now called Kilauren, who had been brought up by well-to-do adoptive parents and had dabbled in modelling and art but never entirely found her way in life. Since being awakened to the fact that Joni Mitchell had a long-lost daughter by an article published in Canada in 1993 she had used her nascent internet skills to establish the likelihood that it might be her. If their eventual reunion in Los Angeles in 1997, as a result of which Mitchell suddenly found herself with an adult daughter and two grandchildren, had been the plot of a novel you would not have expected that to lead to a simple happy-ever-after, and that was not the outcome in this case.

Being a parent shapes most of us through tiny increments of experience, in which the sorrows sometimes seem to be outweighing the joys. Being suddenly plunged into the delicate negotiation which is parenthood after thirty years of being able to get her way by just picking up the phone and announcing herself cannot have been easy. Even those closest to Joni Mitchell would be obliged to point out that diplomacy is not always her strongest suit. In 2000 the police were forced to attend her Bel Air home following an incident in which the vexations with her daughter turned physical. No charges were pressed as a result. When quizzed about it in 2013, Mitchell put it down to her daughter's 'abandonment issues' and said that there had been tension between the two of them and, as is so often the case with families, the granddaughter had been 'conscripted' against her. She added that the two of them were now over it.

There isn't a musician in the world who thinks they've been given their proper due, and over the years Joni Mitchell has been no exception. She's been particularly forthright about the fact that Bob Dylan got the coronation which should rightly have been hers. She never forgave him for coming along to a playback of her album *Court And Spark* in 1974 and falling asleep. She has even claimed that he's an unpleasant person to harmonize with on account of his reluctance to brush his teeth. She has bitterly pointed out that Dylan seemingly invented his musical persona and puts it on like a suit, not really noting that this is what most rock stars do. Dylan would certainly be the first face chiselled on rock's Mount Rushmore, but in the days when his kind of fame was invented they didn't call it hero worship for nothing.

However, game recognize game, as they say in hip hop. Joni Mitchell liked to say that it was when she first heard Dylan's 'Positively 4th Street' that she realized songs could be about anything, that you could maybe use them to settle scores or to describe your own life as a series of set-piece dramas in which the last word would always be yours. Here you could place your elbow on the scales of life and include the stories you wanted to and leave out the ones you'd prefer not to share. The longer the careers of these troubadours continued the more long-time followers grew accustomed to connecting the songs with the lives, and the more misled they could be.

At one stage Mitchell claimed she was working on her autobiography, but nothing appears to have come of it. She may have found, like Mick Jagger, who took an advance for doing the same thing and then paid it back, that the idea of doing such a book is more attractive than the reality. For most of her time in the spotlight she was keeping a secret from the world. Maybe it's not the only one. After all, in 1990 George Michael collaborated on a ghostwritten autobiography called *Bare*, supposedly to indicate how revelatory it was. It didn't mention the fact that he was gay. Brian Wilson has published his autobiography twice, which strongly suggests even he doesn't know which is the true version. In the twentieth century it was possible to appear to be spilling one's innermost secrets while still hanging on to some private life. This was proved by Mitchell's peer Bob Dylan who secretly married the singer Carolyn Dennis in 1986, divorced her six years later, and neither the press nor the far more formidable force that is the worldwide tribe of Dylan watchers knew anything about it.

That would prove impossible in the new century. Facebook would launch in 2004, YouTube the year after, and in their wake would come a succession of products that would bring about the greatest changes in human behaviour seen in the last three quarters of a century. The next generation of rock stars are digital natives, so-called because they have never known anything but life in the panopticon of social media, and therefore they have never known what it is to have a secret and to hold on to it for decades.

17

The 2000 film Almost Famous, starring Kate Hudson as a groupie with a big heart, appealed to people who believed the seventies were a golden age.

CLASSIC ROCK AS COSTUME DRAMA

Amara's Law, named after a computer scientist of the sixties, holds that when it comes to technological change we tend to overestimate the likely impact in the short term while underestimating the actual impact in the longer term. In the years leading up to the millennium, billions were thrown at attempts to forestall the catastrophe which was supposed to happen when the digital clocks in all our devices clicked from 1999 to 2000. This turned out to be a threat that was somewhat overstated. In the years leading away from that epochal switch of date we still have not fully realized the extent to which the transition to the twenty-first century has had the effect of increasing the appeal of the music and musicians of the twentieth century by lending them the sepia tint of history.

When 124 years ago the calendar moved from the nineteenth to the twentieth century, people were looking ahead optimistically. They had lived through massive technological change which clearly improved their lives. At the dawn of the twenty-first century we were nothing like as optimistic. This applied no less to music than to any other sphere. Musicians who found they could no longer rely on a record company coming up with an advance were more likely than most to look back on the century just departed as a distant land of lost content, and critics and taste makers were increasingly in the market for a romantic view of those people and places. The music of the seventies in particular was seized on in the same way that British jazzmen of the forties hankered after the old style of music that had been played in Storyville before 1917, exalting the old 'traditional' form of playing at the expense of the hipsters of modern jazz.

At the beginning of the movie *Almost Famous*, which was released in the USA in September 2000, the eleven-year-old hero fishes out a bag which his older sister has placed beneath his bed. She, being a child of the sixties, has gone off to look for America and therefore has bequeathed her long-playing records to her brother, who is a child of the early seventies. The boy flips through them, running his hand wonderingly over the jackets of Joni Mitchell's *Blue*, Bob Dylan's *Blonde On Blonde*, the Beach Boys' *Pet Sounds*, Jimi Hendrix's *Axis: Bold As Love* and the Who's *Tommy*. Immediately before leaving, his sister has assured him that if he listens to the latter by the light of a single candle he will see his whole future. She has promised him that if he takes these records to his heart they will set him free. She has further assured him that he shouldn't worry about the painfully gauche stage he's going through because one day he too will be as cool as these records.

Because this is a turn-of-the-century Hollywood view of the seventies, and therefore as far removed from the actual events it depicts as the 1967 film *Bonnie and Clyde* was from the reality of Depression-era America, there's little here that is permitted to jar its soft-focus conjuring of an apparently golden age. Among the sister's records there's no corny old Herman's Hermits album, no *Love Story* soundtrack, not one off-colour comedy record nor even a stray example of the sort of inexplicable one-hit wonders that pitch up in the record collections of actual people in the actual world. The inclusion of even one of these might have marred the fantasy, which was essentially what the film was selling. It was vital that the records the hero was willed by his sibling to listen to were from the classic rock canon, as Cameron Crowe's movie and its many successors would encourage the new century to see it. In cinemas as the year turned into 2001, *Almost Famous* permitted the rock culture of the seventies to be reborn as period drama.

The film was based on the time its director had worked as a young journalist on *Rolling Stone*. This was now an era which had passed through the awkward stage of mere datedness and was emerging into the sunlight of legend. The young actors of *Almost Famous* had a field day dressing up as the hip outsiders of the Watergate era and delivering lines which might have come from a think-piece written in the twenty-first century. Philip Seymour Hoffman presented the real-life writer Lester Bangs as a rock critic who spoke entirely in epigrams, a species almost unknown in the real world. Kate Hudson was delicately pretty as the groupie Penny Lane, which might not always have been the case in the wild. The lead singer of the notional band Stillwater was at one stage supposed to be played by Brad Pitt. This would have been a catastrophic error because even the handsomest rock star is never quite movie star handsome.

Almost Famous wasn't a particularly successful film at the time. In the American box office chart for 2000 it achieved a modest eighty-second place. It was nothing like as critically acclaimed as *American Beauty*, winner of five Oscars that year (including Best Picture), or as bankable as *Gladiator*, released just a few months earlier. But in the years since then it has become one of those films that has steadily grown in popularity, turning into the kind of picture people go back to watch again, the sort they cite approvingly because as time goes on it seems increasingly to chime with a way they prefer to see its world, its very title slowly and almost imperceptibly shimmering into a kind of shorthand for a way of repackaging Rock Past so that it may meet with the approval of a mass market in the present. A successful outfit for the chic young thing attending a rock festival in the twenty-first century would be described as 'very *Almost Famous*'. Lester Bangs, a man who in his lifetime was known only to a few thousand very devoted students of bylines, is now known to a far greater number of people who have not read him but have picked up an idea of what he is supposed to represent. Cool, a word hardly ever employed in the seventies, is now, as Cameron Crowe said, 'a mass concept', and *Almost Famous* helped make it so.

Almost Famous had two things going for it when it came to cool, neither of which involved the actors, the script or anything that actually happens in the film. The first is the old music on the soundtrack and the power that music has, as Woody Allen memorably observed, to make a film look better. Simon & Garfunkel's 'America', Rod Stewart's 'Every Picture Tells A Story' and Led Zeppelin's 'That's The Way' provided the true heart of the film. The scene where the entire tour bus ends up chorusing Elton John's 'Tiny Dancer' as though it were an immemorial anthem like 'Abide With Me' popularized a song that had slipped out of his repertoire at the time and gave even Elton's career a fresh boost as it was entering its fourth decade.

More significant even than the music was the look of the film. By the late nineties it was clearly no longer sufficient to send a bunch of actors out in jeans and T-shirts and hope that they would achieve the look which rock people seemed to have achieved unconsciously back in the early seventies. By the time it was being made, the kind of past this film needed was no longer available off-the-peg. The film's costume designer, Betsy Heimann, who had already been responsible for rehabilitating the looks of the recent past through various Tarantino films, designed every outfit in *Almost Famous* from scratch. She even went to the extent of getting permission from Neil Young to design a T-shirt featuring the Stillwater lead singer which looked like a similar shirt featuring the real-life Neil Young.

More significant than anything worn by the male characters was the wardrobe Heimann designed and made for Kate Hudson to wear as groupie Penny Lane. The centrepiece of her look, a shearling-lined coat, was designed to make the actress appear to be glowing from the inside. This outfit was as far removed from seventies reality as the costume worn by the actor playing Darth Vader in *Star Wars*. Heimann looked far and wide for a garment that would frame Hudson's features and allow her to appear appealingly vulnerable. Unable to find one, she used part of the film's $80 million budget to purchase five household rugs from Urban Outfitters, instructing her team to dye them in different shades of white until she found one that worked best with the lighting. Judging by the fact that twenty years after its release young fashion mavens not even born at the time still understand precisely what is meant by the Penny Lane coat, it was worth every bit of Heimann's trouble.

The last quarter of a century has produced many hugely popular acts, acts that fill stadiums whenever they choose to tour – Coldplay, the Arctic Monkeys and their like. Yet it sometimes seems that their fame cannot quite outshine that of bands like Oasis who came along in the era of physical product when success was visible in every shop-window display and through every plastic bag being brandished on the way home.

Sales of CDs were at their peak in 2000. Fortunes were still being made. Eight years later sales of CDs had declined by more than 50 per cent. This was not all down to Napster-style file sharing and other forms of theft of copyright. Technology was taking the music business's most profitable format, the album, and unbundling it. Once people were at liberty to buy just their favourite tracks from albums and leave the rest at the edge of their plate, that is precisely what they did. The music business, which had once liked to think it could bend its consumers to its will, now had to adapt quickly to the changing habits of the audience, habits which were usually shaped by changes in tech. The same thing applied to the performers, who used to pride themselves on the fact that they knew what the kids would do next, and were suddenly exposed as equally hopeless and helpless. They flipped, they flopped, between the future and the past. After a brief period during which they entertained the fantasy of selling their product directly to their fans they decided they would prefer record companies to exist if only to have somebody to get a big cheque from when they delivered their new album and then somebody to blame when it didn't do so well. The record business continued to exist but it was only half the size of what it had once been. Even the big record companies were seeking buyers or partners for mergers. What had once been the prince of packaged goods businesses was now having to settle for some scraps from technology's table. Tech ruled the world. Steve Jobs's biography, the story of a man who ran an IT firm, was a massive best-seller with which no mere entertainer could compete.

The biggest rock star of the year 2001 was a small white box. When it was first unveiled to the world on 23 October it was described as being about the same size as a packet of cigarettes. At the time 15 per cent of adults in the UK smoked, a proportion which had more than halved since 1985, the year of Live Aid. This was only one of the major behavioural changes that took place in the period of time covered by this book. The small white box would usher in its own.

Since this invention would swiftly become as ubiquitous a feature of daily life in the twenty-first century as the cigarette packet had been in the twentieth, the comparison was strangely apposite. The man doing the unveiling, Mr Jobs of the computer company Apple, showed what the small white box could do by pressing the button which made it play a song called 'Building A Mystery' by the Canadian singer Sarah McLachlan. This was followed by Bob Marley's 'Could You Be Loved', Yo-Yo Ma playing one of Bach's cello suites and, inevitably, something by the Beatles. This apparently serendipitous mix was either a happy accident or a harbinger of the changed attitude to music consumption which the box would soon bring about. It was explained that these were just a few of the thousand recordings that could be housed in this one pocket-sized white box, which would be known as the iPod. The iPod would change many things about the music business. For a start it would make the past every bit as easy to access as the present. The world of *Almost Famous* was now just a click away.

More than twenty years after its release *Almost Famous* still inspires regular think-pieces, many of them from twenty- and thirty-somethings who confess that the film infected them with the craving to live the life of the rock journalist as played out by the film's young hero. This career, which was once lived by a fortunate handful, was already becoming a fantasy by the time the film was released. The life of turning up at the stage door with a winning grin, a notebook and a paper copy of your fanzine in a tote bag, hoping to 'hang' with the band and to be whisked off on their tour bus in search of pointless freedom, was as difficult to achieve in the real world as a job as a Spitfire pilot. The economy that supported such roles, which was based on the physical distribution of records, on industrial combines that purchased ink by the barrel and paper by the ton, was already beginning to slip away by 2000, and in time would take those dreams over the horizon. Ironically, in the twentieth century, when the job 'rock journalist' could at least have been said to exist, there were no academic courses teaching it. In the twenty-first, when the job no longer exists, there are hundreds.

While this book was being prepared, Cameron Crowe, noting the success that jukebox musicals were having in attracting middle-aged music fans to the theatre, launched *Almost Famous* on Broadway. It closed soon after in the light of reviews that pointed out that it's impossible for on-stage cover versions ever to match the pangs people felt when they went to the cinema and heard Led Zeppelin and Cat Stevens coming over the soundtrack. No young person in their right mind ever thought they would be able to improve on those records that had been made so long before they were born in a world they couldn't help feeling they missed out on. One representative of that generation, Hannah Ewens, writing in *The Times*, had a nice way of describing the *Almost Famous* effect and the spell it cast on a younger generation of music fans like her. It had made her, she wrote, 'livid with nostalgia'.

18

THE NOT ENTIRELY LONESOME DEATH OF JOHN ENTWISTLE

The Who bassist spent the periods between money-spinning American tours among the optics and bass guitars at his country pile in the Cotswolds.

Bob Geldof described the experience of persuading the members of the Who to come together to play at Live Aid as being like getting four ex-wives together. In 1985 it was impossible to say with any certainty whether the Who still existed, and, in Britain at least, it was debatable whether anybody cared. When they toured the USA in 1982 they had said it would be the last time, which probably didn't do any harm when it came to filling two further Shea Stadium shows. Three years later Geldof felt they had to be on his bill in order to satisfy the interests of the American audience, where they had always been more popular than they were in Britain. With his customary sense of decorum he told Townshend that if the group didn't appear the fundraising efforts would be a million dollars down and therefore children would die as a consequence. As susceptible as ever to hearing an argument underlining his band's place in the march of mankind, Townshend agreed.

Most of the performances that day went eerily well. The Who's was an exception. They had problems with Entwistle's bass, the satellite feed carrying their performance to America failed for two numbers, they missed cues and they had clearly come along thinking that it wouldn't be possible to do a great deal of damage to their reputation in the course of four numbers. In this they were mistaken. It was doubly bad because while the band that had been performing an hour earlier, Queen, had taken the trouble to distil their essence down to a show reel for the ages and thereby provide a launching pad for a new stage in their career, the Who were all over the place and were in truth never the same force again. It was only at the last moment that they decided against using the occasion to unveil a song Townshend had written about the famine, a song which clearly nobody would have wished to hear. One of the reasons Cat Stevens' offer to play at Live Aid was not taken up was because he too had written a song for the occasion, which clearly nobody would want to hear.

The Who emerged from the Live Aid experience feeling as if the band had been handed its coat. At this stage the individual members probably still felt they had other options. In 1985, principals Pete Townshend and Roger Daltrey still entertained the idea that the qualities which had made them a success within the band might turn out to be a success outside the band. The jury was still out on solo careers. Mick Jagger had only just released his first solo LP, *She's The Boss*, and it was not yet clear that when the hardcore of a band's fanbase went out and bought a member's first solo effort in the first week of release they were merely being polite and definitely wouldn't be back. It took a while for bands to realize that fans liked people who knew their place, that place being within the band. There was also the question of the attitude of individual members to substance abuse. The cover of Townshend's 1980 solo record, *Empty Glass*, contained a mordant thanks to the makers of Rémy Martin cognac 'for saving my life by making the stuff so expensive'.

However, as the band's leader and primary songwriter, Townshend could at least claim to have his fate in his own hands. The same didn't apply to drummer Kenney Jones, who had replaced Keith Moon following the original drummer's death in 1978. It certainly didn't apply to John 'The Ox' Entwistle, who had been their bass player since the beginning and was a crucial component in their sound but didn't appear to actually do a great deal. This didn't alter the fact that he was a fundamental character in the drama of their continuing existence. Once bands have been established a few years they are no longer just a collection of musicians: they are living tableaus, walking, talking reminders of what is, was and ever shall be. In this role they also serve who only stand and appear unimpressed. It was observed that Entwistle stood stock-still on stage because if he didn't, the rest of the band would fly away altogether.

The problem that Entwistle faced – one in common with many other members of major bands who didn't write many of the songs – was the fact that he needed to be able to rely on a new album from the Who to provide his share of a big advance from a record company. This release would inevitably be accompanied by a mammoth tour of the United States. All this would earn him enough money to stay ahead of his creditors. It would also get him out of the house.

The image of a rich rock star rattling around in a sprawling mansion in the country, attempting to get the hang of the country sports favoured by the local aristocracy but never entirely fitting in and eventually being driven mad by isolation, is a standard part of our view of what happens to musicians who suddenly find they can afford to live anywhere and are advised to invest in property by accountants understandably fearful of the cash burning a hole in their wallet. These homes are usually so cavernous that every corridor seems to be begging to be enlivened by the introduction of a suit of armour. The economic trajectory of their occupants is such that said conversation pieces begin life amid baronial splendour and eventually have to be accommodated in modest semis following a period of retrenchment. The new owner comes home from a period away on tour and celebrates by shopping. Every additional square yard of lawn seems to scream for a ride-on lawnmower. The garage space is so generous that it seems a shame to have fewer than ten cars, the majority of which serve no practical purpose. After five years most of which the owner has spent away on tour, it resembles a pharaoh's scrapyard, its public areas a museum to abandoned fads.

Some rock stars develop a taste for domesticity. The man they called the Ox was not one of them. He and his first wife left their first house in a prosperous suburb of north London for a Gothic pile in the Cotswolds, which was an odd place for a man who had no talent for solitude. The house had no fewer than fifty-five rooms. There were so many he was still discovering new ones many years later. He required many of them to house his collection of 250 guitars, an accumulation so vast it might be regarded as a cry for help. Entwistle wasn't the first rock star who liked spending money on toys. He had many vintage cars and employed a chauffeur to take him out in the Rolls-Royce or the Bentley whenever he felt the need for retail therapy. He spent more money installing two studios in the house in the mistaken belief that the availability of these facilities would make him more productive. He spent a year noodling about with other musicians who were similarly at a loose end, coming up with an album nobody wanted to put out.

He installed a bar he called the Barracuda Inne, which he liked to feel was the heartbeat of the house. This is the kind of domestic statement that rarely bodes well when made by a retired footballer, and it was no different for Entwistle. There were skeletons in the bedrooms for the rich amusement of the many guests who passed through. He installed his elderly mother in one of the five houses in the grounds. When his first marriage broke down his son ended up living there too. He eventually took up with a twenty-something American girlfriend he had first run into at the Rainbow Bar and Grill, a charmless speakeasy on Sunset Boulevard where cocaine bores go in search of ageing legends seeking the Viagra of attention, a quest in which they are rarely disappointed. Visitors to the house, which was called Quarwood, came away with impressions of a life that was morphing into a lampoon of rock star excess. Spying foxes on the lawn on one occasion a visitor drew it to his host's attention and was then taken aback to see Entwistle immediately reappear with a shotgun and a bandolier of cartridges, by which time the foxes had sensibly withdrawn.

Consider the life of such a member of rock royalty as he slips towards his Third Age in the early part of the twenty-first century. Being such a rock star is clearly more than a hobby. It is a calling from which there is no possibility of retirement. On the other hand it doesn't involve quite enough of your time to be described as a full-time occupation. Even on those rare occasions when the band are supposedly recording, most of the musicians in that line-up are rarely called for. They record their parts then wait until the leader has done the rest and summoned up the courage to declare it finished. Every now and again they will emerge from the state of gilded idleness in which their being normally resides, doing whatever their neighbours do to pass the time, and then for a few months, as the band go on tour, they are bulleted into a world of private jets, motorcycle outriders, blacked-out people carriers, presidential suites and warm currents of approbation being wafted in the direction of their fundaments night and day. Every night they put on the costume they have been wearing since they were nineteen to step out into the carnival of light in front of tens of thousands of (in some cases) teenagers, who roar their full-throated approval of not so much what they do as who they are. That is heavy medicine from which nobody can recover.

Entwistle took no exercise, ate neither fruit nor vegetables, drank and smoked, and not surprisingly suffered with his blood pressure. He tried running a band of his own but had trouble adjusting from the grand luxe style in which the Who did things to the more modest fees and running costs of a band that was, for all the bass player's lineage, just starting. Then, when he was at his lowest ebb in the mid-eighties, the inevitable tax bill arrived. Like so many musicians he found himself paying for the fat years from the proceeds of the lean. He was fortunate that the other two members of the band hadn't had any solo success since the last break-up and so they were happy to tour the United States. At the end of that tour Townshend formally said it was all over. Entwistle, who had come away with $3 million, didn't seem to mind so much.

Whereas the US Marines are said to assume their new recruits know nothing and consequently make a point of teaching them everything from scratch, life in a band operating above a certain level is calculated to achieve the exact opposite, which is to kill the smallest ability to do the tiniest thing for one's self. One further respect in which rock bands resemble the military is in encouraging the individual's tendency to identify with the pack. Entwistle had a fear of being on his own which was reminiscent of Elvis Presley's. When the Who set out on their latest pension top-up tour in 2002 he had left his girlfriend back in Britain and therefore it was out of the question that he should go to bed in the Hard Rock Hotel, Las Vegas, on the night of 27 June without company. The bedmate in this case was one Alycen Rowse, who was either a stripper or a groupie depending on how she was feeling. She was thirty-two and had hooked up with the fifty-seven-year-old Entwistle before. When she awoke the following morning it was to find that the man with whom she had checked in was dead. She later recalled that he had prepared for sex by folding his trousers over a chair and taking out his hearing aid.

Following Entwistle's death the house in the Cotswolds was sold. It wasn't an easy deal to push through because, as the agent said, Quarwood would only suit certain people. The profile of these people had changed. When the first generation of rock gods bought their piles in the country the original owners were generally look-ing to downsize and cash-rich rock stars were an attractive source of new money. Come the twenty-first century there were dotcom billionaires, hedge fund tycoons and mysterious oligarchs, all of whom could readily afford to take them off their hands. John Lennon's old house Tittenhurst Park, the same one in which he imagined no possessions, was eventually bought by the ruler of Abu Dhabi. Entwistle's fifty-five-room house went to a Dutch millionaire for almost $4 million. As it turned out that would be just about enough to pay off the death duties.

19

ROCK GOES TO LAS VEGAS AGAIN

Celine Dion's 2003 show, A New Day, established the new template for hugely lucrative Las Vegas residencies: high production values, social media photo ops and an audience primed to whoop and holler.

Not long before his death in December 1980 at the age of forty, John Lennon was heard to reflect that the worst fate that could befall any rock and roll musician was to end up playing the old hits in Las Vegas. At this point the former hero of his youth, Elvis Presley, had been doing just that for ten years, and to the mind of Lennon and many of his contemporaries this glittering strip in the Nevada desert had become the place where youthful promise went to die. In fact Las Vegas was less a place than a descriptor, a handy way of summoning an entire world of gilded decay. No other location occupied such a distinctive place in rock and roll's mental map. The gambling town in the desert was essentially a departure lounge for middle-of-the-road TV favourites like Liberace and the occasional rock luminary like Presley who had, to Lennon's mind, somehow lost their way. Playing there, he thought, was tantamount to giving up.

A great deal changed in the decade following Lennon's death. He died before MTV, before the compact disc and the iPod, let alone the internet and the smartphone. He didn't live long enough to walk down the street listening to music on a personal stereo. The year he died, guitarists in performing rock bands were still tethered to their amplifiers by snaking co-axial cables, properly balanced live sound was rare and the first jumbo screen to be employed at an outdoor event was only just being trialled. When he was alive, the live

presentation of pop music had very little use for choreography, costume changes, special stage sets, lighting design, elaborate illusions
or expensive pyrotechnics. You could count the number of female
rock stars on the fingers of one hand. This was more than would
have been required to count the number of openly gay entertainers
because there simply weren't any of those.

Were Lennon to come among us today, many of these things
would surprise him. He, who had started with skiffle, learned his
trade in Hamburg, become a star in the package tour era, been
entirely inaudible at the zenith of his career, and had only really
tasted the arena experience which was now the bread and butter of
his peers when playing with Elton John at Madison Square Garden,
would have been forced to concede that his experience was strictly
small time. Few things would surprise him half as much as the
transformation in the relationship between rock stars and Las
Vegas: in the years following his death they would collapse into
each other's arms, united by their shared enthusiasm for the latest
presentational technology and a powerful lust for money. For the
generation of rock stars that lit out for Las Vegas in the twenty-first
century it turned out to be anything but the last-chance saloon that
Lennon had in mind. For many of them Las Vegas turned out to be
the best payday they ever had.

There was a long history of Vegas being able to attract performers from unexpected quarters. In 1955, when it was first becoming
established as America's premier tourist destination, the owners
of the Desert Inn, some of whom did not encourage close scrutiny,
approached Noël Coward with what he described as 'an offer from
another planet'. Coward, who needed the money at the time, assented.
(The fact that even the most famous, most successful and most
apparently wealthy performers are from time to time in need of
urgent replenishment of their funds is a factor insufficiently borne
in mind even to this day. The rich have the same money problems

as we do; the only difference is these involve larger figures.) Coward signed up for a month of appearances and evidently enjoyed being able to use the facilities of the venue to provide the audience with a thoroughly five-star production. Out of it came a very distinguished live album in which he can be heard paying heartfelt tributes to the quality of the staff who were running his Vegas show.

These high-calibre people were attracted to Las Vegas by the same thing as the stars. As veteran historian of the city Marc Cooper observes, in Las Vegas the sole currency is currency. In the fifties and sixties the entertainers were paid big bucks in order to attract the gamblers who made the place so profitable. After the eighties, when the mobsters got out of town and the big entertainment conglomerates moved in, the city continued to trade on its louche reputation – in 2001 George Clooney and Brad Pitt starred in a remake of *Ocean's Eleven*, the 1960 heist movie in which Frank Sinatra and Dean Martin sold the world on the dream of Las Vegas as a place where bad behaviour was granted a weekend pass – but was increasingly keen to attract people who would pay handsomely to see shows featuring their favourite musical names. These could be new or they could be established. All that mattered was that they could fill a ninety-minute set with songs everybody in the audience knew. Vegas was no place to unveil your new album. As if anyone would be interested in your new album.

It was no longer a question of playing to people more concerned with dining, drinking or gambling. In March 2003 the Canadian singer Celine Dion pointed the way when she began a residency at the Colosseum, the four-thousand-capacity theatre attached to Caesars Palace. When Sinatra had played the Sands in 1966 the only back-up he needed was provided by Count Basie and his band. By the time Dion was playing Caesars Palace the expectations of audiences had changed, meaning there had to be troupes of dancers filling the vast stage and small armies of people bearing the title 'director' behind it. The show was called *A New Day*, presumably in order to counter the unspoken identification of Vegas with the twilight of a career and also to chime with a new Vegas tradition whereby shows of any kind always had some pretensions to a concept. The chief conceptualist here was Franco Dragone, who had worked with Cirque du Soleil, the French-Canadian outfit whose extravagant approach to presentation was making the efforts of the music people look strictly end-of-the-pier.

This was what the public demanded. Whereas the people who had gone to see Sinatra at the Sands had been primarily attracted by the pull of music, something other was demanded in the Age of Spectacle. What the new century called for was a show that was a celebration of its star, a show that was utterly intoxicated with its own sense of importance. Dion's production was devised for the twenty-first-century audience, for whom polite applause could never properly express their enthusiasm – a feeling better articulated by a barrage of whoops and hollers. The early reviews of the extravaganza tended to point out that its least impressive parts were those where the singer was alone on stage just singing. This didn't seem to bother the customers, who were happy to pay just to be in the same place as anyone who was both famous and fabulous. The original plan was for Dion's residency at the Colosseum to last a year. It was eventually extended for five years, during which time she performed for over three million people and grossed just under $400 million. This kind of turnover unsurprisingly got the attention of those artists who might previously have looked down their noses at the idea of playing Vegas.

In 2004 Elton John moved into the same venue to alternate with Dion with a show with the conceptual title *The Red Piano*. This was designed by the extravagant fashion photographer David LaChapelle who, remarked Elton, had reached the point in his career when he couldn't take so much as a holiday snap of someone without getting them to dress up like Jesus. LaChapelle's production turned even the essentially sedentary prospect of the fifty-seven-year-old Elton running through his Greatest Hits into a visual feast by having every song accompanied by specially shot videos, most of them featuring actors who were younger and more toned than any of the musicians who were on the stage. Still playing the drums behind Elton was Nigel Olsson, who'd been doing the same job since 1970 when an Elton John gig meant hauling your kit up the stairs to play above a furniture shop in Birmingham.

Vegas appealed to performers who liked some fuss along with their money. Cher was planning her sixty-second birthday when she began her 2008 residency at the same venue by unobtrusively descending from the ceiling in a golden chariot. During her set she did seventeen songs. Designer Bob Mackie had devised a different costume for every single one, each of which had been created to recall the look that accompanied the video at the time of the original hit. As far as the audience was concerned, this was money well spent. Nobody asked for their admission back because they had come for spectacle rather than music. In fact they weren't so much attending a concert as being granted an audience. And since these already wealthy artists were hired to perform exactly the same set every night in front of what was effectively the same audience in the same room in a city they would ordinarily go to considerable lengths to avoid, it's safe to assume these shows paid them the kind of money that even the rich with their retinues of employees and other dependants find impossible to refuse. At the time of writing, Cher, now seventy-seven, is due to play another residency in Las Vegas. This is more than twenty years since she announced what was supposed to be a modest fifty-date tour of the USA at the end of which she planned to retire.

A Las Vegas residency meant that the kind of artists who could no longer rely on a steady stream of royalty income from record sales could earn big money from live performance without having to submit to the exhausting and spirit-sapping business of touring. Furthermore, in such a Las Vegas 'sit down' it was possible to control every element of the production and have the audience come to you rather than you having to go to them. The companies vying for paying customers on the Strip were always building new venues, each of which had a sound-and-light system which redefined state of the art, and hence they could approach big-name acts, challenging them to invent a show for their venue, the kind of show that couldn't be done anywhere else.

This combination of the massive cultural footprint of Boomer idols with the new technology of entertainment and the generous budgets that were available in Las Vegas would redefine the big show for the twenty-first century. When the deal was struck between Cirque du Soleil and the Beatles to bring the Beatles' songs to Vegas in a show called *Love* they constructed a special building in which to house it. *Love* began in 2006 and is still running at the time of writing. It seems fair to assume everybody got their money back long ago. This show pointed the way to a future in which you would be able to charge superstar ticket prices without requiring the superstars to be involved at all.

In the days when Vegas was earning its reputation, the audiences wore their best clothes as a mark of respect for performers in tuxedos. They admired high-kicking showgirls and similar militaristic displays of synchronicity. In the twenty-first century the audiences, who were if anything more prosperous than their forerunners, would turn up in expensive branded sportswear and there would be as much plastic surgery in the stalls as there was on stage. They preferred shows with the dream-like quality they had found in pop videos. To satisfy this craving Vegas invested more and more in screens until in 2023 U2, a band which on the face of it ought to have been even less likely to warm to Sin City than John Lennon, inaugurated their sixth decade as a live act with the residency at a new Vegas venue called the Sphere, which seated almost twenty thousand people within what was effectively the world's largest LED screen. The kinetic phantasmagoria on the outside of this giant globe was sufficient to distract the pilots of planes coming into Las Vegas airport; the deserts, skyscrapers and cloudscapes, which formed the background to the band's performance, provided ticket holders on the inside with an experience certainly more expansive than rock shows had ever been able to provide. This, its boosters promised, would bring the band's music to life in entirely new ways – a statement which conceded that the Age of Spectacle was entering a new phase. The promise of music alone was no longer enough; as U2 entered their golden years, reaching the age where the members of a band curse the advent of the high-definition camera, their fans would be invited to Las Vegas. Here they would pay top dollar effectively to watch them on TV.

The most telling part of the show came towards the end when the house lights went up and they played 'Beautiful Day'. At this point, because the Sphere's seating is steeply banked, it was suddenly possible for the members of U2 – all gentlemen from Dublin in their sixties who, for reasons best known to themselves, perform indoors wearing sunglasses and woolly hats – to have face-to-face contact with their actual audience, who were of course a largely white bunch of real estate agents, insurance executives, school teachers and retirees, the bulk of whom were only slightly younger than the band on stage and no longer moved with the easy, unselfconscious grace of youth. They say you should dance like nobody is watching. They did their best, swaying without total commitment while keeping an eye on their purses and phones. Bono tried encouraging them; he told them they were beautiful. In fact both band and audience looked faintly embarrassed to be caught doing what they were doing in, of all places, Las Vegas.

20

LED-ZE

When Led Zeppelin played Knebworth in 1980, you could get a ticket for less than £10. When they played the 02 in 2007 somebody paid £83,000 for a ticket.

LED ZEPPELIN'S HOT TICKET

At the end of 2005 the music business trade magazine *Billboard* listed the acts that had made the most money from touring in the previous twelve months. It wasn't simply dominated by those who had made their names in the previous century, it was monopolized by them. In that year the Eagles, Bon Jovi, Paul McCartney, the Rolling Stones and U2 all had tours which grossed many millions of dollars. All were nominally connected to new albums of one kind or another, but it was no longer expected that the exposure of a cross-country trip would be justified by sales returns. In fact Bon Jovi's was in support of a record which sold about a thirtieth of the numbers they had sold back in the eighties. Nobody was coming to hear anything new from these bands. They were hoping the bands would, in the words of a popular T shirt slogan, 'play some old'.

The economy of the music business was in the process of shifting from a model based on the selling of recorded music to one based on how much money you could take out of the market in exchange for live appearances. The record business was fading away but the music business seemed to be in ruder health than it had been for years. This was thanks in part to the fact that acts were no longer constrained by the feeling that their products were being bought by 'the kids'. They were now selling to middle-aged adults. The business they were in was no more price-sensitive than the market for high-end restaurants. The people making bets on this business had long felt that concert tickets were undervalued. They had been priced artificially low because it was felt that the primary job of live appearances was to publicize a record and because no band wishes to be seen to be charging the kind of money that the market would clearly bear.

Live was once the poor relation of the music business. The big names of the sixties and seventies had come up playing repurposed cinemas such as the Finsbury Park Astoria, university canteens like the one where the Who recorded *Live At Leeds* and even engine-turning sheds such as the Roundhouse in north London. When the Rolling Stones played their Farewell to Britain tour in 1971, prior to reorienting themselves towards the United States, the venues were predominantly Victorian town halls where the capacity would be no more than a couple of thousand. When on 20 November of the same year Led Zeppelin took their show to Wembley, the cavernous venue in the outer suburbs of north London was still called the Empire Pool in reference to its original use for Olympic swimming events and seasonal spectaculars on ice. Over two nights in this space, which was so vast that fans unaccustomed to this kind of scale spent a lot of time looking around them, they sold over twenty-five thousand tickets. The following night they were back in the old routine, playing the Public Hall in Preston, Lancashire, for an audience whose tickets may have cost them as little as a pound.

During the subsequent decade inflation raged every bit as much for music fans as it did for everyone else, but the relationship between the price of live music and the price of recorded music remained much the same. Simply put, live music was cheap and recorded music was expensive. Consequently fans would pay twice as much for Led Zeppelin's new album as they might to see them live. By the time the original line-up of the group had played what proved to be their final show together in 1980 in Berlin it was in front of a crowd of six thousand who were paying less than £5 each, which was by then roughly comparable with what they might have paid for their most recent record release, *In Through The Out Door*. When they had played Knebworth earlier in the summer of 1980, tickets for the whole day's entertainment had cost £7.50. By the time Queen played the same open-air show in 1986, the price of a ticket had doubled but they could still be bought on the day. This was still a business where the majority of transactions were made in cash. It wouldn't be long before it would no longer be sensible to carry around the amount of cash it would take to buy a ticket for a prestige live show.

The prime mover in this change was Bob Sillerman, an American businessman who took advantage of changes in regulation to buy up the radio stations which were vital to making sure people knew which shows were coming. Having done this, he did the same with the regional promoters who would bring the big acts to your city. Then he bought up the actual venues. By the end of the nineties it was no longer possible to tour the United States without dealing with Sillerman's companies. Having built up this enormous business he sold it to the radio chain Clear Channel Communications in 2000 for more than $4 billion. Five years later they spun it off into a company with the misleadingly folkloric name Live Nation. Five years after that, by which time live entertainment had become all about credit cards and online sales, they merged with Ticketmaster, and the modern live music business was born. In this steely new world there would be no room for mavericks and visionaries.

Between 1996 and 2003 the average price for a concert ticket in the United States rose by 82 per cent and it didn't stop there. A ticket for a seat on the floor when Bruce Springsteen played Giants Stadium in the latter year was $77. The internet changed the game.

Tickets for music shows had once gone to those who queued up all night or sent the right cheque with the right stamped addressed envelope to the right box office on the right day. It was never free from profiteering. The internet suddenly made scalping a game anyone could play. Order your four-ticket allocation from the comfort of your own home on your own credit card or your parents' and if you were successful in securing them you could sell two of them and make enough money to cover your outlay. The internet introduced dynamic pricing long before it was dignified by a euphemism. Managers quickly realized that people were paying far more for the tickets than they were charging and they didn't see why their acts shouldn't have the difference.

These giant companies would often pay the artists over the odds, knowing they could pass on the increased cost in ticket prices, purely because their priority was securing the tour and being able to sell high-value sponsorship on the back of it. This would increasingly be a business where the performer would take all the money from tickets, and the promoters would make their living out of the additional revenue streams, from parking to merchandise to alcohol sales. Jimmy Buffett achieved legendary status in this new dispensation by demanding and getting 105 per cent of the ticket income on the basis that his parrot-headed fans had such a powerful thirst that the promoter could do quite well out of beer sales alone. When Clear Channel spoke of their customers, they were referring to the blue-chip advertisers and sponsors rather than the people who bought the tickets. Suddenly everybody had dollar signs for eyes. Michael Cohl, who had revolutionized the rock and roll touring business with the Rolling Stones' Steel Wheels tour in 1989, was proposing to buy 80 per cent of the Stones – live music, publishing, merchandise and all – for $280 million. In the end the market wasn't convinced and Mick and Keith decided they weren't comfortable entering into such a long-term arrangement when they were still in their sixties.

When work began in 2003 on building the twenty-thousand-capacity indoor arena which was to be known as the O2 inside the shell of what had once been the Millennium Dome, it was the first time a building had been erected in London for the purpose of live entertainment since construction started on the Royal Albert Hall in 1867. After more than a hundred and thirty years, here was a venue designed with the requirements of twenty-first-century light and sound in mind. No wonder the three living ex-members of Led Zeppelin chose this as the place to pay tribute to their late mentor Ahmet Ertegun, raise money for charity and compensate for those rather half-baked reunions they had staged since they closed for business in 1980. For this December 2007 show they rehearsed properly, once again with the son of their late drummer supplying percussion; this time there would be no last-minute squabble in the wings about whether it was a good idea to play 'Stairway To Heaven'. It was a straight Greatest Hits. No funny business.

The *Guinness Book of Records* gave them a prize for having attracted twenty million requests for tickets, which meant there were a thousand people wishing to occupy every single seat. Kenneth Donnell paid £83,000 for a ticket in an auction for a British children's charity. He was twenty-five at the time and explained that he was gutted he was not born in the sixties and had not been able to see them in the seventies. People came from all over the world – an early indication of how some people now planned their travel around prestige shows. The guest list included Paul McCartney, Mick Jagger, David Gilmour, Noel Gallagher, Dave Grohl and Priscilla Presley. The reviews remarked on the fact that they didn't seem at all rusty. The writer from the *New Yorker*, one of the many high-toned media outlets covering the event, publications which would have given them the shortest of shrift back in the days of their pomp, pointed out that this was more remarkable in the case of Led Zeppelin because they had always advertised the extent of their horniness and the fullness of their trousers and it was difficult to do that with a straight face when a group's collective age amounted to 224.

It was widely assumed that this would be the precursor to a world tour in the course of which for the first time they would earn as much respect as cash. When they had been storming the world in the seventies, fashionable opinion was utterly against them. Now that decades in the A&R laboratory had failed to produce a hard rock band capable of getting anywhere near their cavalier swagger and the producers of hip hop records seemed to be reaching for the Led Zeppelin pill whenever they needed something with the requisite quality of heaviosity, it seemed as good a time as any to pronounce them the originators, most distinguished practitioners and owners in perpetuity of an entire category of music. Surely this one night of vindication would be just the beginning of a worldwide lap of honour.

It wasn't to be. It turned out they had done enough to make their point and to erase the memory of previous reunions which had not been as satisfactory as they would have liked. When they were asked about a return to full operations in interviews they obfuscated as though they had never really discussed it, as if none of them had the diplomatic skills it would take to forge some kind of working agreement that would allow them to do so without it taking over their entire lives. It was widely felt that the reason it wasn't happening was because Robert Plant, who had the most developed solo career of the three, didn't relish the idea of the scrutiny he would inevitably come under as the man out front. It's a lot easier to age in a dignified fashion when you're securely behind an instrument than it is when the only thing between you and the audience is a pair of trousers and, in theory at least, underwear. In one interview talking about

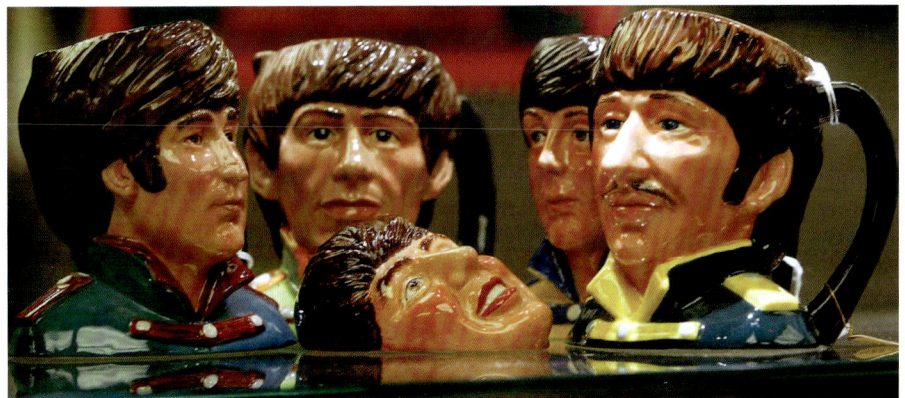

As the trade in rock-associated memorabilia raged in the twenty-first century, smart auction houses in Bond Street and Manhattan were only too happy to bring their gavels down on anything from Royal Doulton Beatles mugs (**above**) to Freddie Mercury's extensive collection of kimonos (**below**).

As recorded music became impossible to avoid and effectively free to consume, initiatives such as the annual Record Store Day underlined how much some people hankered for the scarcity of old and the scratch-prone reassurance of what were now known as 'vinyls' (**right**).

*For heads of state the honouring of old rock stars was a win-win. President Barack Obama presented Led Zeppelin (**above**) with a Kennedy Center honour for their 'lifetime contribution to American culture', while the then Prince of Wales waved the traditional sword over Sir Ivan Morrison (**below**).*

*When Elizabeth II came to the British throne in 1953, the rock revolution had not begun. When she celebrated fifty years in 2003, the likes of Paul McCartney, Tony Iommi, Cliff Richard and the Corrs (**above**) were part of a new establishment, and the national anthem could be performed by Brian May of Queen from the roof of Buckingham Palace (**below**).*

In politics as in pop, when you're hot everybody wants to be your friend; in 1993 Fleetwood Mac, whose song had been a campaign theme, reunited to perform at Bill Clinton's inaugural celebrations (**above**).

Brian Wilson posed with Paul Dano (**left**) and John Cusack, the actors playing him at different ages in the 2014 film Love & Mercy, while Taron Egerton (**below**) pointed out how keen the real Elton John was to promote Rocketman's version of his life, which came out in 2019.

The organizers of rock museum exhibits sought to overcome the ephemeral nature of the form by showcasing Pink Floyd through *Their Mortal Remains* at London's V&A (**above**) and glass-casing what remains of the piano on which 'Like A Rolling Stone' was written at the Bob Dylan Center in Tulsa (**below**).

*Whereas twentieth-century Glastonbury Festival-goers saw roughing it as part of the experience (**above**), their twenty-first century children and grandchildren have the option of paying a supplement and glamping their way through it (**below**).*

*Via the Sunday afternoon slot at the Glastonbury Festival senior citizens of showbiz such as Dame Shirley Bassey (**above**), who paired her £50,000 dress with a pair of diamanté-encrusted wellingtons, could be reborn as absolute legends.*

*In 2001, on the thirtieth anniversary of Jim Morrison's death in Paris, fans gathered at his graveside in Père Lachaise Cemetery (**below**), some of them wielding unexpectedly religious symbols.*

*Among the mourners gathered for the 2023 funeral of Shane MacGowan of the Pogues were President of Ireland Michael D. Higgins, Johnny Depp, Bob Geldof, the former leader of Sinn Féin Gerry Adams and representatives of an entirely new generation of fans (**above**).*

*And then there were three (**above**): on the occasion of the release of* Hackney Diamonds, *their first record of new material in nearly twenty years, Ron Wood, Mick Jagger and Keith Richards made a point of looking animated.*

the O2, Plant spoke about the effort it had taken to get, as he called it, 'in character'. And of course the character he had been trying once more to occupy was that of a twenty-four-year-old man in tight trousers who had sung as though he wanted to get the world into bed. Now he was sixty-five and, it seemed reasonable to assume, had a different agenda.

Washington politicos line up for Glen Campbell's autograph after a Library of Congress concert to raise awareness of Alzheimer's disease.

21

GLEN CAMPBELL FORGETS

On 30 November 2011, Glen Campbell played the Ryman Auditorium in Nashville, Tennessee. The audience sat, as they had always done, in hard church pews. The Ryman had been opened in 1892 as a tabernacle for a famous revivalist preacher. In 1943 it became the home of the Grand Ole Opry, the regular radio show which became to rural America what *The Ed Sullivan Show* had been to the America beyond the pick-up truck.

Campbell was never strictly a country star but his appeal certainly stretched into the country of country. Although he came from Pike County, Arkansas, Los Angeles was where he did his work and made his name. He had moved there in 1960 to play guitar on recording sessions. Here he was just as likely to be called for Frank Sinatra as for Sonny and Cher. Happily Glen's talents went beyond the guitar. He could sing too. In fact Glen was such a good singer he could make terrible material sound like gold, which was why publishers paid him to cut demos of the often third-rate songs proffered to Elvis for inclusion in his movies. When Glen was unleashed on good material he could make it sound brilliant. In these endeavours his key partner was writer Jimmy Webb, another country boy who had pulled up those roots at the first possible opportunity, gleefully embracing a far from righteous life in Hollywood's fast lane, all paid for by singing the praises of Phoenix, Galveston and Wichita.

In a country where so much music is also about geography, Glen's was a good business. A very good business. In fact in 1968 Glen Campbell sold more records in the United States than the Beatles. In the early seventies he had his own high-rating TV show. Glen made a lot of money, but like many stars he also spent a lot of money, much of it on three divorce settlements. He accumulated a great deal of responsibilities. Beginning when he was seventeen, he fathered nine children. All these obligations didn't make him a natural home body. According to Alice Cooper, who has some claim to be an expert in these matters, nobody did more cocaine than Glen Campbell. None of this would have been evident to the outside world. On the surface, Glen maintained the clean-cut choirboy exterior he had presented when replacing Brian Wilson in the touring Beach Boys in the mid-sixties.

When in 2011 at the age of seventy-five he told the world he had been diagnosed with Alzheimer's he wasn't the first popular musician to do so. He was however the first to announce alongside such news the schedule of a 150-date farewell tour which would take him to three continents. Was this a cruel and unusual punishment to inflict on an elderly man of failing health or was it the greatest gift one could possibly bestow on him?

Most of us don't get to continue doing the thing we love right through till the end. The touring musician, even one with Alzheimer's, is different. He has more chance of being able to persevere with his calling than the accountant who looks after his money or the nurse who takes his temperature. When he goes among his people it's often hard to decide who is deriving the greatest benefit from the experience. The audience secretly enjoy the delicious sadness of a near-deathbed meeting with somebody they have never really known; there's a certain cachet in being able to say you saw this or that person during their last go-round. From the other side of the footlights, the performer savours the milk of human kindness in the form in which he has grown to prefer it: applause.

Campbell's final tour was only possible because most of the people involved in it were either family or had been working for him so long they might as well have been. They had all begun the tour apprehensive in different ways about what might await them. For the professionals there was the standard concern about whether the star would let the show down. For those connected to him by ties of blood was added the more pressing concern that their father or husband would let himself down in front of thousands of people.

Then there was the audience. Would they show up? The tour manager at first feared that people would only come in the secret hope of seeing a legend fall apart in front of them. But then, after seeing the crowds, the old fans who flocked to see him in the heartland and the hipsters who came when the tour reached the coasts, he decided that maybe he should have given his fellow man more credit. If there were nights when Glen happened to play a song twice because he had forgotten he had already played it they were prepared to regard it as one of those charming things that big stars do.

Might it be possible to justify his staying on the road as the best way of managing his condition as it continued its inevitable process of deterioration? Being a touring musician is often compared with being in the armed forces in that the question of what to do today, the question that occupies most people in their senior years, is taken out of their hands by a tour schedule and a road manager, and in Campbell's case, by his wife – his fourth, Kim, herself a former Radio City Rockette. She understood that being able to exercise the performing muscles could play a vital role in keeping depression at bay, filling every hour of the day with something which urgently needed to be done exactly as it had been done the day before. She also knew that those who have been carried through life by the loudly expressed love of live audiences find it hard to do without them. No matter how badly the rest of the day may have gone, whenever eight o'clock rolled round once more they had the opportunity to go out and repair their life again. Most of us aren't granted that privilege. If we were we would probably keep doing it as long as Glen Campbell did.

Music, particularly American music, is above all a business and therefore this was no gentle farewell. If he had completed the whole itinerary he would have played the full 150 shows, a Stakhanovite work rate for a semi-retired person in need of medical care. But this is how the economy works, particularly in the streaming era. Since he didn't write 'Rhinestone Cowboy' or 'Wichita Lineman' and he was no longer a big seller of records, the only way he could make money was by going on the road. His wasn't the only mouth to feed. The beneficiaries would not just have been the star. There were also the three young family members who were in his band, for whom backing Dad was simply taking part in the family business.

There were additional duties on his 2011/12 tour. Since he had gone public on his condition politicians and policymakers were keen to enlist his celebrity to spotlight the slow-moving health emergency represented by the coming reckoning between the Baby Boomers and the various ways in which they could lose their grip on the world. Campbell visited Congress and listened while Nancy Pelosi talked about what a priority this ought to be for the nation. On the film that recorded the tour the likes of Bruce Springsteen and Chad Smith of the Red Hot Chili Peppers popped up to mention their own family experiences in dealing with dementia and their understanding that this was something likely to affect them and their audiences. The Edge of U2 pointed out that the way musicians with some form of mental impairment can still play music is a form of magic. Certainly Campbell never lost his place in a guitar solo. He might forget the key, but once he set out on a solo his fingers still delivered him safely to the close. He still had the gifts. What might give him more of a problem was to know where and when to deploy them. He could do 'Duelling Banjos' with his daughter because she played the lines first and he followed them. Muscle memory didn't seem to let him down. Like an athlete, he had to make sure he didn't let his mind get in the way of his body. The voice might not be quite as golden as before but it was still uniquely noble.

Inevitably, however, it went wrong from time to time. During that show at the Ryman Auditorium in Nashville, the performance had to be stopped when something happened that would never have befallen Roy Acuff or Merle Haggard or any of the army of performers who had trod the same boards in the past. During the opener, 'Gentle On My Mind', the John Hartford song which he had played every night since he recorded it in 1967, the teleprompter from which he was reading the words failed. There was an embarrassing pause. The band stopped. Glen stood awkwardly centre stage and wondered aloud if anybody had brought with them the means of getting around the problem. He had difficulty communicating what he wanted. He couldn't remember the word for words.

The longer the tour went on the more dependent he became on that teleprompter. As more and more shows of all kinds have to be synchronized with lighting cues or special effects, more and more live acts use teleprompters as a way to make sure the star doesn't go off-script. Stars of any kind are accompanied by courtiers whose job is to reduce the amount of time they have to think for themselves. This is even more the case if that star has Alzheimer's. Eventually Campbell could only introduce his own children by reading their names on the teleprompter. When Paul McCartney came backstage to congratulate him on his appearance at the Grammys he was gratified. But it was not clear that he understood who his well-wisher was.

The tour did not complete its projected 150 dates. By the time he had done more than a hundred shows he was getting increasingly erratic, wandering out of the lights, mangling the cues, complaining of the cold and succumbing to temper tantrums in the face of the slightest reverse. His wife thought it would probably help if people avoided the terminology of modern medicine and just talked about Grandpa getting forgetful, the way people used to do in the old days. On the other hand, when you're in showbiz every life event, whether happy or not, is also a promotional opportunity and nobody ever got a Lifetime Achievement Award from the Grammys with the full build-up from star du jour Taylor Swift just because Grandpa was getting a little forgetful.

Thus it was that on 30 November 2012, Glen Campbell, seventy-six years old and a professional musician since his teens, played his last show at the Uptown Theater in Napa in the wine country of northern California. He wasn't aware this was his last show because by this point on the farewell tour, which had begun early the previous year, he had trouble processing any but the most concrete aspects of his daily life.

Campbell went home and retired, eventually moving into an assisted living facility near Nashville where he died in 2017. Following his death three of his children from previous marriages took legal action because they weren't beneficiaries of his will. It was only too easy for lawyers to cast his fourth wife as the schemer who had sought to promote her own children at the expense of the offspring of these earlier unions, at least one of whom was by now a great-grandparent. Similarly it was easy for the *Daily Mail* to pluck a figure of $50 million out of the air when they sought to estimate how much his estate was worth. As Eamonn Forde points out in his book about musical estates, *Leaving the Building*, this was on the fantastical side. The Probate Court put it nearer to $1 million. As in rock star life so in rock star finances: the truth would have been somewhere between the two extremes.

22

Following his cancer diagnosis in 2013, the Dr Feelgood guitarist found himself feted by the likes of Elton John as he embarked on a nine-year lap of honour.

WILKO IN THE
VALLEY OF
THE SHADOW

As the advertising on which newspapers had depended for so long migrated to the internet, the early decades of the twenty-first century saw the printed media in the grip of a crisis of confidence. As its erstwhile readers appeared to be able to get along without many of the things it had traditionally provided, it increasingly fell back upon those editorial elements its readers clearly couldn't get enough of. One of these was the rock star obituary. In this period, those keeping a weather eye on the relevant pages of the formerly heavy papers had an opportunity to reflect on what appeared to be the newly broadened church of rock's glorious dead. This was educational. Performers who would have had some trouble getting arrested by the arts pages while they were actually walking around and plying their trades were, once they were dead, considered perfectly good for eight hundred words among the obits; here, in the magnificent equality of death, the fallen foot soldiers of rock took their place among the nation's great and the good, cheek by jowl with deceased military officers and former government servants, attesting by their presence to the newly elevated status of these former patrons of the Speakeasy or the Blue Boar.

In the year 2013, for instance, this kind of treatment was accorded the following, among many others: Reg Presley of the infallibly entertaining Troggs, the man whose colourful views on drummers passed into history along with the *Troggs Tapes*; that early employer of Paul McCartney and John Lennon in Germany, Tony Sheridan, who spent his last days designing coats of arms; that languid Lothario of the Canterbury Scene Kevin Ayers; and the man whose sheer fretboard velocity on the show-stopping 'Going Home' at Woodstock had made him the briefly world-famous Alvin Lee; Richie Havens, the man who opened that same festival by pounding up and down singing the single word 'Freedom' again and again; that singer of bar-room laments George Jones, who enjoyed legendary standing among people who had never actually heard him sing thanks to the story about him setting off to the local bar on a ride-on lawnmower, this being the only vehicle to hand at the time; Ray Manzarek, the man who imprinted himself on the consciousness of more than one generation with that one solo on the Doors' 'Light My Fire'; Trevor Bolder, the dewlapped bassist from Hull who appeared puzzled by his costume as he stood alongside David Bowie on the one edition of *Top of the Pops* that everyone remembers; the great rhythm and blues singer Bobby Bland, who defined the singing style that others such as Rod Stewart went on to emulate; Jackie Lomax, the old mate from Liverpool that George Harrison brought into Apple; Junior Murvin, the reggae singer whose big tune 'Police And Thieves' was covered by the Clash; Noel Harrison, that scion of Hollywood royalty who had one hit called 'Windmills Of Your Mind' – but what a one hit; and Lou Reed, of whom you might say very much the same. All, it seemed, were honourable men and colourful characters.

It wasn't just the heavy papers that latched on to rock star death as a fruitful area. It also soon became a staple of the micro messaging site Twitter, which was just starting to reach critical mass around the same time. Assuring your followers that you were personally broken up about the passing of a sleeve-note name from the past fulfilled the double purpose of social media: it reminded others of your existence, while advertising your own good taste and sensitivity. Death appeared to have the happy effect of making everyone seem simultaneously cooler and more popular. People seemed to be attracted to artists who were no longer in a position to let them down. This particularly applied to solo singer-songwriters such as Nick Drake, under-appreciated in his time and over-venerated as a consequence many years later.

There was a tourism angle as well. Of the ten most-visited graves in the USA, just one is the resting place of a president. The rest are all the graves of entertainers. The majority of those are musical entertainers, with whom we seem to have a stronger bond than their peers in other spheres. Their popularity speaks volumes for the fact that fans feel they are somehow members of their family who were unaccountably never invited round when the distinguished cousin was alive; these people are far more likely to turn up to pay tribute to a member of a band whose single they once bought than they are to do the same thing for any actor they once bought a movie ticket for. Whatever their avowed attitude to organized religion, music fans rather like the idea of having a grave to visit. In describing their journeys to the same they rarely resist the parallels with pilgrimage.

Sadly they do not always know how best to conduct themselves in these places. When guitarist Duane Allman was killed in a motorcycle accident in 1971 his grave in Rose Hill Cemetery in Macon, Georgia, began to attract people who thought it was the appropriate place to 'hang out' and smoke weed. When the Allman Brothers' bassist Berry Oakley, who also died in a motorcycle crash, was buried there the following year his grave was nearby. Once that had been done, the pilgrimage was on. Some of the alleged mourners who visited exhibited a puzzling compulsion to demonstrate their grief by leaving things behind. When Oakley's widow visited she found that some people had left beer cans and even used condoms at the grave site. Over the years that followed the Allman Brothers Band broke up, re-formed and broke up again but nothing seemed to stem the tide of visitors to the cemetery. Many of them were people who only grew up and heard the Allman Brothers many years later. For them a visit to the graves seemed as natural a part of the fan experience as joining the fan club might have been in the sixties. The detritus eventually became such a problem that the Rose Hill custodians were forced to take steps. When Duane's brother Gregg died in 2017 and was buried in the same place the graves were fenced off so that mourners could no longer use it as a place to hang. They were compelled to pay their respects from a distance.

When Doors singer Jim Morrison died in Paris in 1971 and was buried in the Père Lachaise Cemetery, the graveyard was primarily famous for being the resting place of Oscar Wilde and Edith Piaf. In the years immediately following the Lizard King's death it became more commonly known as the Jim Morrison Cemetery. It was not until 1981, when Morrison was effectively relaunched as a pop culture icon with his face on the cover of *Rolling Stone* alongside the line 'he's hot, he's sexy, he's dead', that the crowds really began coming. In 1991 his grave, which had originally been anonymous, was given a larger headstone with a bronze plaque. In a learned essay called 'The Social Construction of Sacred Space', Peter Jan Margry described how the so-called 'espace Morrison' had become a place where fans 'drank excessively, smoked, took drugs, removed their clothes, had public sex, slept and put into practice the non-conformist ideas and lifestyle championed by Morrison'. In 2004 the Père Lachaise authorities said they were so tired of the behaviour of some of the many visitors who came every year they would happily transfer Morrison to another cemetery if they could find one to take him. Having been unable to do so, they put a fence around his grave. Some fans complained that they were no longer able to touch the headstone. Is this an excess of reverence or the same sense of entitlement that makes some fans feel that their evening is not complete unless they have climbed on stage? Even the custodians of the quiet grave of Nick Drake, which is in a remote country churchyard in the Midlands, got so tired of having to sweep up the guitar picks left as votive offerings that they erected a sign telling visitors that the only acceptable tributes were floral ones.

In all these cases these custodians are having to respond to the fact that their charges have become more popular in death than they could ever have been in life. Whoever originated the apocryphal tale of a rock star's sudden death being applauded as a great career move was simply reacting to the clear and obvious fact that rock fans love nothing more than a dead idol. Once that idol is under the sod they are no longer likely to let their fans down and therefore they can instantly become more popular. Their approval index goes through the roof. At this point the previously uncommitted can join the fun. Everybody can rush to recap the part, however fleeting, the idol played in their life. It's a form of exhibitionism. The person who is known for being a long-time fan actually enjoys the sensation of being showered with condolences without having suffered any actual bereavement. The departed is ushered into the hereafter to the accompaniment of hosannas they never quite heard during their time on earth.

When Elvis Presley died in 1977, America's foremost celebrity magazine, *People*, did not put him on the cover because they no longer considered him a big enough celebrity. At the time it was still assumed that being dead made you a less appealing celebrity. This was of course the reverse of the truth. The deaths of John Lennon, Ian Curtis, Kurt Cobain and other cover-worthy idols were enormously good for business when the world was dominated by print. Then came social media. Death and social media were made for each other, making it possible to mourn without putting yourself to even the smallest inconvenience.

For the first three weeks of 2013 nobody in my social media timeline had mentioned Wilko Johnson, erstwhile leader of Dr Feelgood and at the time widely regarded as a charismatic has-been. Then he gave an interview on the BBC radio programme *Front Row* and everything changed. He used the occasion to announce that he had cancer and had been told that he had at most a year to live. An ultimatum of this kind makes anybody news, and when the subject is somebody who is simultaneously clearly a legend but also uncelebrated it seems particularly apposite. In the parlance we were just beginning to get used to, the sixty-six-year-old guitarist and band leader from Southend suddenly found himself trending.

A feeding frenzy followed, led by the professional media operatives, each of whom hurried to plug their new issue in which they had published an 'inspirational' interview. Even the people who couldn't get an interview with him – Wilko had so many requests he was having to fight them off – could point to some archive item from two years earlier which they were 'so proud' to have published. This was always declared to be 'uplifting, inspiring, sad', which had become the holy trinity of keyboard mourning. Wilko, meanwhile, suddenly had gigs to do. More than he could manage in fact. In raising their prices to reflect the unexpected rush of demand for these shows, ticket touts were accused of being callous. But they were only responding to demand, and demand was suddenly through the roof. Clearly many who previously had found they had better things to do when his annual caravan came around suddenly discovered that his progress through the valley of the shadow of death had made Wilko a very hot ticket. Everybody hurried to get in on the fun. A group struggling with the name Henry's Funeral Shoe masked their delight at the prospect of playing in front of more than three men and a dog with a tweet saying they were 'thrilled' to be supporting Wilko at the Fleece in Bristol.

Then things moved up a gear. Wilko began to be given awards. Nobody had bothered to give him awards before. *GQ* even asked him to present Elton John with some Genius award. He made a record with Roger Daltrey. They had talked about it many times before and never got round to it, but now, as Wilko said, you could never refuse a dying man, so they started. Wilko never expected to survive to see it released. But he did, and even went out and did all the publicity. Cab drivers began offering him free rides. He got a slot at Glastonbury. 'It seemed I had to get terminal cancer to be deemed worthy of their attention,' he reflected in what seemed no more than the truth.

The faint tapping of the Reaper from the corridor outside gave everybody free rein to place Wilko Johnson in a new frame which suddenly put him among the grown-ups of the world of art and religion. Julien Temple made a film called *The Ecstasy of Wilko Johnson* in which Wilko sat on the sea wall at Canvey Island and played chess with fate, Ingmar Bergman-style. The *Guardian* welcomed the film's message of 'rocking against the dying of the light', Dylan Thomas-style. Wilko Johnson, a man who since Dr Feelgood had been eclipsed by the Sex Pistols and been of interest only to hard-core pub rock holdouts, was suddenly being gushed over by everyone from daytime TV to the style magazines, all of whom love a bit of mortality.

When his diagnosis was first delivered, Wilko decided he should go and visit Japan to see the cherry blossom one last time. Between that announcement and his eventual death at the age of seventy-five in 2022 he was to return to Japan five further times. If ever a musician could be said to have enjoyed his own obituaries, that man was he. He could see the funny side of this sudden rush of attention. If this was the only way he could keep his datebook full he would, like most musicians, take it. Prior to Wilko's extra-time episode this was a privilege that could only be claimed by folk-rock fiddler Dave Swarbrick. He it was who had sat up in a hospital bed in 1999 and read the *Birmingham Mail*'s account of his apparent death. It was, he remarked, not the first time he had died in Coventry.

23

BILLY JOEL'S SATURDAY NIGHT

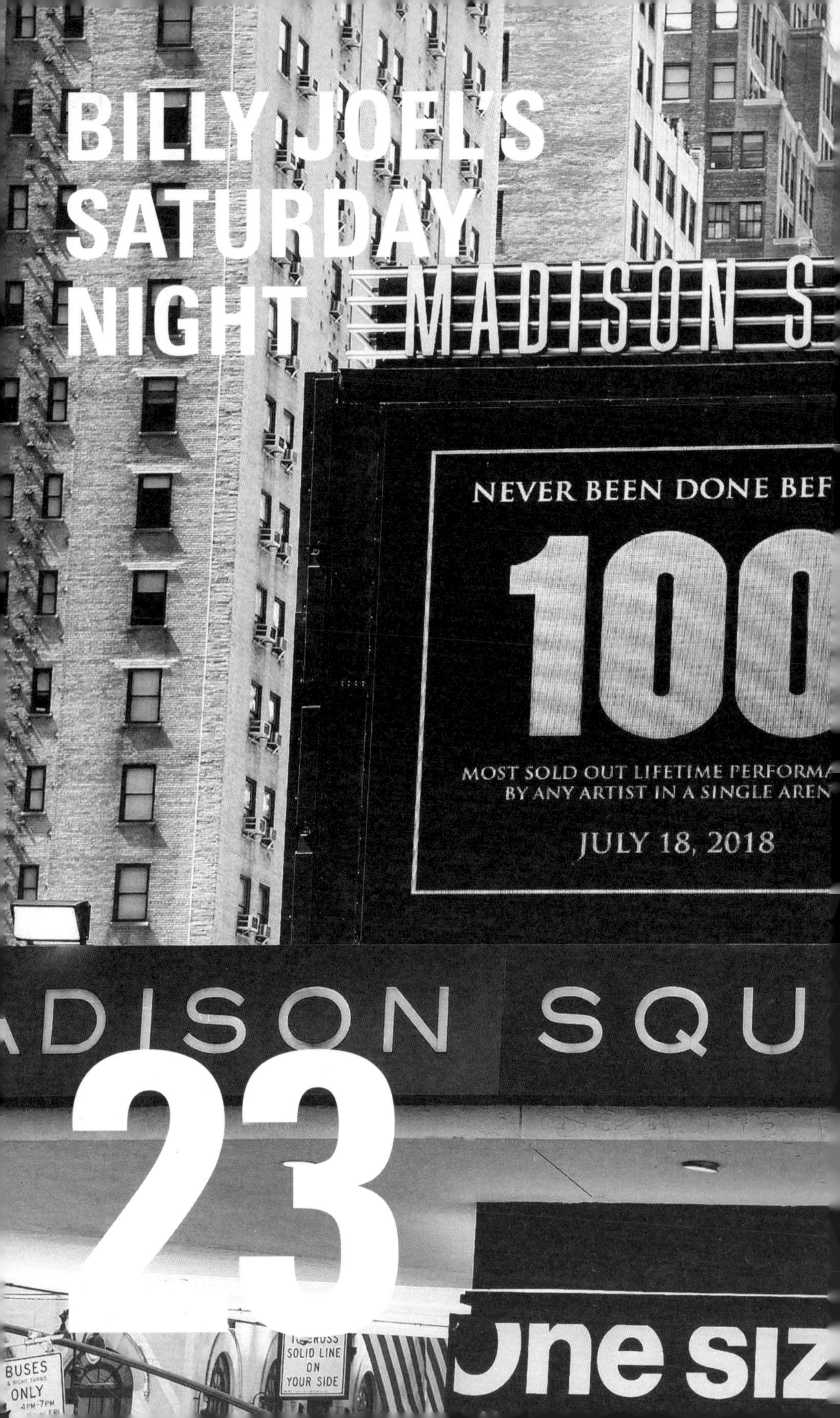

In 2014 Billy Joel announced he would be playing Madison Square Garden once a month, 'as long as the demand continues'. The series did not conclude until 2024.

Mike was born in Long Island in 1971. As a child he spent a lot of time in hospitals. Like many other young patients who would grow up to be musicians – people such as Joni Mitchell and Neil Young – he directed a lot of his youthful energies into practising and playing. By the age of thirteen Mike was a good enough piano player to be able to perform shows for money. The songs he played at those shows were learned from his parents' record collection; these were the songs of Paul McCartney, Elton John, and also Billy Joel, who had himself grown up in Long Island twenty years earlier.

As a young man, despite his obvious talent, Mike had little suc- cess with his own songs and his own albums. It was even more competitive trying to make a name in the music business in the nineties than it had been for Joel twenty years before. Approaching the age of thirty, with his wife and children still living in a trailer, Mike decided that the price of staying in the music game might be an adjustment of his expectations. An idea suggested itself. During his fourteen years playing piano bars night after night for people who weren't really listening, he had become particularly adept at performing the songs of Billy Joel – 'Just The Way You Are', 'She's Got A Way', 'Piano Man' – songs with which his audience could identify, songs they liked to join in with late in the evening. Tribute bands were just getting traction in the United States at the end of the century, and so he thought he might give one a go. American bar bands had always paid the bills by playing the hits, but a tribute band, which promised to deliver a complete evening of songs by an established favourite, was something else.

The idea of the tribute band had been born in Australia, which had always been far enough removed from the beating heart of stardom to feel that if you couldn't get close to the original then the next best thing was an act dressed up to look like the original, and rigorously enough rehearsed to sound, in many cases, better than the original. Furthermore a bunch of unknowns doing their best to entertain by sounding like the original was bound to be preferable to any other band playing some tracks from their new album. The very best of these bands enhanced the prestige of the acts they so lovingly sought to emulate. The first of them to break through in Europe were Björn Again, who came to the UK in 1991 when Europe wasn't entirely sure how they felt about Abba. For ten years following their break-up in 1982 Abba were an apparently broken brand. It was only in the early nineties when they were adopted as gay icons via covers by the British synth duo Erasure and use of their music in movies like *Priscilla, Queen of the Desert* that their record company decided the time was ripe to release a definitive compilation of their biggest tunes, which has remained in the charts ever since. David Gilmour was so enamoured of the Australian Pink Floyd that he invited them to perform at his fiftieth birthday party, claiming, in all seriousness, that he had never seen Pink Floyd before. Some, such as the Bootleg Beatles, who have been together four times as long as the band on which they're based, dress up to pay their tribute, while others, such as the Dutch group the Analogues, pride themselves on the eerie verisimilitude of their recitals of complete Beatles albums on original instruments.

Mike decided he would do the same thing for his Long Island local hero. Rather than apologizing for playing the songs of Billy

Joel, Mike formed a group that did nothing but. In honour of a Billy Joel song the group was called Big Shot.

It went well. The discovery that the public were more likely to turn out for an evening's entertainment that was guaranteed to involve songs with which they were familiar than to submit to the usual lottery of a live show came as an invigorating surprise. Big Shot soon became a way to make a living rather than just a way to keep the wolf from the door. Soon they were booking residencies, tours, special events and private parties, as many as a hundred dates a year. It went so well in fact that some of the original members bowed out because it was too much work. By then Mike was able to replace them with a couple of members of Joel's band who were looking for work between rare Billy Joel tours. Their involvement was a true vote of confidence. After that, things moved up a gear.

When Billy Joel was due to undertake a European tour in 2013 there was a need for a musician to come in to play the Billy parts during rehearsals. Mike was hired to do that job. During one such rehearsal, Joel, who was in his dressing room, heard the music coming from the stage and assumed they were playing one of his records through the PA. They weren't. What Billy was hearing was the sound of Mike being Billy. After that, Mike was signed up to play piano, and guitar, and to contribute harmonies – effectively to be a member of Billy's band. He was there to provide a second Billy Joel, albeit a younger one who could manage the tenor of Billy's early hits. When he hired him, Joel thanked him for his work over the previous thirteen years during which, he said, 'you've been keeping my songs alive on the island'.

Sex appeal had never been one of Billy Joel's calling cards but that had not prevented him from having a colourful romantic career. When he divorced his first wife, who had been his early driving force, he retained her brother as his business manager before falling out with him too, in a costly manner. His second wife was the supermodel Christie Brinkley, the very model of the 'Uptown Girl' of his biggest hit. The fact that she stood five inches taller than him meant this was one case where a rock star marrying up was more than a figure of speech. After getting hitched to his third wife in 2004 he became rather less keen to get involved in prolonged tours overseas. By 2014, a year before marrying a fourth time, to a former Morgan Stanley executive, he had come to terms with the fact that the world could get by without hearing any of his new songs, but was still very keen to hear his old ones. They were particularly keen to hear them in New York, the city with which they were so strongly identified. Therefore, in January 2014 he began a monthly residency at New York's most iconic venue, Madison Square Garden.

Billy, now in his mid-sixties, still lived on Long Island, albeit the part of Long Island with which Jay Gatsby would have been familiar as opposed to the Levittown in which he had grown up. Intriguingly, the new arrangement envisaged a season exclusively comprising home fixtures and involved a novel routine. Each Saturday evening of his Madison Square residency would begin with Billy sitting on his dock surveying the view of Oyster Bay. The house, which was on an island, sat on twenty-six acres and had been bought for $22 million in 2002. There he would wait for the vehicle that would take him to the show. After a while, he would discern the distinctive thock-thock-thock of an approaching helicopter. This would set down on the property's helipad, prior to scooping him up and then conveying him in the direction of the world's most glittering skyline. Over the months he came to love the journey, not merely because it meant not getting held up in traffic but also because the sight of those familiar canyons increased his heart rate and prepared him for the show. Clearly, if you can make it there you can make it anywhere.

At the end of the flight he was set down near the United Nations building, where a blacked-out people carrier would be waiting to whisk him directly across town and into the very bowels of the Garden. Here an elevator could convey him almost directly on to the stage in front of which representatives of the bridge and tunnel crowd, their New York Giants caps in place, high on pre-show drinks and the occasion itself, would already be as primed and whoop-ready as twenty-first-century audiences who've paid top dollar were tending to be. He would begin with 'Miami 2017 (Seen The Lights Go Out On Broadway)'. This was a song he wrote in 1975, at a time when the city was on the verge of bankruptcy and the *New York Daily News* carried the headline 'Ford To City: Drop Dead'. The passing of time and the events of 9/11 had transformed it into an anthem in celebration of the city, and nobody seemed better placed to sing that anthem than the short, wise-cracking guy with a face that seemed to belong on a cab driver's ID badge.

As the residency wore on, Billy Joel at the Garden settled into a ritual celebration of the enduring bond between an ageing audience and the pop music of their youth. The people came, as most audiences past the first flush of middle age do, primarily to validate their life choices. On a grand scale they were able to gather around the piano of the man who soundtracked their adolescence and young adulthood and simply enjoy a good wallow. Songs like 'Say Goodbye To Hollywood', 'New York State Of Mind', 'Just The Way You Are' and 'Scenes From An Italian Restaurant' acquire an extra frisson when sung in front of an audience in the heart of New York. And there's something extra in the air when a reasonable proportion of that audience have gone through a divorce or otherwise had their fenders dented by life. Finally, there's the choral catharsis of joining in. And when the audience doing that joining in are north of fifty, everything they sing ends up sounding like 'My Way'.

On occasions like these the traffic across the footlights goes in both directions, which can be difficult for both parties. Just as the eyes of the people in the audience are raking from top to toe the performers they've come to see, searching for signs of the march of time or their hearts no longer being in it, so the performers are looking out at the audience and being forcibly reminded of their own age by the fact that they are staring at a sea of faces that long ago whooped and hollered during their own fiftieth birthday celebrations. Rock stars of pensionable age understand fully that they are there for people who are in their late middle age, but that doesn't always mean they like to look at them in the front row. It can be tricky to convincingly summon the spark of some song you wrote when you were young when you're evidently singing it to the kind of people you might run into at the golf club or in the car park at the supermarket. Billy Joel was not the only performer to get round this problem by leaving parts of that region unsold and then getting his people to go and find deserving young people in distant seats and conducting them to places close to the stage that were directly in the star's eyeline. If the happy beneficiaries also turned out to be attractive and female, that was a bonus for the boys in the band.

The crowd would still be applauding the final encore when Billy's car ascended the ramp out of Madison Square Garden, headed for the United Nations building and the helicopter home. They would be flooding out of the venue and heading for the parking garage as he looked down on the estates of the robber barons of the Gilded Age. As they were joining the queues on the Long Island Expressway, Billy would be out on his porch with a small cigar as a late-night snack was prepared. In layman's terms he had ended the evening significantly richer than he had begun it. Twenty thousand people laying out the price of a good dinner for a ticket comes to a significant amount, particularly when so many of them buy a souvenir T-shirt as well. Joel came to call it 'feeding the elephant' because he understands that scores of people depend on him working to earn their daily bread, from Mike on the backing vocals through the long-serving members of his crew to the courtiers and retainers who travel in the train of a superstar. He understands that whether he likes it or not he, a long-established rock star, is also an industrial concern. It probably suits him to think that because, like most of his generation as they approach their seventies, the thought that over the years he has become psychologically dependent on the buzz of being on stage in front of twenty thousand people is faintly embarrassing to have to confess. Even though he claimed back in 1999 that he was playing his final show, more than twenty years later it's clear that there are bills to pay and urges to satisfy, and as long as that remains the case the power to retire is not within his gift.

24

David Bowie would increase the chances of passing through New York unnoticed by carrying a Greek newspaper.

ALL THE OLD DUDES

n the spring of 2006 I happened to find myself one day in Tate Modern. I happened to be in the company of Bryan Ferry. That afternoon, like most during term time, the huge gallery on the bank of the Thames was full of school parties of teenagers. None of them recognized my companion, who was sixty at the time. However, they were all accompanied by their art teachers, every single one of whom most definitely recognized him.

This was an instructive lesson in how not every pop icon of the late twentieth century automatically graduated to become one of the legends of the twenty-first, one known even by the teenagers of the time. Some people transcended their era. Others didn't. While Bryan Ferry could wander through world capitals unbothered by fans, David Bowie, who had been his peer in the middle of the seventies, had been forced to discover that the secret of merging into a crowd was to wear a hat and carry a Greek newspaper, having learned from experience that his carrying the latter would persuade those who were wondering if they might have spotted him that they were most likely to be mistaken.

Close examination of the sales charts for the period would not explain why Bowie was sustained by an aura which seemed almost godlike while Ferry turned into just another musician heading for retirement age. In truth, neither of them did great record business in the twenty-first century. Bowie did slightly better but most of his post-2000 releases had the kind of brief showing in the chart which usually indicates hardcore fans buying something out of duty and a record company keen to be able to show radio that their senior artist was still getting some traction. The full economic truth is, the only thing that counts with charts is how long you remain in them. Bowie's first chart album in 1972 remained in the list for years. Nothing after that did half as well. It's your early hits that define you for the ages. For all the talk of shape-shifting and restlessly questing, most of the people who turned out for Bowie's later tours were every bit as keen to hear the old favourites as the most conservative fans of Cliff Richard.

This was not the way it was supposed to be. David Bowie used to say he couldn't see why Mick Jagger still did 'Brown Sugar'. He reckoned he would go mad with boredom if he did the same thing. Most performers have similar love–hate relationships with their most popular songs, resenting the fact that the audiences clearly adore them more than they do. Most artists prefer to think the reason they're there is to write and record new songs – songs which, they always say in interviews, are among the best things they have ever done. That may or may not be the case. Even though careers can continue for a long time and you can still be in great demand and even score new recording contracts (very often from companies run by people who were your fans when they were teenagers), it is very unusual for an artist to go on selling records beyond their second decade. In the last decade or so of the twentieth century David Bowie put out a series of albums which were accepted with reservations by hardcore fans, respectfully noted in the public prints and pretty much ignored by the uncommitted. This was getting to be standard for those whose celebrity no longer translated into sales. There's a sense about it. Despite the assumptions the record business operates on, the number of people who want to own more than six long-playing records by a particular artist is actually quite small.

These records would be marked by interviews in the heavy papers – interviews generally conducted by people who wished they had been there before the parade had gone by – a few days of fuss on the radio and very little in the way of proper follow-through. They would go in the charts, stay there for a few weeks, then drop out, never to return. Without a hit single there was no reason to bother the wider public with them. The crabbed, unlovely format of the CD made it even tougher to make that instant magical connection with the curious record shop browser which had been made when they slapped eyes on the twelve-inch canvas that was *Low* or *Station To Station*. The market was way more crowded and it became more and more difficult to get that sort of cut-through. Bowie albums with titles like *Black Tie White Noise*, *Earthling*, *Tonight* and *Never Let Me Down* both looked and sounded like punches which didn't quite land.

Bowie knew this. When he gave interviews during his 1995 tour he described his decision to tour an album that nobody had yet heard plus a number of obscurities from his back catalogue as 'commercial suicide'. When he toured in 2002 it would be with a set that was made up of old favourites. He was only doing what all the old stagers were doing by this time. On the Rolling Stones' 2003 tour they played pretty much the whole of the accompanying retrospective album *Forty Licks*. Paul McCartney was by then appearing with a band who were to all intents and purposes a Beatles covers band, kicking off each show with a bunch of copper-bottomed smashes from the sixties, all played on the Hofner violin bass which still had pasted to it the set list from the Beatles' last show at Candlestick Park. When the Police got back together in 2007 they didn't pretend it was anything other than a last chance to make sure that they and their offspring should never know want. If, as was widely rumoured, they were mainly doing it for money and couldn't abide being with each other, they were clearly made of strong stuff to be able to rise above that antipathy for no fewer than 150 shows. Why were all these acts undertaking such massive tours at the point they should have been winding down? Because neither they, their relatives, their dependants, their interior decorators nor their investment managers could possibly conceive of passing up the chance to earn more cash than they had ever earned in their lives up to that point.

The new century opened up new vistas of money making. If you belonged in that select group of acts that had the right kind of brand recognition then you could go out and play the old songs to more people in more countries for more money than you ever would have made back in the days when those songs were burning up the chart. Phil Manzanera of Roxy Music tells the story of that band's 2001 reunion tour in his autobiography. He, Bryan Ferry and Andy Mackay had been idly toying with the idea of getting back together until the promoter offered them £7 million for a seventy-date tour, at which point it was inconceivable that they wouldn't go ahead; the only question was how big a cut of that money Ferry would get on the grounds that he was the biggest star. And was his insistence that they be joined by a troupe of glamorous dancers the ageing singer worrying that he no longer had the sexual magnetism to hold centre stage on his own?

This was the three Ages of Pop in action. We all know about the First Age, during which names are made, screams are screamed and all your audience is under the age of thirty. The Second Age takes in the middle years with their attendant embarrassments. Your old audience is too busy with work and family to bother with you. The test is to hang on for the Third Age, which is the golden one. This is when your old fans come back, bringing their children with them, paying prices that would have been considered comical when they were back in their teens, eager to have their youthful passions validated on an appropriately massive scale.

Our relationship with the pop music of our youth is unique. Its roots are sunk at a time when the clay of our personalities is at its most malleable; these roots stay as deep within us as our inclinations in the matters of religion, politics and football. Turning out to see these heroes when you are in your fifties or sixties is a perfect opportunity to demonstrate to the world that the fourteen-year-old you made the right call all those years before. You like to think you chose the right music when the truth is that the music chose you.

As these acts were heading into their golden years they began to realize, if they didn't realize it already, just how much they owed to those early songs. These were very often the songs they had written in a tearing hurry when they were in their early twenties and under the gun, in need of a new single to play on the TV show they happened to have been booked for. Even the biggest, most successful songwriter finds that when it comes down to it, all the value in his life's work amounts to about half a dozen songs he wrote when he was a kid. These would be, more often than not, the songs that gave you the right to book the big tour. They would also be your pension.

David Bowie was one of the first to take steps to realize the value of these songs. In 1997 he had been approached by an investment banker called David Pullman with a plan for safeguarding his future. The idea behind these asset-backed securities, which got a lot of exposure on the financial pages as soon as they were called Bowie Bonds, is that an insurance company would loan Bowie $55 million which he would then use to buy out the 50 per cent of his material owned by his old manager Tony Defries and thus have complete ownership of everything he'd made before 1990. The interest on the loan would then be paid from the royalty income from those records.

The bonds had a seven-year life at the end of which he had to pay the money back. The tours that he undertook during those seven years suddenly leaned a lot more on the old classic material he had previously seemed less keen on. It wasn't all smooth sailing. The arrangement went through bumpy phases. In 2004, when sales of physical product had fallen off a cliff, the bonds were re-rated by the agencies to just a notch over junk. Thankfully everyone's embarrassment was saved when iTunes steadied the market and they resumed their previous rating in time to pay back the money in 2007, thus ensuring that Bowie had hay in the barn and no longer needed to tour.

That was a relief because he no longer had the stamina required. After a lifetime of almost insane overindulgence he was beginning to look after himself, as befitting the middle-aged parent of a small child. He had even stopped smoking in 1999 and now, like most of his peers, lived his life in close consultation with his doctor, his chef and his personal trainer. Nonetheless he was forced to stop a show in Prague in 2004 after feeling chest pains. He apologized and left the stage, returning later having taken some medication; he attempted to resume from a stool but then left the stage for good saying that he was in too much discomfort to continue. It seems inevitable that in the future we will be able to go on YouTube and see a rock hero dying on stage while the audience whoops on oblivious to the fact that at such a moment they really shouldn't be there.

Fortunately, that wasn't the outcome on this occasion, and David Bowie was able to treat it as a warning sign of what was bound to happen if he kept on touring. Which is why he was able to spend the last ten years of his life pleasing himself and his family. He seemed to spend a lot of that time impressing other celebrities rather than the public. The former group always appeared intrigued by the fact that somebody who had seemed to devote such energy to styling himself as an alien should, when encountered in person, be such a regular fellow from south London. Neil Tennant of the Pet Shop Boys was impressed that Bowie's lunch was the same sandwich shop baguette as everybody else's. All these stars went into their first encounter with him thinking they were the biggest David Bowie fan on the planet, and came out of the encounter disarmed by his normality.

During those later years of doing nothing but reading, spending time with his family and looking at pictures, Bowie's stock rose all over again. The widespread assumption that he had retired into private life and would not be heard from again meant he was now securely established as an immovable item of the cultural furniture, suddenly familiar far beyond his hardcore fans, quietly invested into Britain's select company of 'national treasures', the titles of his old songs being repurposed for movies and TV series, his sartorial history plundered for a best-selling collection of budget clothing at Target, his cameo on Ricky Gervais's *Extras* outshining the other, far more box-office names, an exhibition of his worldly goods selling thousands of tickets for London's Victoria and Albert Museum. It seemed he was never bigger than when he was doing nothing.

After ten years he suddenly felt the urge to make a record again. He called his old collaborator Tony Visconti and they were in the studio the very next day. During the time it took to make the record word never got out, partly because the musicians had to sign non-disclosure agreements and partly because Bowie knew he wasn't in a tearing hurry to put it out and wasn't keen to get involved in the usual pre-release process of overplanning. *The Next Day* came out without fanfare in 2013 and was better received as a consequence of its lack of fanfare. Three years later he put out another one called *Blackstar*. Even his producer and closest collaborator didn't know how ill he was. Just days after its release he died of liver cancer. He was sixty-nine.

In the wake of his death it became almost a cliché for professional writers, and also the millions of other scribblers publishing their opinions on social media without benefit of payment, to muse that when David Bowie died the world started going wrong, linking his demise with events like the election of Donald Trump and the UK's leaving the European Community. This process of beatification, through which a human being of average complexity and above-average ambition is recast in the harsh light of mortality into some kind of benign spirit presiding over his fellow human beings, demonstrated just how much the deaths of rock superstars satisfied some people's need to feel sorry for themselves.

A week after his much-noticed death in New York, one of the legion of contemporaries who came up with David Bowie died in a nursing home in a small town in Wales.

Dale Griffin, who had long been known to his band mates as Buffin for some reason lost to history, was one of those many grammar-school boys who were bitten badly during the beat boom of the sixties. His parents bought him the biggest drum kit hire purchase could afford and he played it with a number of bands near his Hereford home. There was the Silence and the Charles Kingsley Creation, Yemm and the Yemen, the Doc Thomas Group and the Shakedown Sound – all names that sound absurd for the simple reason they failed to happen.

Dale's next band, Mott the Hoople, had a name that was scarcely less absurd but which turned out to be a good deal more memorable. Since this name came to be associated with a few hits, it's the one that reverberates down the years; it gains further lustre from the fact that the band's success was never quite enough to spoil their position as admired mavericks with heavy appeal to lost souls. In the mid-seventies the membership of their fan club included a young Morrissey and Benazir Bhutto. The last thing fans like these want is for their favourites to be adopted by everybody else.

Mott the Hoople had some success, and this changes things. Once they've reached first base with Lady Chart very few musicians ever give up entirely. A sizeable minority step back into non-performing roles within the industry. Dale was one of those. When Mott came to the end of the five years which was a band's allotted span back in the seventies, Dale started engineering recordings for other bands, eventually overseeing sessions for up-and-comers on John Peel's radio show.

In the early years of the twenty-first century he did what many of his contemporaries did, which was look up his old friends from Hay Grammar School on the new internet sensation Friends Reunited. This is where he linked up with schoolmate Jean Smith. Jean had carried a torch for Dale ever since he disappeared to London in 1967. That year, when he was at the peak of his youthful glamour behind that oversized kit in his sleeveless vest with the star on the chest, he was all that a girl could desire. They arranged that she was going to come to a Mott the Hoople gig, but then her lift didn't show and they went their separate ways, each thinking the other had let them down. Again thanks to the internet they put their relationship back together, and in 2002 he went back to the Welsh Borders to be with her.

By 2009, when he was barely sixty, he had been diagnosed with Alzheimer's and Jean slipped into the role of carer. She found it irksome when people remarked that his condition might be linked to the lifestyle he must have lived. Mott, she said, was never really that kind of band.

The same year the band got back together again for a reunion tour. This climaxed with five nights at the Hammersmith Odeon, which was more audience than they would have commanded in their stack-heeled pomp. Dale's condition meant that he was unable to play a full role in the shows, although he was brought on for the encores to play drums alongside Martin Chambers. Kris Needs, who had run their fan club back in the day, recalls him remarking that it seemed like old times even though he may not have realized quite where this fitted into his own personal history. Once on stage he seemed happy. People commented that he appeared particularly serene when playing along to 'All The Young Dudes'.

This seemed to be the final last chance in a career that had been strewn with them. When Ian Hunter had been invited to lead the band in 1967 he was already twenty-eight years old (Ian was born when Neville Chamberlain was prime minister and wore a wing collar) and had reason to believe his chance had passed. After five years of stirring up nothing but apathy, they were about to give up following a particularly traumatic show in Switzerland. When one of them called David Bowie to enquire about a job, the singer, flush with his recent success, persuaded them to try one more time with his song 'All The Young Dudes'. They did, it was a hit, and they enjoyed a couple of years in the First Division before giving up again.

The original coining of the T-shirt slogan 'the older I get the better I used to be' has been attributed to everyone from John McEnroe to Van Dyke Parks; it would certainly apply to Mott the Hoople, whose best songs seemed to be about the sadness and glory of generations changing hands. Their nostalgic summoning of the shade of the Saturday gigs, of the Bradford Singers and the Orioles, of the TV you wanted and the T. Rex you got, their insistence that it was indeed a mighty long way down rock and roll, was potent enough when it was describing events that had taken place the day before yesterday. With the passing decades it seemed to grow even more affecting.

Thus in 2013, when Mott the Hoople came together again, this time to play even bigger venues than they had done during their previous reunion, Dale was too far gone to be involved, even though he was only sixty-four. When he died in 2016 in the same week as David Bowie his tributes were sparser and justified via a smattering of bold face names. Mott the Hoople were always Buffin's band, said Ian Hunter. Queen had been their support early on. David Bowie rated him. John Bonham had once tried to borrow his drum kit. He had produced an early session for a group called Nirvana. Even in death it was all a matter of who you knew.

Paul Simon, seen here playing at the White House, put out an album called Seven Psalms *which was widely interpreted as a farewell.*

25

THAT DIFFICULT
LAST ALBUM

Popular music being by now nothing if not a broad church, the list of the missing that was being compiled as this book was being written encompassed veterans of the sixties like Jeff Beck and David Crosby, old enough to remember when bands wore matching outfits; longhairs like Gary Rossington and Robbie Bachman, who came to prominence in the excessive seventies; a few, such as Sinéad O'Connor and Andy Rourke, who rose on the indie wave of the eighties; a handful, like Otis Redding III and Lisa Marie Presley, whose fame was owed to a long-gone predecessor; musical giants on the lines of Wayne Shorter and Robbie Robertson, stars with a capital letter such as Tina Turner and, in Burt Bacharach and Tony Bennett, two men born in the twenties who were old enough to have been enlisted into their country's armed forces. The latter kept on performing into his tenth decade, even after being diagnosed with Alzheimer's. His family reported that during these years there were occasions when he would appear momentarily puzzled by his surroundings until he heard the band strike up the intro to the opening number and the announcer call his name. Once that happened he would stride smiling towards the spotlight, take the microphone from the stand and go into his act just as he had done a thousand times before. It's a truism among people who treat Alzheimer's patients that even when they no longer recognize their own children they can slip into an old favourite song. How much more is that the case if you're the one who's been performing it for decades?

In May 2023, Paul Simon released a record called *Seven Psalms*. This was his fifteenth solo album. The first, which had come out in 1965, was recorded in London. At the time he was making £25 a night playing the folk clubs, a sum which made him think he had reached the top of that particular tree.

While he was there he heard from old high-school friend Art Garfunkel that a track the two of them had recorded in New York before he left had been reworked with an electric band and was bubbling under the *Billboard* chart. Realizing that this might pay even more than £25, Simon returned to the United States where by the beginning of 1966 that first Simon & Garfunkel record, 'The Sounds Of Silence', was competing for the number-one spot with the Beatles' 'We Can Work It Out'. What he didn't know was that the world of pop was entering a new phase and he was on his way to earning the kind of sums of money with which songwriters had never previously been associated.

By the time Simon & Garfunkel were thirty their names were on *Bridge Over Troubled Water*, at the time the biggest-selling album ever. The styles of the songs herein married a musical curiosity which was authentic rather than affected with a song merchant's ear for the hook. Thus *Bridge Over Troubled Water* remains the only multi-platinum album that begins with a slowly unfolding gospel ballad, proceeds through an adaptation of a traditional song from Peru, takes in a heavily coded song about Simon's fracturing partnership with Garfunkel, and even includes a song named after an avant-garde architect. In years to come such obscurantism would lead to the lower regions of similarly obscure charts. In Paul Simon's case it led to the very peak of the biggest one of all, versions of which were displayed behind the counter of every record shop in Britain and America.

THAT DIFFICULT LAST ALBUM

Despite his success down the years, Simon clung to his old way of working, remaining happy to let music and words come to him rather than go chasing them. The best part of two decades later, when he was talking about his new record, *Graceland*, which was to be as big a success in the new-fangled world of the compact disc as *Bridge Over Troubled Water* had been in the era of microgroove, he assured me that the lyrics still arrived mysteriously from what he called his 'tumultuous sub-conscious'. This was apparently still the case over thirty years later when the idea to make *Seven Psalms* came to him, he said, in a dream. He didn't question this mysterious injunction and began to play with chords. After a while words began to arrive, words which apparently belonged with the chords. The words came to him between three and five in the morning, an hour when, like many men on the verge of their ninth decade, he found himself regularly waking.

This wasn't the first time he'd felt that the songs were flowing through him and it was his job to take dictation. It had happened in the past but he hadn't always felt the ideas worthy of capture. When a writer has reached his eighties, when he has lost the hearing in one ear and realizes he may no longer tour, he is apt to think differently about the messages that are coming through. Simon denied that the tracks on *Seven Psalms*, which were presented as a suite of songs running from one to another without the divisions of track marks, and the majority of which contained at least some reference to the bourn from which no traveller returns, were directly inspired by his contemplation of his own mortality.

It's not easy to persuade fans that records aren't in some way autobiographical. Whether they're overtly so, as in John Lennon's songs about his life with Yoko Ono, or, as is more often the case, like the products of a musical word-association game, they are taken to reflect the stages of a journey. For sixty years the songs of Paul Simon had reflected the twists and turns of a personal life lived in the public square, from affairs with teenage sweethearts who appeared on the covers of albums to divorces in middle age from women who didn't, from the simple drives of a young man on the make to the unquiet conscience of the senior citizen; that journey was, assuming it went well, always going to reach this place.

Listing great first albums is a long-established pub game. The great last album has even more responsibility. A certain consciousness of the weightiness of the moment is called for. Leonard Cohen's final bulletin was called *You Want It Darker*, a gift for those among his fans who could imagine nothing finer. If the record Randy Newman made in 2017 proves to be his last then there would be no regrets about calling it *Dark Matter*. David Bowie's *Blackstar* appeared two days before the announcement of his death. This was never going to discourage critics from the view that the songs were all about his contemplation of that end. Glen Campbell finished his final album with his recording of 'These Days', a song about the putting away of foolish things. Jackson Browne had written it at the age of fifteen.

There were times when the fates did not cooperate with the career plan. In 2000 the singer-songwriter Warren Zevon, who had charged through life with a reckless abandon which caused even Keith Richards to raise an eyebrow, made an album called *Life'll Kill Ya* which finished with a song called 'Don't Let Us Get Sick'. The irony of this was not lost on his friends, who knew that he was so frightened of doctors he always took whatever symptoms he had to his dentist. Two years later, when he was diagnosed with cancer, he joked that he had already made that album and contented himself with sprinkling his remaining records with grim, foreboding titles like 'My Ride's Here', 'I Have To Leave' and 'You're A Whole Different Person When You're Scared'. He died in 2003, enjoining his friends to enjoy every sandwich.

In the case of Paul Simon's *Seven Psalms* it was particularly difficult for the lifelong fan, aware that they were listening to what may well be the last will and testament of somebody they had been singing along with since their teens, and noting how many of the songs are about various versions of finality, to find Simon's argument that he is not religious wholly convincing. The Second World War aphorism states there are no atheists in foxholes. Any rock stars in their eighties, as Paul Simon was when he wrote his fifteenth solo album, could be said to occupy just such a foxhole.

26

Patti Smith sang Bob Dylan's 'A Hard Rain's A-Gonna Fall' at the Stockholm ceremony to mark his Nobel Prize in Literature in 2016.

BOB DYLAN'S NOBEL PRIZE

At every prize-giving a bargain is being struck. The body giving the prize hopes to gain as much in terms of profile as the recipient earns in prestige. When in 2016 the eighteen members of the Swedish Academy plumped for Bob Dylan as the winner of that year's gong for Literature they must have hoped they could win some publicity by tempting the seventy-five-year-old Dylan to attend. The incongruous sight of the never appropriately dressed Dylan as a guest of honour at academic gatherings had been guaranteed its share of play in the press since he accepted an honorary doctorate from Princeton University in 1970. He had picked up his Légion d'Honneur in Paris in 2013, but that was because the French government were prepared to arrange it around his European tour schedule. The plan of the Nobel committee didn't work out the way they had hoped. When on 10 December 2016 the great and the good of Sweden gathered in Stockholm to hand out the annual prizes, Bob Dylan wasn't there. He pleaded 'previous commitments', which was a bit thick. Since for once he wasn't due to play a show on that day we can only wonder what those commitments might have been. The *New Yorker* wondered if it might be a family wedding. You wouldn't have been surprised; then again, you wouldn't have been surprised to discover he was staying at home, watching *Coronation Street*. Bob Dylan's enduring mystique, sixty years and counting, is an unparalleled advertisement for the 'never apologize, never explain' approach to conducting a life in public.

The Nobel committee did eventually get their full value out of the resulting controversy on the arts pages of the heavy papers all over the world. This turned on whether it was appropriate for a man who had described himself back in the day as 'a song and dance man' to be presented with a prize that usually went to people who sat in their cells and agonized over what precise order to put their words in. There was no shortage of supporters, from the former Poet Laureate Andrew Motion to every retired English teacher who had ever tried to invoke Dylan's name as a way of getting reluctant readers to think about poetry. There were also detractors. According to novelist Irvine Welsh, who clearly didn't harbour any thoughts of picking up his own Nobel in time, it was 'an ill-conceived nostalgia award wrenched from the rancid prostates of senile, gibbering hippies'.

But even Welsh would have to applaud Bob Dylan's power to attract interest. If you believe that the key characteristic of a rock star is that his fans should wake up in the morning and wonder what he might be doing and why, Bob Dylan is by some distance the greatest rock star of them all. He doesn't feel the need to share. There is always far more held back than is confessed. He has managed to maintain his privacy while staying in plain sight. Even his show business friends never get to see the inside of his house. On the other hand, he's an inveterate visitor to other people's homes. It's rare a year goes by when a story doesn't emerge of him turning up on a doorstep, whether it's paying for a tour of John Lennon's childhood home in Liverpool or knocking on the door of the house in Crouch End he thought belonged to Dave Stewart. The door was answered by a woman whose husband had just gone to work. It didn't help that he was also called Dave. That anecdote went round the world.

If anyone has good reason to fear the madness of fans it's Bob

Dylan, who has spent sixty years looking into their eyes. He moved his family out of Woodstock in the late sixties to protect them from people who felt justified in breaking and entering to get closer. It's instructive to turn round during one of his concerts to look at the audience and for a moment to stand inside his shoes, as he himself wrote. In any gathering there will be a sprinkling of people whose eyes shine with the same misplaced adulation as the disciples in the *Life of Brian*. There will be people moving in pantomimes of abandon. In every audience there will be a certain number of people who were there the night before and will be there the night after, noting every detail and measuring him against some mysterious standard of their own. No wonder he keeps the lights so low.

As the most inscrutable luminary of rock's golden generation, Bob Dylan is like China. We can see what he's doing but we can never work out why he's doing it. We've been wondering for a long time. Once the members of this generation were past their thirties the question most often asked of them was, why are you still doing it? Given that the people posing that question have been posing it for almost as long provides its own answer. The one thing we can never bring ourselves to believe is that they're more like us than we thought.

The thing that we seemed to find most puzzling was the fact that in the second half of his career Bob Dylan, a performing musician, should spend so much time performing his music for the public. The fact that so much of this work took him to places the music business terms, with lordly condescension, secondary markets only added to the general mystification. The idea that Dylan was actually on a project called the Never Ending tour dates back to an interview the music journalist Adrian Deevoy did with him in 1999. He was trying to get at how Dylan's attitude to playing live had more in common with the way Hank Williams would have played than with the event tours everybody else was doing at the time. It was Deevoy who came up with the idea that it was a Never Ending tour, and Dylan agreed. But still the questions remained. Why would this man who never needed to work again bother to play so often? Surely he could put his feet up? And shouldn't he? He couldn't possibly be the same as the rest of us, could he?

As David Geffen wisely observed in the mid-seventies, having dealt with thousands of musicians, he found Bob Dylan to be every bit as interested in money as the most acquisitive of them. People from his record company, intent on devoting their minute of face time with him to explaining how much of a difference he had made to their lives, are always wrong-footed by his tendency to cut across them with a question about why this or that release under-performed in this or that territory. Presumably he figures that since these are people who work in the record business, the business of records is what he should be discussing with them. He has always identified with the great artists of American vernacular music, people such as Hank Williams and Lead Belly and Louis Armstrong and Frank Sinatra, and therefore it wouldn't be surprising if, like them, he had made quite a lot of apparently creative decisions based on nothing more than how much money he would make for how much labour. This, after all, is how his fans interrogate their own daily work. Why should he be any different?

This could account for many of the ways he chose to direct his efforts in the twenty-first century. Is it possible that he started out writing sleeve notes for the reissues of three of his old albums, found that, like most rock musicians, once he started writing he didn't know where to stop, realized he would get a whole lot more money by selling this written work to a book publisher, and thus was born the compelling but curious *Chronicles*, which spent eighteen months on the *New York Times* best-seller list on its publication in 2004 and must have made him more money than any of his records in recent years?

Between 2006 and 2009 he was the star of the much-admired *Theme Time Radio Hour*, in which he played the role of a nighthawk of the airwaves, introducing old country and rhythm and blues recordings organized around themes like baseball and divorce. All the records were chosen by somebody else and his links were clearly read from a script. This is no criticism. The twenty people on the production team did a better job of providing the kind of show Bob Dylan would do than he would have done had it been left to him. What they were really doing was producing a show that was consistent with Dylan's brand values, which are all about antiquity, wisdom and valve amplification. They did three series, during which whatever they paid Dylan must have been justified by the number of new subscribers he drove to their radio station. As soon as the contract expired, Dylan's interest in broadcasting stopped with it.

In 2004 brows were furrowed all over academe by the news that he had licensed one of his songs to Victoria's Secret; he actually appeared alongside a scantily clad lovely in the resulting ad. Why had he chosen to do this? Presumably he had been persuaded by the proximity to beauty, the resulting news value and, clinchingly, the cheque.

The musical *Girl from the North Country* opened in London in 2017, and was running on Broadway before the pandemic happened because Bob Dylan wanted it to. He had noticed the number of long-running productions in theatres all over the world, earning for the songwriters significant revenue and also the recognition of a new audience. It was Dylan's manager Jeff Rosen who sent Irish playwright Conor McPherson all Dylan's albums and asked him if he could make a play out of them.

Beginning in 2002, his shows began to be opened with a recording of a member of his staff intoning a rather over-coloured potted biography. This was heavily indebted to a piece that had appeared in an American newspaper, and began by describing him as 'the voice of the promise of the counter-culture'. Deep-end Dylan disciples, always tortured by the worry that he may be cracking a joke they have failed to recognize, speculated that he did this purely for its humour value. Since he retained the announcement for ten years, it seems more likely that he was using it as a way of introducing himself to the members of his audience who hadn't had the privilege of growing up with him.

One of the things they called him was 'the poet laureate of rock & roll'. This is a curious handle because it rather assumes that rock and roll must be in want of a poet laureate when in fact it's about as necessary as a lead singer in a string quartet. This kind of thinking has historically hovered over all attempts to pat pop music on the back for being something other than pop music. When Dylan got his honour from Princeton back in 1970, he wondered how come they put so much emphasis on his words when no less an artist than Duane Eddy had just recorded an album of Dylan instrumentals? However, just as he did nearly fifty years later, he went along with the plan.

There may have been another reason in 2016. Nobel Prizes aren't purely about the glory and the respect of the establishment. There's a sizeable cash prize attached. The drawback is that to get the money you have to deliver a lecture, and you have to do it before the deadline or you don't get the jackpot. Dylan took his time. At least, somebody took their time. Six months later he turned in a twenty-minute essay in which he repeated some old familiar stuff about Buddy Holly and then some more surprising stuff about *Moby-Dick*. He claimed that when he'd seen Buddy Holly play, their eyes had met and something passed between them. This is about as credible as his claim to have read *Moby-Dick* while in high school.

Failing to properly note that Bob Dylan's greatest creation is Bob Dylan, and this Nobel gave him an opportunity to add to that many-layered self-portrait, the internet had a look at his essay and broadly approved. They liked the idea of Dylan as rock's craggiest old soul. Then somebody pointed out the signs that some of it had been lifted from CliffsNotes study guides. Nobody was exactly indignant, but this isn't what people expect of Nobel laureates. It would on the other hand be entirely what we expect from a song and dance man like Bob Dylan who operates in the world of performance rather than poetry.

It's possible if you're the kind of person who was impressed by Dylan winning a Nobel Prize that his borrowing of a few sentences out of a revision aid might come as a surprise to you. If you're the kind of person who prefers to be impressed by the fact that you can close your eyes now and listen to fifty old Dylan recordings playing in the jukebox of your head, it won't. What makes Dylan interesting is less the songs than the way he sang them. His art is measured in minutes, not words. Duane Eddy knew.

More important than all this, in exchange for that essay he was paid £700,000. Not bad for a seventy-five-year-old man. Age clearly has its compensations.

Toto have had fourteen different line-ups in the forty years since they recorded 'Africa', the single song that makes them still a festival favourite all over the world.

27

TOTO AND THE HUMAN JUKEBOX

Back in 1985 James Taylor wrote a song about what it was like to be really well known for a song. Part of the lyric referred to people who 'pay good money to hear "Fire And Rain" again and again and again'. The bemused tone of this reflection on the lot of the famous musician suggested that playing even such a well-loved song can become a bit of a chore. At the time of the new song 'That's Why I'm Here', his classic 'Fire And Rain' had been in his repertoire for a mere fifteen years. At the time of writing, which is fully fifty-four years since he first sang 'Fire And Rain', he is due to go on tour, when he will sing it again. That's still why he's there. If an artist like James Taylor, who has written and recorded many songs that could justifiably be regarded as standards, can reconcile himself to the fact that every artist in his Third Age is on some level called upon to do duty as a human jukebox, then so can everybody else.

In the sixties and early seventies, when it was assumed that their best years were still in front of them, some acts would play a medley of their hits, which is the single most infuriating thing a performer can do. The next most irritating thing is to do what many acts do, which is play them too fast, as though they can't wait to get them over with. The Rolling Stones have not played 'Satisfaction' at its proper tempo since 1965. Then you can just play them in a way that renders them unrecognizable, which has been Bob Dylan's policy for forty years. He has the excuse of having cussedness as a brand value. Often, acts can disappoint audiences out of absent-mindedness. When George Harrison toured Japan in 1991 a deputation from the band came to him and begged him to play the solo from 'Something' the way he played it on *Abbey Road* because nobody in the world wished to hear anything other.

It's not unusual for acts to go through a stage of hoping the audience is going to grow out of demanding a hit the band never liked, such as Radiohead went through with 'Creep', but when an act is playing for what might be the last time for some members of both band and audience it seems churlish to deny them their wish. The bigger the crowds and the higher ticket prices creep, the more the audiences tend to get their own way. The more connected an act is with fans, the more sensitive they have to be to their demands, with some bands polling their fanbase before a tour to find out what songs they would like to hear. Fans holding signs above their heads naming a particular favourite have been a feature of Bruce Springsteen shows in the last ten years. Many acts have managed to make the playing of an old favourite seem less of a chore by announcing shows where they play the whole of an old album in its proper sequence. In 2008 Sparks, who can claim the unique distinction of trading under the same name with the same personnel since 1966 – an achievement even more remarkable for a pair of brothers – did a run of twenty-one shows in London where they played all of the albums they had made since 1971 in sequence. On the final night they played their new one. When the band are veterans and the fans are too there's an acceptance that the paying public will only eat their greens in the shape of new tunes if their favourites are guaranteed as the main course. In the latter stage they know that he who pays the piper literally calls the tune. Furthermore, the tune won't always be one you expect. When standing on the verge of their careers, bands prefer to give the impression that all will proceed along the lines of a grand plan of their own devising. When looking back many years later they realize that whatever longevity they achieved was most often because of something that happened to them for reasons entirely beyond their control, sometimes hilariously so.

Toto, the band put together in 1977 by a bunch of first-call session players from the Los Angeles studio system, all highly rated musicians who eventually grew tired of providing the catchy bits for better-known and often less musical performers, were, at the time of their establishment, scorned for their polish and earnest professionalism. In 1977 these were the very qualities nobody wished to be seen to be buying. At this time bands who could actually play their instruments found it best not to draw attention to the fact. This was a time when a casual reader of the music press could have been forgiven for thinking it was acceptable for a punk rock legend to murder his girlfriend but was in no doubt that you absolutely couldn't call yourself a 'muso' – and Toto were nothing if not musos. The most important quality any band could claim was 'attitude', a quality in which Toto were manifestly deficient.

However, the world turns and pop turns with it. Twenty years later, following the Guilty Pleasures movement and the belated elevation of the likes of ELO into the pantheon of rock legends, it was suddenly better to be perceived as being above such shallow considerations as 'attitude'. Twenty years later it was their very *vorsprung durch technik* qualities that saw Toto embraced by a new generation, a generation that wasn't born when they had first come along. Unlike those bands who had sustained a career by continuing to appeal to their original fans, Toto were by no means alone in getting a third-stage boost by attracting people who had no prejudice about them for the simple reason they had never previously heard of them.

That's because in that time Toto had become, in the words of guitarist Steve Lukather – one of the two members of the band who was there when they formed, around the time the presidency of Gerald Ford gave way to Jimmy Carter; they were still there when the presidency of Donald Trump unwillingly moved over for Joe Biden – 'the "Africa" band'. In a 2020 interview focusing on Toto's unlikely late-career renaissance, Lukather talked about when they had headlined a festival in Australia in 2018. 'We played one of these kids' festivals where we were the only ones on stage who were actually playing live. There were twenty thousand kids in the audience, and all they knew was that the "Africa" band was playing.' Toto had been deliberately booked by the organizers of this festival as their meme act. They had about as much comprehension of the world of the younger acts as the younger fans had of theirs, but it didn't matter. 'Africa' bridged that chasm.

Toto had known other hits, but 'Africa' was more than just another chart entry. That one record turned out to be their lifetime meal ticket, and like so many of the songs that bands grow to depend on, it had come about entirely by accident. At the time of their fourth album in 1982, which they christened with characteristic flair *Toto IV*, they thought so little of the song that they made it the last track on the running order. This usually indicates either that nobody in the group had a great deal of ambition for it or, as is frequently the case, there were members who actively campaigned against it. In the previous year the Sheffield synth pop group the Human League had done something similar, consigning 'Don't You Want Me' to the same position on their album *Dare*, as though daring the public first to locate it and then to warm to it. Which they did, ensuring that the Human League would have to play it live for the next forty years.

The words of the song 'Africa', which touched foggily upon the magnificence of Mount Kilimanjaro and the wild dogs yearning in the night for 'some solitary company', were firmly in the tradition of those produced by gentlemen who are familiar with more than three chords and consequently feel that if they're going to write a song it must have a lyric aspiring (if only foggily) to dignity. The recording that they made of this rather ponderous song was very pleasing to the ear. Since the members of the group had previously played on the likes of Boz Scaggs's *Silk Degrees* and Michael Jackson's *Thriller*, in the course of which they would have been charged with magicking up all manner of earworms, this wasn't surprising. But clearly there was something about the plain silliness of 'Africa' which spoke to people's depths. CBS Television even decided it was just the thing to use during their coverage of the funeral of Nelson Mandela in 2013.

This attractively silly confection, together with a couple of others, has fed, clothed and shod the various members of Toto over the forty-plus years since, during which time they have cycled through no fewer than fourteen different line-ups. Their unflagging facelessness, the very anonymity which is the session man's calling card, meant that they have been able to survive the passage of three lead singers, two bass guitarists and three drummers. Members have come, gone and even returned, often on less advantageous terms. Steve Porcaro, the brother of original drummer Jeff, left the band in 1987 and rejoined over thirty years later, this time as a salaried player.

Given the amount of time Toto has functioned it's no surprise some of the original members have exited the ranks permanently. Jeff, who in the eighties was the most in-demand session drummer in Los Angeles, died in 1992 of a heart attack at the age of thirty-eight. His death was initially thought to be linked to his inhaling the insecticide that had been recently sprayed on his lawn. Deep-end rock scholars seized on this as a sign that finally at least one percussion great had, as was claimed of John 'Stumpy' Pepys of Spinal Tap, succumbed to the bizarre gardening accident of legend. The Los Angeles coroner, however, decided it was actually due to hardening of the arteries connected with excessive cocaine use. In the hectic, round-the-clock world of the Los Angeles session man of the time, excessive cocaine use could have qualified as an industrial injury.

Underlining the point that it is a mighty long way down rock and roll and the most unlikely events are likely to come to pass, in the year 2018, over forty years and seven US presidents after Toto's original formation, Jeff Porcaro's widow, Susan, by now married to the head of Tupperware and presumably more cognizant than most of what may still be earned by brands long past the first flush of novelty, instigated legal action against the remaining members of the band, claiming her late husband's estate and his children should benefit from the revenues still being earned by Toto, the band he had been such a key part of several decades earlier.

This was one of those cases, bitterly contested and quietly settled out of court, in which legal precedents established in the world of business are brought to litigate a form of social organization which has never behaved like a business. Few would argue that the heirs of band members who played on a band's records should continue to benefit from the earnings of those records for as long as copyright pertains, but should the same thing apply to the earnings that come from the efforts of the surviving members? If it's Lukather and singer David Paich who have been keeping the band's flag flying through corporate gigs, county fairs and the thousand and one indignities that lie in wait for any act before and after their hot streak, should they have to share the proceeds of their sweat with members who have left the ranks for reasons of either pique or death?

There are few precedents for deciding the legacy of a band anywhere else in life, let alone in show business. Lukather's feelings about the issue were raw and may possibly have spilled into a song he subsequently wrote called 'Along For The Ride', which accuses person or persons unknown of 'riding on my bloody coattails'. From John Lennon's 'How Do You Sleep?' to Liam Gallagher's 'Don't Brother Me', disputes between members of bands are apt to find their way into songs of singular bitterness, made worse by the fact that, as is the case with many bands, there never was a written agreement in the first place. Rock bands were formed in the hope they would enjoy the fruits of a flaming youth. For a small number of them there was the distant prospect of a comfortable middle age. What nobody planned for was the Third Age that Toto and many other bands were living through.

The two remaining members of Toto were living in a future that nobody had predicted. They had continued to plough on after Porcaro's death, albeit with fewer entries in the Top 40. Their prime mover was guitarist Steve Lukather, by his own admission one of those musicians who will go anywhere for a gig. At one stage the anywhere even encompassed a show in the Faroe Islands. This was in 2017, by which time the music world was all about streaming and the majority of people doing the streaming had little knowledge and less interest in the creation myths that bands had so assiduously tended in the past. This new audience frankly drew no distinction between Toto and U2. Both bands had come along at roughly the same time and both had similarly enigmatic two-syllable names. Furthermore, both had front men who once sported mullets and now concealed their hair loss beneath a succession of increasingly preposterous hats.

All bands, if they're lucky, end up as jukeboxes, hired to trot out a small number of songs that were once on the chart. That handful of hits endures long after anyone in the audience has ceased being impressed by how tight they are or wishing to sleep with any of them. It's a wise band that manages to reconcile itself to this fact. If a band sticks around as long as Toto, it's not impossible they might find themselves the beneficiary of one of those paroxysms of taste that restores them to the spotlight, possibly at the expense of their own dignity. When a bunch of Hollywood writers with time on their hands and too many records decided to rehabilitate a particular stratum of Los Angeles pop music which they dubbed 'yacht rock', Toto's 'Africa' was high up in the mix. It steadily came back into focus in the twenty-first century in classic twenty-first-century fashion, first as a sample in hip hop, whose practitioners have always been the first to champion anything whose catchiness exceeds its unhipness, and then via animated series like *Family Guy* and *South Park*. In the new dispensation, 'Africa' became something more than a hit. It became that essentially twenty-first-century phenomenon, 'a thing'. Only that could explain the decision in 2018 of a Bristol nightclub to play 'Africa' and nothing but 'Africa' for five hours.

There was clearly something in its nature that drove people to unaccountable extremes. Mary Klym, a fourteen-year-old from Ohio, heard it on the soundtrack of the Netflix series *Stranger Things* and decided she would like to hear it covered by her favourite band. Her favourite band were Weezer, who seemed to occupy the opposite end of the taste spectrum from Toto. This being 2017 and there being such a thing as Twitter, and Weezer suddenly having to operate in a world where bands no longer lead the fans but instead do their bidding, eventually the band had to give in and record their own version.

When Weezer's version went to number one on the iTunes chart Lukather was invited to perform it with them on *Jimmy Kimmel Live*. On that occasion he detected that the success of the song hadn't gone down well with Weezer's leader, Rivers Cuomo, who resented the fact that people wanted to hear somebody else's song. 'I saw him wince,' said the sixty-year-old Lukather of the forty-seven-year-old Cuomo. 'They initially did it as a goof, but now they realized they'd have to play the song for a lot longer than they thought they would. This whole business runs on hit records. If you get one, you'd better be prepared to play it for the rest of your life.'

In the twenty-first century the guitar has lost its pre-eminence as the iconic rock instrument. Fender bosses are pinning their hopes for a revival on Taylor Swift.

28

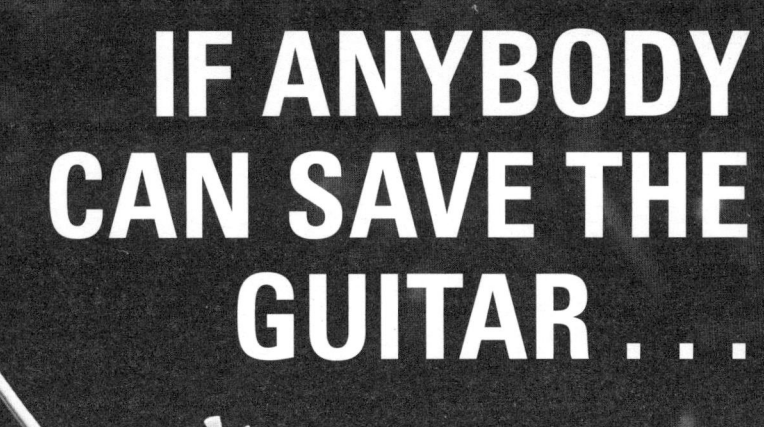

IF ANYBODY CAN SAVE THE GUITAR . . .

When the Californian accountant Leo Fender began making electric guitars in the years following the Second World War he took it as an article of faith that a guitar's looks were every bit as important as its performance. That was because guitars were not as other instruments. Buyers of guitars, particularly the buyers who happened to be young men, didn't want simply to take the guitars down and play them. They also wished to wear the guitars like garments. It was important to them that they liked the way the guitars made them look. Furthermore, they had to like the way the guitar made them feel about themselves.

At the time, in the post-war America of Eisenhower, of TV which broadcast through the night, of cars with bench seats and fins, in a country where everything needed to look like the future, that meant guitars with jet-age names like Telecaster and Stratocaster, each realized in designs that emulated the contours of the tabletops of Californian diners, finished in colours with names like Candy Apple Red, pigments as deep and throbbing as sin.

No wonder, then, that in 1959, when Cliff Richard sent away to the United States in order to import the first Stratocaster to Britain for Hank Marvin of the Shadows, London-based lovers of beautiful things would foregather whenever the instrument was taken out of its case, purely in order to gaze in awe at what appeared to them to be a visitation from the future.

In the sixties, Leo Fender's career was dogged by health problems. At the end of the beat group boom he sold his company to a corporation. That corporation moved manufacture to Japan and began to compete on price. They introduced new models such as the Starcaster, most of which didn't have the requisite charisma.

A minority of people might have mourned the passing of the old Fender guitars but by the eighties they were all but forgotten, eclipsed by the new 'pointy' styles favoured by the hard rock bands that capered in spandex on MTV with little thought for either their own dignity or the roots of rock and roll. The shock-haired shock troops of electro pop, who preferred to perform from behind their stand-up keyboards like check-in staff at an airport, passed over these redundant, finger-torturing stringed instruments entirely.

Some dreamed of reinventing the guitar for what was seen as the modern age. A company called Steinberger had some success marketing futuristic-looking instruments fashioned from carbon fibre. These had digital displays rather than knobs and switches. Most eerily, they had no headstock at the end of their necks. This made them seem, to some eyes at least, disturbingly abbreviated and aesthetically incomplete.

These 'headless' guitars were for a short while taken up by well-funded performers of the era, people like Mark Knopfler, Sting and Eddie Van Halen. At the time there were good practical reasons for preferring them: they were lighter, they were easier to keep in tune and they would even go in the overhead lockers on flights. However, even their early adopters found the headless guitar as difficult to love as their toilers in the band's engine room found the simultaneously marketed syndrums difficult to warm to.

Practicality had never really been the point. Not where guitars were concerned. Steinberger's new generation of apparently circumcised instruments simply no longer looked right. For a start, they

weren't nearly big enough. They appeared to be like toys; real guitars, on the other hand, with their chromium extremities, their
dangerous curves, their hazardous edges and their divine heft, were
more like guns.

A counter-revolution was at hand. In 1987, in the nick of time,
American guitar man Bill Schultz headed up a management buyout
of Fender from its previous corporate owners. Bill had a bold strat-
egy. He thought the future of Fender might be in its past. More
specifically, he felt it might lie in rekindling the romance of the
guitar.

Fender began making guitars for famous musicians. These so-
called signature models, which started in 1988 with a family of
Stratocasters tailor-made for Eric Clapton, available in his preferred colours Ferrari Red, 7Up Green and charcoal grey, led to a
range aimed at the increasing number of weekend players for
whom an instrument named after their guitar hero was an acceptable alternative to the motorcycle which traditionally announced
the mid-life crisis. Eventually the signature guitar business would
grow to such an extent that one would even be named after Bono,
who was famous for not playing the guitar, the blues man Robert
Johnson, who died in 1938, and Kiefer Sutherland, who is better
known as an actor.

Even more significant was another of Bill's initiatives. This was
the Fender Custom Shop in Corona, California. Here, American
craftsmen, the best of whom were known by name and would leave
their names on the neck, would make instruments to the blueprints
of musicians. The demand was no longer for the instruments of the
future. It was far more often the case that they would ask for something that felt like an instrument they had once loved, played or
merely coveted from afar at some point in the past.

Guitarists are like golfers in that they are prone to believing they
are only one piece of equipment and one pro tip away from realizing

their full potential. As such they were the natural client base for the Custom Shop. As the orders came in and the Custom Shop grew, it was no longer building brand-spanking-new replicas of famous instruments of the past. In fact no self-respecting gearhead was ever in the market for anything that gave the remotest appearance of being new. New was the very last thing a guitar should be. Anything that was new couldn't possibly have the qualities of soul or cool or whatever currency one preferred when it came to measuring that mystical property, cred.

Ideally the Custom Shop would hand the customer a product that felt anything but box-fresh. If the instruments didn't have a past then one could be invented for them. To achieve this, guitars would be fitted with rusty screws that made them appear reassuringly old. They would be finished with paint which as far as possible looked and felt like the original cheap patina. Finally they would go through a process known within the company as 'relicking', from which they would emerge with the appearance of having endured a lifetime of club gigs, transit abuse and tough love. The makers would even develop back stories for the instruments, such as the gunslinger's belt buckle that had been responsible for the scratches on the back of the body. Cigarette burns would be applied to the headstocks to imply this instrument had once been loaned to Keith Richards. Every last scar and love mark on the guitar had to look as though it had been earned. Particularly if it hadn't been.

In 1969 Graham Nash bought a Fender Stratocaster in a pawn shop in Phoenix, Arizona. It was already fourteen years old by that time and had passed through many hands. Nash gave the guitar to Jerry Garcia of the Grateful Dead as a thank-you for the guitarist playing on his solo album *Songs For Beginners*. Garcia liked the way the guitar looked and felt and he used it on stage throughout 1971 and 1972. It was featured prominently on the triple live album the band made of their concerts in Europe in 1972. By that point it had been extensively modified by the band's technicians. They improved its performance and handling but were careful not to do anything that interfered with its image as an old guitar. The last thing they wished to do was bring it up to date.

Neither did they wish it to appear pristine. Impressed by the quality of the stickers they found on tour in Europe they bought a few and applied them to the body of the guitar. The most prominent among them was one featuring a grinning alligator, which led to the guitar becoming known by Deadhead cognoscenti as 'the Alligator Strat'. Garcia stopped using it in 1973 but by then its mystique was assured. Grateful Dead fans still revere the last live version of 'Dark Star', which was played on the Alligator Strat. After Garcia's death in 1995 the guitar was auctioned and bought by a Dead fan and film maker for almost half a million dollars.

That wasn't the end of it. In 2022, Master Builder Austin MacNutt of the Custom Shop arranged to borrow the instrument, took it apart, examined it minutely, photographed every inch of its innards and measured the precise distances between every part. He did this so that he could produce a limited edition of one hundred replicas, each one with the sticker Garcia's guitar tech put on the original in 1972. The same alligator sticker is now on sale from the website known as Garcia Family Provisions for $5. The site does everything from a key ring to a beer glass, all bearing the beatific image of the portly guitarist. You'll pay about the same for that replica sticker as you might have paid to be in the hall for one of the three-hour concerts which are on the triple album *Europe 72*. The hundred guitars in the Alligator Strat range now sell to gentlemen of a certain age, the kind who would otherwise be wasting money on motorcycles, for almost £20,000.

Most of those people are buying in order belatedly to fulfil a dream of a youth when they spent hours with their nose pressed to the glass of an instrument shop yearning to look as cool as their guitar-wielding heroes. Only a select few stars have moved the dial where the purchase of musical instruments is concerned. At the time of the boom in folk music in the United States and skiffle in Britain, huge numbers of young people, temporarily under the spell of Joan Baez or Lonnie Donegan, nagged their parents for cheap acoustic guitars. The boom in electric guitar ownership, initially driven by the Beatles and then by Led Zeppelin and Oasis, established that instrument as the most powerful symbol in what used to be referred to as youth culture.

Early in the twenty-first century it began to slip from that position until in 2017 the *Washington Post* was announcing that sales had plummeted by half in the previous decade. The smart kids were at home playing with their computers. The owning of guitars no longer conferred instant envy. A lot of that was ascribed to the fact that it still required a considerable investment of time before a guitar could be mastered, and kids raised on the instant gratification of digital toys were not inclined to put it in. On the other hand, the growth of *Rock School*-like tuition in how to play songs from (in most cases) decades before the kids were born had produced a generation of pre-adolescents who could master Metallica, encouraged in their studies by parents who wanted to feel that they were somehow passing on their culture.

An increasing proportion of those students were girls. In the third decade of the present century observers began to notice that something was happening which nobody had previously thought possible: for the first time since the early sixties, sales of acoustic guitars were outstripping sales of the electric variety. There appeared to be two drivers behind this trend. One was the desire of many people to take advantage of Covid lockdown to master C, G and

F. The other was Taylor Swift. The boss of Fender called Swift 'the most influential guitarist of recent years'. 'I don't think that young girls looked at Taylor and said, "I'm really impressed by the way she plays G major arpeggios,"' he added. 'They liked how she looked, and they wanted to emulate her.'

A product of the grungy nineties, Phair has learned to adapt to a twenty-first-century world where music stars stride down catwalks and automobile companies pay the bills.

LIZ PHAIR IS STILL IN THE GAME

29

iz Phair was born in Connecticut in 1967 between the releases of the first Velvet Underground record and *Sgt Pepper's Lonely Hearts Club Band*. At the time many of the musicians featured in this book were already established adults. Unlike most of them, she attended university and, as the offspring of a comfortable, well-established family, had options. The one she chose was to be a singer-songwriter. Not a folkie singer-songwriter, not a stool percher. Instead, she played the electric guitar, wore mini-skirts and cowboy boots, made much of her mane of hair and moved in a fashion that, whether she meant to or not, exerted a fascination over indie boys which was more than merely musical. There are pictures of her performing in Chicago in the mid-nineties where her audience is entirely made up of lonely young men, all standing on their own, dreaming of what it would be like to have such a woman of the world at their side.

By the time Liz came to make her first album, the basic blocks of rock's rich tapestry had been established and therefore one of the few things that was left to the artist to do was play with that established picture. This Liz Phair did, with *Exile In Guyville*, which came out in 1993 when she was twenty-six, and was purported to be a track-by-track feminist response to the Rolling Stones' 1972 album *Exile On Main Street*. This idea that you could base a new record on one that was twenty years old and assume that your audience would get at least some of the references was an indication of just how heritage-conscious rock and roll was becoming at the time; the further notion that albums could be feminist statements as well as everything else was an early sign of the fact that the majority of records were now, for good or ill, being bought by graduates and therefore could be marketed at them as though they were improving paperbacks.

Liz Phair was not in any sense born to be in any form of show business. She had never been on a stage of any kind. When she was writing that first record neither her friends nor family knew what she was doing. When her mother heard *Exile In Guyville* she said, 'I never realized you were so sad,' which caused her daughter some twinges of guilt. A certain amount of artful sadness went with the territory. Indie records were rarely about happiness. Ideally they would hint at great pain, bravely borne.

Exile In Guyville was widely celebrated rather than commercially successful. It won for Liz Phair a level of fame which is shared by hundreds of indie acts that do well at festivals but would have difficulty being recognized on your local high street, a level of fame that has been termed 'cool person famous'. Phair benefited from the fact that she was attractive, articulate and ready to engage the media on the subject that they preferred to talk about above all, which was sex. She seemed to come along at the exact moment when women performers began to talk about sex, which they never had done in the past, while male performers, who had talked about it freely in the past, suddenly found they had nothing to say on the subject.

In the nineties, in the last days of print magazines, this combination of forthrightness and being photogenic won a lot of ink for Liz Phair. Like other female performers such as Alanis Morissette and Björk, she crossed over from the music press through the women's titles to the lifestyle supplements of the heavy papers. *Rolling Stone* put her on the cover with the line 'A Rock Star Is Born', which was the wishful thinking of a title looking for new banker cover stars. Such treatment made her seem more famous than she was. People made the mistake of thinking that since she was famous she must be wealthy – even her father, who cut her out from the family health insurance because he assumed that since she was well known among certain sections of society she had to be newly self-sufficient. People back in the smart Chicago suburb where her parents lived expected her to be like Madonna.

The sales, however, were never at the Madonna level and therefore, following the obligatory three albums on the hip label, she was cut adrift, as tends to happen in these cases. Her third album, made at the age of thirty-one, was about becoming a mother, which was probably not what the indie boys wanted to hear. But there was no question of giving up. She settled to the work much as she might have done if she had been writing novels or making sculptures rather than in the business of pop, which traditionally calls for more in the nature of physical commitment. She lived in the Chicago suburbs. She took her son to school. This was the life she'd signed up for and you didn't stop just because you were no longer the new thing.

She tried making commercial pop records. She tried film music. She tried. No reasonable offers refused. Her old record company made a compilation after she left and called it *Icon*, which was a recognition of the fact that the fame she had won around *Exile In Guyville* was still her most valuable asset. The picture on the cover showed her in her late twenties; at the time she was actually forty-seven and divorced. She reflected in interviews that this disparity between the image the world still had of her and the reality meant that she was probably doomed to stay single. 'I don't want to be a notch on a belt. I think it's hard, once you've set a persona, to go back and get to know the person.'

Liz Phair had come up in the twentieth century, when pop said the first thing that came into its head. She has had to make her way in the present century when pop has learned to keep its mouth shut for fear of becoming collateral damage in the latest scandal. This is a change that takes some getting used to. In 2019, at the age of fifty-two, she was ready to make a new double album based on the Beatles' White Album when its producer, the indie hero Ryan Adams, was suddenly disgraced by allegations of his sexual harassment of younger female musicians. Adams was cancelled about as abruptly as anyone can be and Phair had to abandon the project. She wrote about it in the first volume of her memoirs without mentioning him by name. Of course he had tried to get her to sleep with him, she said, but that didn't mean she'd agreed.

Liz Phair continues to make albums. In some cases they are good ones, but their main reason for being is to reassure Liz Phair that she is still in the game. She moved to Los Angeles and lives with her son, who is now about the age she was when she started writing the songs for *Exile In Guyville*. That was an album about trying to make it in a world where all the stars were men. In 2024, most of the big stars are women. The biggest male rock stars are Harry Styles and Ed Sheeran, who aim themselves squarely at the female audience. When Liz plays live the audience is no longer dominated by horny adolescent males. It's more likely to be women.

She is still asked about the things she was asked about when she started. What she thinks about men. What she thinks about famous women. Sometimes between the lines of these pieces it's possible to detect a faint whiff of disapproval of the way she, a woman in her fifties, presents herself, but then, as she says, she'll be buried in a mini-skirt. She notes that it's a lot harder to make an impact when you're in your fifties because you don't stand for the same things. Her last album was called *Soberish*, which is hardly the kind of banner people gather around. She's thoughtful enough to have entertained the thought that a lot of rock and roll only makes sense to people who haven't seen a lot of life and haven't thought particularly deeply about it.

'To be rock, you've got to go, "Fuckin' A, this is what the fuck it is!" I don't have a lot of that anymore. Time and experience has burnished me. I'm gentler on human beings, and I'm less sure that I know better than you. I need the songs to express the truth of my inner soul, and my soul has wisdom, and it has patience, and it has room for differing opinions and differing viewpoints. It has perspective. I miss being able to point the finger and be, like, "Fuck you!" You have to own that – you have to believe it. You can't fake that.'

Exile In Guyville came out in 1993. It was reissued in a special edition to mark its fifteenth anniversary and then again in another special edition to mark its twenty-fifth. Over thirty years after its release it's still inconceivable that Liz Phair could ever be introduced in any context without its being mentioned. One of the themes of her autobiography is how that little bit of indie fame made it impossible for her ever to take up a normal life again and left her stranded between being a star and a civilian. Looking on the bright side, she has a good chance of getting to the end of her working life on the power of that original boost which established her as a public personality. The security provided by once having been part of people's lives was not what anybody expected of a pop career. In the end it's a living.

'Sometimes I feel like I work for Liz Phair,' she says. 'And I have years off but then, like, I work for her.'

The singer–pianist (second left) left Fleetwood Mac in 1998 after almost thirty years but then found she wasn't cut out for retirement, returning for a 2019 tour.

30

CHRISTINE McVIE'S LAST HURRAH

Most of rock's golden generation grew up with parents who expected their children to consider certain things when choosing a profession. Ideally it ought to be steady. It should also last long enough to see them through to retirement. At which point, if all had gone well, there would be some kind of modest pension. That was the pot of gold at the finish line.

Many of those professions didn't set a great deal of store in job satisfaction, and the idea of enjoyment wasn't very high on the list of priorities. You could see this in the way the movies depicted work. The happiest day in your working life was the day you left it, the day you retired, picked up your carriage clock, listened to some kind words from the boss and then went off to tend your roses or improve your golf. If you found that boring, that wasn't a problem: the retirement years wouldn't last long because life expectancy wasn't very high in those days. For our parents' generation, there was no mistaking work and play, duty and diversion, serious business and fun and games.

If your child had a mind to run away from adult responsibilities and be a rock star, that was regarded as a foolish notion which a couple of years would be bound to get out of their system. This generation of parents and guardians weren't enrolling them in *Rock School*. This was the age of John Lennon's Aunt Mimi saying, 'The guitar's all right, John, but you'll never make a living out of it,' and

Bruce Springsteen's father raging about the fact that his son was upstairs playing 'that goddamn guitar'. Nobody thought they were in this for the long run.

Of course, for some of them, it wasn't to turn out that way. But it would turn out that the niche that could sustain a handful of people making a living playing their own songs, making albums regularly, following their own creative impulses, pontificating to the music press, high on their own supply of self-importance, was a bigger niche than anybody would've thought. Of course, only a tiny proportion of the occupants of that niche could have been described as comfortably off, but there were many others who somehow found the means to carry on.

This was the job from which it would appear nobody ever retired. Rock stars never said, 'I've done enough, these trousers are too ridiculous, I can no longer pretend that my hairline and waistline are as they were when I was twenty-eight, I can no longer climb on stage and sing a song about a girl who was a year above me at school. This is no job for a grown man or woman. Bring me the carriage clock. I shall now sit back and let a new generation take over.' No rock musician ever said anything like that. That, of course, is a sweeping statement, but it's broadly true.

The number of rock stars who were prepared to say that they had retired is a select enough group to make the listing of them a game that can be played using your fingers.

John Deacon of Queen decided there was no point going on after the death of Freddie Mercury in 1991, and since then he has lived a private life, not joining the others when it's come to any of the money-spinning efforts to keep the brand going, while maintaining his quarter share in the business and by all accounts checking in regularly on the health of that firm.

Bill Withers walked away in 1985, feeling he had more than done his bit, and that his patience with record companies and the energy it required to maintain his career was at an end. He can't possibly have foreseen that the handful of perfect jewels he had created up to then, such as 'Lovely Day', 'Lean On Me' and 'Ain't No Sunshine', would go on and on putting food on the table thanks to their use in the marketing of everything from Campbell's Soup to Planters Peanuts.

Mark Knopfler resigned from Dire Straits when they were still one of the biggest bands in the world, has refused offers to re-form, didn't turn up to be invested into the Rock and Roll Hall of Fame, and since that time has devoted himself to smaller projects from which he derives satisfaction. The same thing applies to Roger Hodgson of the seventies band Supertramp. Grace Slick retired from music after a 1990 reunion of Jefferson Airplane and devoted herself to the visual arts, saying there were things a twenty-five-year-old could do that it was best a seventy-year-old should avoid.

Those are the exceptions to the rule that musicians will keep going as long as there is a date in the diary. As this book was being completed the ninety-year-old Willie Nelson was announcing tour dates that were six months away, and the Sun Ra Arkestra was being led by the ninety-nine-year-old Marshall Belford Allen. There are many reasons why musicians never give up. One of them is they're as addicted to the buzz of the job as are top sporting coaches who fear that once they leave there will be no going back.

A rare exception to that rule was in one of the biggest bands in the world.

The year was 1967. The place was Swinging London. The twenty-three-year-old Christine Perfect was working as a window dresser at Dickins & Jones in London's Regent Street when two men she knew from her home town of Birmingham asked her to join their blues band, Chicken Shack. They didn't want her to be the pretty lead singer, which was the role occupied by most women in rock bands at the time. They wanted her because she could play the piano – her father was a classical violinist – and sing a bit.

HOPE I GET OLD BEFORE I DIE

In those days even a blues band needed a hit single and so when they released 'I'd Rather Go Blind' the singer was Christine. The record was a minor hit and at that time women singers were so thin on the ground that Christine found herself voted the best of the year in the *Melody Maker* poll for 1969. Not long after that she became Christine McVie when she married John McVie of another blues band, Fleetwood Mac.

Christine tried being a solo act, but it didn't suit her. She effectively retired. By the time Fleetwood Mac decamped to the proverbial house in the country to reorganize themselves in the wake of the departure of Peter Green in 1970, she had become a housewife, albeit of the hippy variety. She was cooking stews and tie-dying T-shirts. During this phase, the band was so unsure of its direction that Christine slipped into the strength and began adding her songs.

For a few years the band trod water before deciding to invite Lindsey Buckingham to join. He said he would only come if he could bring his girlfriend, Stevie Nicks. Because there was no precedent for a band having two 'chicks' on the strength, Christine, by now in her thirties, was given the right to veto the recruiting of the younger singer. Christine said she didn't mind because she had no desire to be out front, she was quite happy behind the piano. Stevie could get out there and hoover up the male gaze.

From her position at the piano, Christine composed and sang many of the songs that made Fleetwood Mac by the end of the seventies the biggest band in the world and a byword for an entirely new strain of popular music, highly polished and popular with adults rather than kids, and subtly reflective of the fascinating soap opera being played out among the members of the band, who appeared to spend all the time they weren't in the studio coupling and decoupling, falling out and reconciling, and writing infernally catchy songs about it.

CHRISTINE McVIE'S LAST HURRAH

By the end of the eighties they appeared to have reached the end of the road. It was only the adoption of Christine's song 'Don't Stop' as the campaign theme of presidential candidate Bill Clinton that made their music once more ubiquitous and meant that it was almost a patriotic duty to re-form to play Clinton's inaugural ball. Twenty-five years after she'd been draping a mannequin in Dickins & Jones's window, Christine McVie was inviting the new president and his First Lady to come on stage and dance along rather awkwardly while the band played on.

In 1998, at the age of fifty-five, she decided to leave the band. She had a fear of flying, which is a pressing problem when at times you're expected to take a flight every day. Her father had died and she felt the need to reconnect with her remaining family and, as she put it, feel her feet on English soil. She'd initially gone to America for three months which had turned into twenty-three years. She had no children but she wanted to put down roots. To that end she bought a rambling period property in the Kent countryside and adopted the magazine lifestyle of a country lady of independent means, strolling around the locality, patting horses, enjoying anonymity and feeling blessedly untethered from the dramas that inevitably attended Fleetwood Mac.

Retirement didn't turn out to be easy. She had been divorced from John McVie since the mid-seventies and now she split from her Portuguese second husband. Then the solitude began to get to her. She drank a little more than she ought. She began to miss the buzz of the city, and thus moved back into a splendid apartment overlooking the Thames. She even toyed with the idea of making a solo record. She thought about going out and playing music again, but then decided there was only one band she wanted to play with. Hence, after fifteen years away, and nearly fifty years since that encounter in the window of Dickins & Jones, she rejoined the group at the age of seventy.

'I now realize where I belong,' she said. 'It took me fifteen years of not being with them to realize it.'

She did two further tours with the band. On the latter one Lindsey Buckingham was replaced by Neil Finn and Mike Campbell. This time the rest of the band were not prepared to wait until Buckingham was ready, not least because Fleetwood Mac were enjoying yet another lease of life thanks to the fact that the records they had made forty years earlier sounded perfectly fine alongside the new one from Taylor Swift and a new generation of female fans wished to salute a band they saw as outriders for the twenty-first-century's feminization of pop music.

Christine McVie died in November 2022 at the age of seventy-nine. Back in the band.

SUPPOR

The erstwhile leader of Creedence Clearwater Revival, who could never be reconciled with his sixties band mates, preferred to employ his own children as backing musicians.

ACME

GREEN RIVER

31

THE BITTER YEARS
OF JOHN FOGERTY

In the early days of Covid lockdown, when the world was, willingly or not, confined to barracks, a number of well-known older-generation musicians began to record performances from home and make them available online. Among the earliest adopters of this folksy new format was John Fogerty, the man who at the end of the sixties had been the voice and songwriter of Creedence Clearwater Revival, at the time America's closest rivals to the Beatles. The Fogerty clips would feature him singing his old Creedence hits around an expensive-looking open fire with the accompaniment of young members of his family.

This was not unique. Around about the same time Nick Lowe performed from his own living room with his teenage son on drums. Crowded House were re-formed with the leader Neil Finn's sons in positions formerly occupied by hired hands. Ry Cooder's son operated as his father's percussionist and musical director as they delivered rousing versions of old folk favourites from home. The babies of the Baby Boomers had been part of the picture for many years. In the 1990s there had been a fashion for offering recording contracts to the sons and daughters of famous singers and writers such as Paul Simon, James Taylor and Leonard Cohen. Many of these people had talent, if not quite enough distinction to stand outside the shadow of their famous parent. As the novelist Martin Amis observed, talent is very often inherited, but stamina is not. On this occasion the appearance of Fogerty in a family context couldn't help recall the fact that when he had originally emerged over fifty years earlier, it had been as a member of another Fogerty family.

His first band was led by his older brother Tom. The difference between the Blue Velvets and other bands in the El Cerrito area of California in the sixties was young John. He couldn't just play, he could sing. He couldn't merely sing, he also looked the part of the band leader hero. What's more, he was the driven one. One of his jobs was packing records in the warehouse of a Bay Area jazz label called Fantasy. Certain qualities made Fogerty stand out from the thousands of young Americans encouraged by the Beatles' appearance on *The Ed Sullivan Show* to form a band. He had, from the beginning, one aim: he wanted to make great records and was prepared to work very hard to find out how you went about doing that.

In the wake of Beatlemania even a record label as far removed from the pop loop as Fantasy thought it could be worth having a toehold in the beat group business. Hence they let young Fogerty's group make a record. At the same time Tom anointed John the leader and strongly suggested to the other two band members, Stu Cook and Doug Clifford, that they should defer to him in all decisions. This they were happy enough to do, because it was obvious even at this stage that John was the person who knew what they should do next. Only he seemed to know where the next handholds were. It was plain as soon as they began making their first proper records, which were covers of rock and roll favourites, that John the singer had already transcended his influences, John the songwriter was capable of imagining his compositions as finished records, and John the producer already knew how to make those records better than anyone else in the world. He could do everything they did but they couldn't begin to do what he did. However, they were yoked together because there was no question that Creedence Clearwater Revival had to be above all things a band. This was something the members, the times and ultimately the audience seemed to demand.

Fogerty's position in Creedence was something like the position of Ray Davies in the Kinks. Between 1964 and 1969, in the greatest hot streak in the history of pop, Ray Davies single-handedly wrote and sang fourteen successive smash hit singles for the Kinks. Beginning in 1969, John Fogerty wrote, sang, produced and – he was most insistent – arranged not many short of that number, and in his case these were hits worldwide. The streak went as follows: 'Proud Mary', 'Bad Moon Rising', 'Fortunate Son', 'Green River', 'Down On The Corner', 'Travelin' Band', 'Who'll Stop The Rain', 'Up Around The Bend', 'Run Through The Jungle', 'Long As I Can See The Light' and 'Have You Ever Seen The Rain'. Those were just the singles.

In time this strength proved to be the tragedy of Creedence Clearwater Revival. John Fogerty wanted Creedence to be a band but the truth is he didn't much need the other three. This couldn't last. It never does. Once a group becomes successful and the non-writers in the ranks notice how much wealthier the songwriting member is they suddenly find that they too are tormented by a ceaseless urge to create. When the songwriting member is producing songs like 'Proud Mary', which was immediately seized upon by everyone from Ike and Tina Turner to Elvis Presley and even James Last, that urge becomes difficult to resist. At first, when the others proposed that the band record some of their compositions, John, who was clearly the gatekeeper, wanted them run by him. He was staggered by how little effort they seemed to be prepared to put in to justify the opportunity. His own brother sent him a tape of a song he'd been working on. John wasn't expecting a full-scale demo. He was however expecting more than a recording of Tom humming.

Unsurprisingly, Tom left the group in 1971. The departure was marked by a statement about wishing to spend more time with his family and make a record in his own right. What he actually felt, which was the kind of burning enmity that can only happen in families, came out years later in a letter – they spent a lot of time communicating by letter – where he accused his brother of believing his own press and the band somehow going from 'we' to 'I'. Here he may have had a point, albeit not the one he thought he was making. His decision proved to be one of the most memorable triumphs of injured pride over common sense in the annals of show business. He slunk off with the air of one who feared he wouldn't be missed. And while the withdrawal of his contribution wasn't apparent, his absence left a hole in the picture that was the band. The subtraction of any member from a four-piece band changes the position the band occupies in the mind's eye, no matter how marginal the musical contribution of that member may seem to have been. The world can never feel quite the same about them again. This is not always immediately apparent to the band.

They broke up in 1972, thinking they could just walk away. They couldn't. The 1969 contract between Fantasy Records and the members of Creedence Clearwater Revival is still taught to students on music business courses as an example of the kind of thing that could only be cooked up between the boss of a jazz record company unable to envisage ever having huge sales to worry about in the first place, and the young members of a band who were not thinking beyond their burning desire to get into a proper recording studio. Looked at from today, it certainly seems far from fair. It's said that the contract was once shown to Allen Klein. The man who had built his reputation on getting money out of record companies that claimed they had already paid, the man who worked on behalf of the Beatles and the Rolling Stones, the man who prided himself on being able to see a way out of the most hopeless situation, looked at the paper the young members of Creedence had put their names to, said, 'There is nothing I can do,' and handed it back.

The case between John Fogerty, the former members of Creedence and the owner of Fantasy, Saul Zaentz, rumbled on for decades. It became the Jarndyce v. Jarndyce of the music business. On one side of this confrontation was Zaentz, who had once been a professional gambler and thrived in the world of independent film production because he took the expenditure of every dollar personally; on the other was Fogerty, who could harbour a grudge for periods of time that would give a Serbian pause. Caught in the middle were the other three, who could barely make their rent as long as the face-off continued. Whenever they reached any agreement with Zaentz over the reuse of their recorded material, John Fogerty would accuse them of betraying him. When they tried to mend fences with him and edge him towards putting the band back together, he made it clear he had no intention of doing any such thing. This went on for decades. From time to time big beasts of the music industry like David Geffen and Bill Graham would try to broker a deal between the two of them. It never happened. In 1985 Fogerty found himself in court having to convince a judge that he hadn't stolen one of his new songs, 'The Old Man Down From The Road', from a song he wrote fifteen years before for Creedence. He won, but even the victory cost him over a million dollars. Zaentz died in 2014. Not long after, Fogerty was asked what he thought. He said that all these years he'd promised himself that when Zaentz died he would stand over his grave and drop his first gold disc on top of the coffin. In the event, he said, he had very little feeling left.

Not counting an al fresco reunion of the four at Tom's second wedding in 1980 and a further performance by the three-piece at an El Cerrito High School reunion, at the time of writing Creedence Clearwater Revival have not existed for over fifty years. In both cases the other guys prayed that this happy event would be the spur for them to re-form. In both cases they didn't dare say anything about it and waited for John to come to the same conclusion. He never did. They are one of the few bands that headlined at the Woodstock Festival in 1969 not to give in to the lure of the massive sums of money that first-generation rock legends can still command in the twenty-first century. There is no band called Creedence Clearwater Revival headlining the Glastonbury Festival or taking its rightful place alongside the Rolling Stones and the Who at the Desert Trip in the California desert. There is no spectacular retrospective for streaming TV, no $100 boxed set of outtakes, no officially licensed T-shirt, no meet-and-greets with dotcom billionaires. There has been nothing new to be heard from Creedence Clearwater Revival since 1972.

In its place was gall and wormwood. Tom Fogerty made four albums, none of which anyone bought. He claimed they had no promotion, which is standard. He split up with his first wife and family, largely because he simply couldn't let go of the idea he had once been a successful rock star, had once been a member of Creedence Clearwater Revival. His wife told Creedence biographer Hank Bordowitz, 'he had quit the band and was miserable because he had quit'. Over time he grew poor. At that stage his only chance of any income at all would come from his portion of whatever Creedence Clearwater Revival might be paid for licensing their music for commercials, where there was still a lot of demand. The other three were always keen to sign these deals but every time John would use his veto. This is the kind of thing that splits up bands and families. In Tom's case it split both. Tom and John Fogerty's mother died in 1988, convinced her two sons would never be reconciled. Tom died two years later. He had been given blood during a transfusion, blood that wasn't screened for HIV. There was even talk of a musical reunion around his deathbed. John rejected that idea too.

Fogerty's face remained set against any reconciliation with the other two. When they were inducted into the Rock and Roll Hall of Fame in 1993, Doug and Stu turned up with their instruments, expecting not only to pick up their award but also to take part in a Creedence Clearwater Revival performance; it was only when they got there that they found that John had agreed to play their songs with Bruce Springsteen, Robbie Robertson and similar luminaries. In the backstage area that night there then ensued a furious exchange between the three former high-school buddies, an exchange many thought was about to turn physical. Watching it with particular alarm and embarrassment were Springsteen and Robertson. This was not the behaviour of elder statesmen of rock. This was the unseemly squabbling of a bunch of teenage boys. They were picking up the threads of an argument that had started two decades earlier and would carry on until the last of them died. On this occasion it was also witnessed by another group of similar vintage that had somehow managed to put their splenetic bygones behind them in order to re-form for the occasion. It is a measure of the bitterness between the three remaining members of Creedence Clearwater Revival that it came as a surprise even to the members of Cream. Also watching on that night was the widow of Tom Fogerty, who had brought his ashes with her.

In 2023, Fogerty finally bought the ownership of his songs back from the company that had acquired them. At the very moment his better-known peers were selling their catalogues and banking the proceeds, he was going the other way. He said he was just enjoying the feeling. For years he wouldn't play the old songs on stage because he couldn't stomach the idea of his adversary profiting from them. He only relented occasionally. In 1987 he found himself on stage with Bob Dylan who wanted him to play 'Proud Mary' because 'if you don't people will think it's a Tina Turner song'. The announcement of the reunion of the old man with the songs he wrote when he was in his twenties was accompanied by the usual platitudes about the inevitability of them lasting for ever, the notion that this might possibly lead to that long-delayed reunion for Creedence Clearwater Revival waved away with the thought 'I miss my brother Tom, who passed at a time when we were not really in each other's lives. I'm looking forward to getting to heaven and playing in God's band, and Tom will be there.'

32

When Elton John began his performing career the concert-going audience was the under-thirties; when he rang down the curtain at Glastonbury in 2023 it was everyone.

GOODBYE
GOODBYE YELLOW
BRICK ROAD

The Farewell Yellow Brick Road tour, which Elton John completed in Sweden in June 2023, had been much delayed, by the star's own health issues and by Covid. Of all the people with whom I had dealings during that time, the ones who seemed most affected by the pandemic were the musicians. Not only were they deprived of their usual way of making a living, which was through live performance, but they found it hard to get through their days without the structure provided by touring. Those days were long and the nights were a good deal harder because they were no longer climaxed with applause. Some even combed through their possessions looking for things they could sell other than their usual services. After all, Don McLean had got more than a million dollars in 2015 for what were apparently the original lyrics of 'American Pie' and a few years later had managed to turn up 'Vincent'. That is what you call a profitable way to publish a song. Many others decided this was as good a time as any to write that long-deferred autobiography. There seemed to be innumerable albums called *Lockdown Sessions* or some variant thereof – at least one of them by Elton John.

By the time Elton's tour had finished it was able to claim to have grossed more money than any tour in history. This was partially because it had involved over three hundred shows but also because it had commanded a high ticket price. Had they played the four hundred shows the agent initially had in mind when it was first discussed in 2018 it would have been even more lucrative. The scale of major international touring in the twenty-first century boggled the mind. In Elton's case, entire nations such as Brazil and Japan had to be scrubbed from the plan for reasons that had as much to do with the fluctuations of currency and the rise in the price of oil following the Russian invasion of Ukraine as any issue pertaining to show business. In 2023, a world tour was dealing with a very different world to the previous century, and it had come to do it in a very worldly way. The period covered by this book began with Live Aid in 1985 when, as I pointed out early on, there were no mobile phones. Two years later I was on a Genesis tour when I saw a laptop backstage for the first time. This now seems Stone Age when set against touring in the new century.

Like all Boomers, Elton had seen a lot of change. The early part of his career had been steered by John Reid, an old-school music business man whose other role in the star's life, as his lover, had to remain a closely guarded secret because of the laws and customs of the time. The latter phase of the same career was guided by David Furnish, a younger man from an advertising background comfortable with talk of footprints, markets and platforms, who was also the star's actual husband. While it might have been Elton's unfeigned enthusiasm for whatever was happening in pop at the time which led him to record with everybody from Eminem to Dua Lipa, it was Furnish's shrewd reading of the research that told him that the aspects of the star's life which most resounded with the social media generations – the sexual history, the addictions, the stirring backstory – should be brought to the fore and that the 2019 film *Rocketman* needed to be a fantasy rather than a biography. In Elton's case, even this long-planned and much-ballyhooed end-of-the-road is unlikely to bring a complete end to Elton John activities. Like most rock superstars he is just one cog in a machine, and that machine will keep on whirring as long as there are opportunities.

His company has a chief operating officer who describes the 'whole immersive space' as very interesting. The Elton John industry is unlikely to stop when Elton John does. In the same year a company with the colourful name Nobby's Hobbies Holdings reported that it had earned £55,000 a day in the previous twelve months and promised that activity in the next few years would include live performances. This is particularly impressive since that company represents the work of George Michael, who died in 2016.

When Elton took the stage at Glastonbury in 2023 for what was regarded as his farewell to Blighty, each different tranche of the audience, each of whom had joined his magic roundabout at a different point in its more than fifty years of revolutions, was seeing the Elton they had come to see: the party animal of the glam-rock days, the sober pilgrim who made rehab a household word, the man who sang a princess to her rest on behalf of the nation, the show business personality who had gone nose to nose with Eric Morecambe, the all-round entertainer with the zany specs, the Bitch, the Rocket Man, the Madman Across the Water, Captain Fantastic, the chairman of the board, the piano-playing Reg and the rest of his teeming host of alter egos, no single one of them any more definitive than the others. This was less like saying farewell to an individual performer than marking the closure of an entire national theatre.

They had all got on the carousel at different points and therefore they remembered him in a different way. For those who recalled the twenty-three-year-old Elton John and some of the same musicians who were still with him at Glastonbury taking the stage of Mothers Club, which was above a furniture shop in Birmingham, or Guildford Town Hall or the Country Club on Haverstock Hill back in the days when the Vietnam war was still raging and the Beatles were still together, the sight of this elderly man in the bacofoil suit gingerly making his way to the piano prior to launching into a song about a deaf, dumb and blind boy who had once shone at an obsolete game of skill and doing it to the apparent approval of a nation grateful for something to unite around was one of those sights for which a lifetime observing pop musicians could scarcely have prepared them.

Did anybody in the crowd remember the Elton John a declining number of us grew up with? That would be the real one who pounded the same pavements as the rest of us, not this walking brand ambassador for the fantasy we all enjoyed in the movie. Would they know the one in the scoop-necked T-shirt and army greatcoat who haunted the import racks of Musicland in Berwick Street waiting for the new Leon Russell album? The one who bashed out all those songs about burning missions and daddy's rifle in his mum's house in Pinner? The one who at the height of his early fame was so far up himself that he dedicated an entire show at Wembley Stadium to songs about the personal lives of him and his lyricist? Not that even this musical autobiography told the truth. This is a man who was allegedly heterosexual for a longer period of time than he has been fiercely gay. A man who publicly sold all his possessions in order to prove he could live without them before replacing them with a fresh set of possessions which cost even more money. A man who was said to buy three copies of each new entry into the chart, each destined for one of the three houses he maintained in three different countries, each of which was supplied with fresh flowers daily, regardless of whether he was there or not. A man who retained members of staff whose sole job was to wrap presents. There is no precedent for the life that Reg Dwight has lived and the career that Elton John has enjoyed. Many rock stars have finished their careers under the management of their wives. The personal journey of Elton John took place against a background of such far-reaching social change that he is the first one to have finished his career under the management of his husband.

For those in the crowd who were born after the release of

Goodbye Yellow Brick Road, Elton John had always been a known quantity, part of the cultural furniture, a superstar, a done deal. A ledge. An icon. For those born before that album, for those who remember the bespectacled troubadour who had made the mistake of signing to Dick James's label, Elton was a story they had followed live as it happened with all its stumbles, reverses and hilarious successes. This is what the present cannot understand. The present star system was not ever thus. The cult of the icon is a relatively recent invention. Some of us remember when they were just ordinary people.

In an interview Howard Stern asked Ian Hunter whether he had been flattered when in 1972 his group Mott the Hoople were offered 'All The Young Dudes' by such 'an iconic artist' as David Bowie. No, said Ian, because back then he was just a little geezer from Beckenham. This is the truth. A geezer from Beckenham. They were all chancers once upon a time. They were all scuffling once, and most of them scuffled in little places that had never expected a great deal of them, places like Beckenham, Dartford and Duluth, Pinner and Ripley, Feltham and Freehold. Most of them came from unpretentious little houses, homes that would, in later years, appear faintly embarrassed to have attention drawn to them through the unveiling of a memorial plaque or a gushing entry in a local guidebook while the boys and girls who had done their growing up in their confined bedrooms were now in their seventies, taking to bigger and bigger stages to play their greatest hits, in the process acting out the fantastic journeys which had been their lives.

33

For audiences flocking to see old favourites like Bruce Springsteen, much of the appeal came from simply seeing old bonds endure.

THE OLD BOYS
OF SUMMER

Bruce Springsteen was touring Britain the same summer that Elton John played Glastonbury. He didn't announce this tour as his farewell but it was conducted with the air of a man who certainly wasn't taking for granted the idea that there would be another one. If he had suffered any reverses on the health front they had not been shared with the public, but some key members of the E Street Band had been gathered in recent years, others had suffered their own problems, and he clearly knew that it was only when appearing with his old gang that he could truly provide the show that people demanded – which was, whatever the material, essentially his life story, the saga of how a nine-stone weakling made himself, by an act of will and with a lot of help from his friends, into the biggest rock act in the world.

In that story he is the star actor, director, producer, writer, juvenile lead, veteran character actor, comic turn, critic and source material. That story tells of how rock and roll came along to transform a no-mark boy from Freehold, New Jersey, a nerd whose passage through high school was so anonymous as to be barely noticed by most of his fellow pupils, and made him the most envied and admired American of his generation – and now he has come among us to raise us too above our troubles through the redemptive power of music.

I saw him first at Madison Square Garden in 1980, back in that vanished world a few days before John Lennon was shot. He was thirty-one at the time and I would guess there was no one in the Garden that night who was more than forty. When he toured the UK in 2023 there wouldn't have been many in the crowd who were less than forty. The records he put out in that time have come and gone but very few of them have supplanted 'Born To Run', 'Thunder Road' or 'Born In The USA'. In truth, people can live without new material from people like Springsteen. It's the old-time religion they go for.

Bruce Springsteen has spent most of the last fifty years telling the story of his generation. Millions of kids thought their lives would be forever changed after they saw the Beatles on *The Ed Sullivan Show*. They all bought the record. Some bought the wig. A few brave souls grew their hair. Bruce Springsteen did more than that. He dedicated his entire life to inventing a band he could lead, a band whose performances could celebrate the fact that their leader never went for the nine-to-five. He couldn't possibly have dreamed how long he would be doing it for. In the gangster movie *White Heat* – released in 1949, the year Springsteen was born – Jimmy Cagney is cut down by the law just as he addresses the mother for whom he has done everything with the words 'Look, Ma, top of the world!' By appearing with the E Street Band in a show that was a celebration of his personal triumph over impossible odds, Springsteen did that every night from his late twenties right through to his seventies and in that time nobody put a bullet, actual or metaphorical, in him. When he played in London in the summer of 2023 he was seventy-three.

He wasn't the only one who had something at stake. A huge amount of the emotional charge that long-time fans draw from going to see their favourite bands performing when both band and audience are in the evening of their days comes from simply being there to watch them walk on stage, to be there to witness them still together with their old friends from their teenage years, playing the songs they first played way back when and still surviving, which is the greatest reward in itself. On stage at Hyde Park he talked about how he was the only member of his first teenage band who was still alive. 'At fifteen it's all tomorrows,' he said. 'At seventy-three it's all yesterdays.'

In most cases star musicians in their seventies tried to re-establish good terms with old friends, and if they had any old enemies, to bury the hatchet. Only the members of Pink Floyd thought it best to bury said hatchet between each other's shoulder blades. But that didn't apply to all of them. While David Gilmour and Roger Waters said deeply disobliging and actionable things about each other on social media in 2023, and while Waters seemed to be doing everything in his power to get himself placed beyond the pale, the band's drummer, Nick Mason, led his own band dedicated to performing Pink Floyd's early works and did it to great acclaim. Waters in contrast remained an unofficial member of that tiny group of veteran musicians who seemed to pride themselves on not fitting in.

Most of the musicians who woke up in their seventh, eighth and even ninth decades to the pleasant news that they were better known than they had been back in the day, and probably better loved as well, took a few minutes to register their surprise and delight and then decided that they would lie back and enjoy it, doing everything in their power not to get in the way of what was transparently a good thing. Van Morrison, who has long been a singularly ungrateful beneficiary of cult status, railed against Covid restrictions on an album, which in the world of TikTok was arguably the least effective way to put over your point. Morrison, who had been knighted after a government campaign to make sure that all the nations making up the United Kingdom had at least one musical knight, seemed to grow more peevish with every garland showered upon him. He had turned up to perform at a special concert staged on the very Belfast thoroughfare he had made famous in song, which is surely as great an honour as any home-town boy may claim, but still wasn't about to give anyone the satisfaction of hearing him sing the song in question, 'Cyprus Avenue'. Morrison campaigned to be one of the first performers to take advantage of the loosening of lockdown by playing a show in London. When this happened, did he say it was good to be back? He didn't.

In the late summer of 2023 queues formed outside the Bond Street showrooms of Sotheby's to see its exhibition of items associated with Freddie Mercury. The singer had died in 1991 when the art trade wasn't exactly in a tearing hurry to showcase a former glam rock star's collection of fifty kimonos. But that was before the Victoria and Albert Museum in London had done extremely well out of an exhibition of material associated with David Bowie and the culture vultures had learned which buttons to press in order to sell the prancing louts of Tin Pan Alley to the carriage trade. 'Freddie Mercury really was visionary,' gushed the lady from Sotheby's at the launch. 'Nobody else at the time was collecting black and queer artists.' It's bootless to point out that nobody else at the time was using either of those adjectives. The present takes the pieces of the past it finds to its taste.

When Record Store Day rolled around in April 2023 it was for the fifteenth time, making it a unique and well-established date in the cultural calendar. It turned out that the twelve-inch vinyl long-playing record, which had slipped away unmourned in the final decade of the previous century, had become, thanks to Record Store Day, reborn in the twenty-first as the music carrier of choice for the small but free-spending minority of people who continued to believe in the specialness of the album.

Record stores, which had previously been found wherever other stores were found – on every high street, in each and every out-of-town shopping mall, even as actual departments in actual department stores – were now reborn in bohemian quarters, this time as heritage destinations, where they projected the kind of antiquarian vibe that might lead a casual shopper to wonder whether they ought to light a candle on entering. On the wall behind the counter would be lovingly tended displays of newly vintage albums, many of which had languished unloved for long years in the bargain bin back in the days when the same patrons preferred CDs.

Like the fictitious shop in Nick Hornby's *High Fidelity*, these outlets seemed to pride themselves on not selling anything that might conceivably be requested by the customer who had just rolled in off the street. Which is why every year the record business strained every sinew to come up with versions of the past to be sold on the day. Record Store Day became a small market in itself, with demand stoked and satisfied by a succession of special edition reissues half of which were snapped up for premium prices by people who didn't allow the fact that they didn't actually own a record player to spoil the fun they derived from being, if only for a day, the kind of people who bought 'vinyls'. The ownership of vinyl suddenly became a way of advertising one's depth of soul. The marketing of the same thing became a way of reintroducing to the market the one property from which so much of the appeal of popular music had historically derived in the past – scarcity.

One of the consequences of this hunger for the soul of the past was that the most passionate evangelists for the music of these bygone eras, and also its best-informed advocates, were the people who were coming upon it forty years after its day. Something similar had occurred with Dixieland jazz, which was rediscovered in the fifties at a time when its original practitioners were fading away. Because the rock revolution of the late sixties left behind it far more traces than the brief recording boom of the late twenties, there has been a stampede to elevate and celebrate names who in their day would have been accorded little more than polite interest. This has led to a kind of veneration inflation where vintage acts are concerned. If Vashti Bunyan's one 1970 record was acclaimed as a deathless masterpiece, how would it be possible to find adequate words for the output of Joni Mitchell?

The latter's re-emergence at the Newport Folk Festival in 2022, playing the nation's foremost acoustic festival for the first time since 1969 at the centre of an ensemble of admirers, had been a timely reminder of the fact that some musicians had been robbed of the opportunity to enjoy their Indian summer by health problems. Joni Mitchell's stock had always been high – in the seventies she was even a staple on the charts – but her critics had never been as kind as they were during the time when she was sidelined by her need to recover from a brain aneurysm. She had always been followed and sometimes loved; only in the present century has she been worshipped. She was also surrounded by women performers, which had rarely been the case when she was in her pomp. When in March 2023 she headlined a show in her honour in Washington State, Annie Lennox described her as 'a genius, a visionary, an inspiration', presumably for the benefit of people who weren't familiar with her work.

In July that year Mick Jagger, the man who used to say he couldn't imagine doing this job when he was forty, celebrated his eightieth birthday with not one but two parties, as befits a genuinely social animal and a family man. He now sits atop a large extended family who all seem to have had the good sense not to fall out with him. As the summer was winding down, the Rolling Stones started banging the drum for *Hackney Diamonds*, their first record of new material since 2005, an event they marked by monopolizing the media for a few days – a phenomenon akin to the media of 1976 being dominated by a story about the reunion of the Original

Dixieland Jazz Band. Then they announced that they were going on tour again. They can still get promoters and insurers to work with them. The old acts are apparently regarded as a good risk because they have learned how to pace themselves. That's why they're the old acts.

Predicting what will outlive a major music act is far from straightforward. The Ramones logo, as seen on many a fashionable chest, has proved more attractive to investors than their records.

34

SOUND
INVESTMENTS

T hat mighty wind called the internet, which blew across the music business from 1990 onwards, swept many people's tables clean. For those who had relied on a steady stream of royalty cheques based on the sales of long-playing records, it was game over. This in itself was nothing new. The history of the music business has been a succession of technological upheavals. Bing Crosby began his career in the twenties, in the days of nickelodeons and singers who sang through megaphones. He died in the seventies when a thing called network television was king and it seemed the long-playing record would never be replaced. Cylinders, player pianos, jukeboxes, wireless, the movies, live performance – all have at one time or another appeared to be the only economy that worked.

So it was with the passing of the long-playing economy. Once it had passed it was recalled as an Elysian era when the living was easy and the cotton was high. This was a state of affairs nobody seemed to comment upon at the time. Once the long-player had been replaced by the streaming economy many artists tried to draw parallels between the money they had previously made by selling records as compared to the money they would make by licensing a couple of tracks from it to be played once. What such parallels failed to recognize was that most of the money most acts previously made was in the form of advances which were paid by record companies in the hope that the next record would join the select company of money makers, a hope that was in the overwhelming majority of cases in vain. Record companies were no longer handing out such largesse.

However, some of the smart money was still prepared to bet on the music of the past. As this book was being prepared, the music story most often occupying the headlines in the City pages told of investment companies like Hipgnosis taking huge sums of money and spending them on the catalogues of people who made their name in the sixties and seventies: Neil Young, Bob Dylan, the members of Fleetwood Mac and others have all been associated with figures in the hundreds of millions in exchange for their songs and in some cases their recordings. For the investors, this appeared to make sense. When interest rates were low and the shine had gone off many of the markets in which they were accustomed to invest, it made some sense to put something into song catalogues. Thanks to the proliferation of music in everything from streaming television to social media, these copyrights certainly keep on earning money. The principal of Hipgnosis said that even if Donald Trump did something crazy, songs would still be played, and as long as the collection agencies were at work the holders of those copyrights would continue to get paid. There was much speculation among cultural commentators as to whether Neil Young's 'Heart Of Gold', Bob Dylan's 'Masters Of War' or Fleetwood Mac's 'Rhiannon' would continue to pull in the royalties further into the twenty-first century. The songwriters who were entering into these agreements may have shared some of their concerns. They may have been advised that they should take the high offers while they were there. They may have reasoned that at least they wouldn't have to think about their heirs having to make the decision following their deaths.

At the beginning of 2024, the first Walt Disney film featuring Mickey Mouse entered the public domain. This was almost a hundred years since *Steamboat Willie* was released. Copyright law, which was originally invented to ensure that the originators of a piece of work would be guaranteed a share of what it earned during their lifetime, has been extended every which way in recent years, largely to suit those who wind up owning those works – usually corporations. In the US, the 1998 bill that extended the already long life of a copyright became known to insiders as the Mickey Mouse Protection Act, so generously did the corporations that have owned that name back the senators who carried it into law, thereby ensuring that you had to be careful copying a fifty-year-old picture of Mickey Mouse for a poster for your kids' school fete. People arguing that more and more works should be covered by copyright are apt to invoke the picture of the impoverished artist starving in their garret and to claim that without its protections no new songs will come forth. What they never mention is the fact that each extension increases the value of the assets on the balance sheets of a handful of large multinational companies which years before purchased them from the heirs of the originators and which are, as a breed, wholly unfamiliar with garrets. What these companies worry about in the twenty-first century is that artificial intelligence may soon make it difficult to get up in front of a judge and argue that the integrity of an original work is at issue; that success in the pop record business isn't largely a question of putting an ingenious twist on something the listener has heard a million times before; and that the really distinctive factor is the musical fingerprint of the act that came up with said twist and is now no more.

The passing of a big rock name inevitably brings their family blinking into the daylight, and all families are dramas in themselves. Some estates are managed by the offspring, which can lead to its own problems. At one stage, two of Frank Zappa's older children, who had more power over his estate than the other one, actually injuncted their younger brother to stop him performing the compositions of his father under his father's name. The many children of Aretha Franklin were still fighting in court a couple of years after her death in 2018. Where a group is concerned it's likely to become complicated as well as bitter. Even in the workaday world it's quite common for the beneficiaries of wills to feel that they have not inherited as much as they should. In the music business it's a lot murkier and uncertain than that. The windfalls can be huge and there will always be a lawyer who thinks you've got a case. Most of the high-profile recent cases alleging infringement of the copyright of acts such as Marvin Gaye and Spirit have been launched on behalf of the musicians' estates or offspring.

As the beat generation died off there were numerous reminders of the fact that no social organization can provide such rich soil for grievances as a band. Unless it's a band with a hit long ago. When Gary Brooker of Procol Harum died in 2022 it was not long after a judge had ruled that Hammond organist Matthew Fisher should also get some revenue from 'A Whiter Shade Of Pale', a record he had played a part in making in 1967. The revenue would not be retrospective but it would still be worth having. In a survey of the most-played records on British radio, 'A Whiter Shade Of Pale' was number one. It was perfectly possible to make more money out of an old record in the modern world than you might have made from it when it was first a hit. The channels down which music is carried are vastly increased since the swinging sixties and will only grow in the years to come.

Because the music doesn't stop when the musicians pass away there are companies that specialize in managing the affairs of late acts. One of them is run by Jeff Jampol. Jampol reckons the work of Kurt Cobain is going to be relevant for centuries. It isn't always the music which lingers or proves to have the value. Jampol's company also handles, among many others, the Ramones. The last of the four original members of the Ramones died in 2014. For years they made the most of their revenue from sales of their T-shirt, which featured a logo designed by fifth member, Arturo Vega. That state of affairs has continued long into their afterlife. Today, an artfully distressed replica of the original shirt might cost almost as much as people would have spent on an annual holiday back in 1976. Indeed the one place you are guaranteed to see the expensive faux vintage rock and roll T-shirt is in the business-class lounge at a major international airport where it seems to form a key part of the travelling wardrobe of a certain species of affluent-looking, leathery middle-aged person. This individual will hold a waxed cup of expensive coffee to indicate that they are on their way to do something very important and will wear a T-shirt featuring Nirvana or the Ramones to hint that they used to be a hellraiser back in the day. It could be that the iconography of these acts might ultimately be worth more than the music. It is often argued that the most valuable asset owned by the Rolling Stones is not 'Honky Tonk Women', 'Angie' or 'Start Me Up', it's the lips and tongue of their logo.

Predicting what music will outlive the musicians who made it is far from straightforward. Bing Crosby was the most successful musical entertainer of the twentieth century and he's all but forgotten now. Frank Sinatra came in second and he is still revered, but as much for what he looked like as for what he sounded like. A hundred years ago Paul Whiteman was the King of Jazz, now he's unknown. Even Louis Armstrong is more likely to be celebrated these days for his sentimental songs that turn up on movie soundtracks of the sixties than for the recordings of his pre-war Hot Fives and Sevens. Giants of the early days of rock and roll such as Buddy Holly and the Everly Brothers are slipping out of the picture as the musicians who were inspired by them slip away. These days oldies radio stations rarely go any further back than the eighties. The 2022 Baz Luhrmann biopic about Elvis Presley made a lot of play of what a musical revolution its subject spearheaded back in the fifties but wasn't brave enough to present a modern audience

with his music without wrapping it first in the comforting habili-
ments of hip hop. This last genre retuned ears around the turn of the
century much as rock and roll had done in the fifties, making everything that came before sound quaint. It couldn't deliver the essence
of Elvis Presley, which was how he made people feel.

The class of 1963, if you care to put it that way, have managed to
make it to the finish of their allotted span without suffering the
indignity of redundancy or retirement. What will become of what
they leave behind? Will their songs really last as long as the songs
Irving Berlin or Cole Porter wrote for the stage shows and musical
comedies of the middle of the last century? The short answer is, it's
difficult to say. Porter's love songs like 'I've Got You Under My Skin'
and 'Night And Day' and Berlin's celebratory anthems 'White Christmas' and 'There's No Business Like Show Business' were designed to
be understood and their longevity is underwritten by their sheer
utility. Anybody sitting at a piano to play them in the middle of the
twenty-first century is likely to get the same result as they would
have done had they played them a hundred years earlier.

The popular music of the first half of the twentieth century was
all about songs. The popular music of the second half of the twentieth century was all about records. What attracted people was sound.
For the overwhelming majority of records that have been to the top
of the charts within living memory, the unvarnished song, that bare,
forked creature, played and sung by one person at a piano, would be
a poor thing indeed. Live performance will continue to go the other
way entirely. Technology will be more and more capable of making
up for the shortcomings of the human factor and, if in doubt, will
eliminate the latter altogether.

Then there are the hygiene factors of taste and decency. The Rolling Stones have already retired 'Brown Sugar'. The witchfinders
general of the twenty-first century will in time get round to 'Stray
Cat Blues', 'Some Girls', 'Hey Negrita' and many more. Here there's

no defence other than the fact that pop music, which was once measured on its ability to stand against respectable values, is now expected to uphold respectable values, and if it doesn't it won't be long before there will be pitchforks and torches coming up the digital drive. The legacy of the Rolling Stones may well suffer from the 'problematic' subject matter of many of their songs. The fact that they have kept going as long as they have means that they don't win the obscurity points which are awarded to Led Zeppelin.

There's also the question of the sound of records. Many people find it hard to listen to records from the eighties because producers of that time were so keen to adopt the latest proven techniques that they ended up with a sound overfull of additives and colourants. A few, such as Bob Marley, have been victims of their own success, spoiled by overexposure. Some others, like Michael Jackson, seem to have survived both that and a level of brand contamination that would have meant curtains for any other product relying on public approval.

Things don't remain as they were in rock Valhalla. Even the dead move up and down the chart in the Hall of Fame. David Bowie's death in 2016 saw him accorded the same saint-like standing as John Lennon had been granted thirty-six years earlier. This was not unconnected with the fact that he died at the exact point when social media had convinced its users they had a duty to tell the rest of the world where they stood in relation to every hatch, match and dispatch. Indeed the spikes in social media traffic which follow the death of any musician may not prove how great a gap they left in our lives, but they certainly bear out a truth the Victorians would recognize – that mourning is a form of public display.

The most widely talked-about musical event of 2023 was a funeral. The death of Shane MacGowan, for years the erratic front man and totem of the London Irish band the Pogues, could be described with confidence as the least surprising death in the annals of music. The funeral, which took place in December at Nenagh in County

Tipperary, was carried live by Irish television and picked up by the BBC, attracted in part by the presence of mourners like Johnny Depp, Bob Geldof and Irish president Michael D. Higgins, and performances from Nick Cave and Glen Hansard and a chorus of Irish folk musicians, as mourners danced in the aisles. Depp and the former Sinn Féin leader Gerry Adams gave readings. In a concession to the A list which was odd in such a celebration of the common man, Bono's contribution was played in off-tape.

People interviewed outside the church said MacGowan's songs would live forever more. Bruce Springsteen, in a statement, said, 'I don't know about the rest of us, but they'll be singing Shane's songs a hundred years from now.' This may or may not be borne out by events, but one thing seems assured. In the future a lot more rock star funerals will be televised and they will be popular because the truth is we will enjoy mourning the passing of our favourites almost as much as we enjoyed tearing our hair and rending our garments over them back in the day. And because we like to feel that our passions are eternal we like to feel that the faces which once looked down on us from our bedroom walls will somehow go down in history.

Orson Welles said it was every bit as vulgar to work for the sake of posterity as it was to work for money. Nobody talks about posterity in the music business. There are no examples of rock stars holding anything back to be released after they are gone. The alacrity with which the likes of Bob Dylan and Neil Young have spent the last twenty years flooding the market with previously unreleased product, the same recordings they previously decried as sub-standard and likely to reduce their standing in the eyes of the public if they were ever allowed to be heard, suggests that most of them prefer the praise and the profit on this earth. Heaven, it would appear, can wait.

THE
IMMORTALITY
BUSINESS

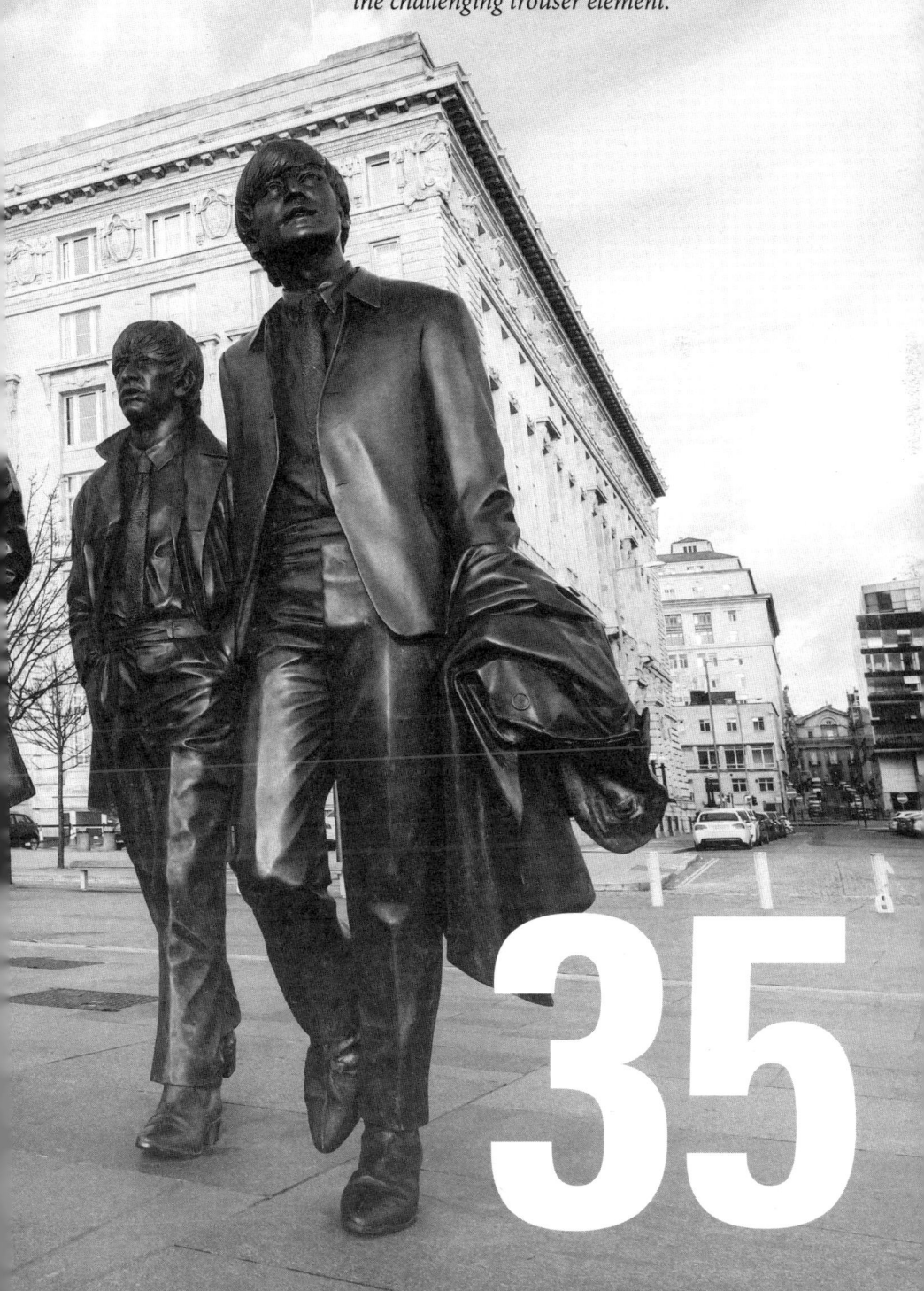

This depiction of the young Beatles striding out to meet the world from Liverpool's waterfront is one of the happier examples of the meeting of music, masonry and civic pride, thanks to its mastery of the challenging trouser element.

35

I n 2013 an exhibition devoted to objects associated with the life and career of David Bowie opened at the Victoria and Albert Museum in London. *David Bowie Is*, as the exhibition was called, subsequently went on a world tour which took it to Canada, Brazil, Germany, France, the United States and Australia. In Paris a school teacher called Sébastien Dormieu was presented with an auto-graphed catalogue for the exhibition to mark the fact that he was its one-millionth visitor. In 2016 a show called *Exhibitionism* opened at the Saatchi Gallery in Chelsea, not far from the flat on the King's Road where the founder members of the Rolling Stones, the group that was the exhibition's subject, had lived when they were poor. One of its most noted exhibits was an attempt to recreate the squalid kitchen of that legendary flat in Edith Grove. In 2017 an exhibition called *Their Mortal Remains*, which was dedicated to relics associ-ated with Pink Floyd, attracted more than three hundred thousand people to the V&A. In 2019 the Metropolitan Museum of Art in New York announced an exhibition 'dedicated entirely to the iconic instruments of rock and roll' at which visitors were invited to gaze upon guitars previously played by Chuck Berry, Bruce Springsteen, Prince and Joni Mitchell among many others. In 2023 the National Portrait Gallery in London celebrated the opening of their new wing with an exhibition of photographs taken fifty years earlier by Paul McCartney. They were hip, they were edgy, they brought in a crowd who would spend freely in the gift shop; there was clearly nothing about old rock and roll stars that the burgeoning culture industry didn't like. However, the most successful example of selling tickets to gaze upon rock relics had a longer history and could be found far from the marble halls of traditional museums and galleries.

When Elvis Presley died in 1977 the probate judge predicted that his estate would be worth $150 million. As Eamonn Forde pointed out in his book about rock estates, it was actually worth only about $7 million and they owed a good deal more than that in tax. Created out of necessity to bridge this gap, the 1982 opening of Presley's surprisingly modest home Graceland as a visitor attraction began the rock heritage business. By the thirtieth anniversary of its opening to the public, Graceland had attracted around eighteen million visitors, making it one of the biggest tourist attractions in the United States. When it opened, admission was $5. These days it begins at $45 and goes as high as $200.

In the early days of the dead Elvis industry, Graceland was surrounded by stores selling cheap unlicensed souvenirs. Over a period of years, as the leases expired, these were taken over by investors working on behalf of the estate and subsequently turned into stores selling expensive licensed souvenirs. Success in the rock memorabilia business, which is not for the easily shamed, calls for the poker face required to argue that the tat you buy as you exit through the official gift shop exists on a more elevated moral plane than the unofficial tat being knocked out by the vendor on the corner.

There's rarely a problem in drumming up interest in any site with powerful rock associations. Footfall is not the problem. What's tricky is monetizing that traffic. For instance, huge numbers of people turn up to Abbey Road every year to have their pictures taken on what is the only listed pedestrian crossing in the United Kingdom. However, the only way the studio's present owners could turn some of that interest into money was by opening a gift shop in the property next door. It's all about putting money in the till.

The heirs of Johnny Cash, who died in 2003, lent his name to the Johnny Cash Kitchen and Saloon in Nashville, where fans can contemplate stained-glass windows recording key incidents in the man in black's journey through this vale of tears without interrupting their consumption of premium-priced country fried chicken washed down with a $14 cocktail called the Folsom Prison Blues. This facility is operated by the same firm that runs similar destinations named after country songbird Patsy Cline, cowboy designer Nudie and, in a most un-Nashville twist, Frank Sinatra.

Country's music city is full of hospitality spaces trading off a relationship with a dead musician, relationships which are often theoretical. They're all operated by companies that look longingly at the figures produced every year by Elvis Presley Enterprises. In life, Elvis blazed a trail; in death, arguably, he has blazed an even more significant one. The shrine to which people flock from all over the world is, unlike Abbey Road, not a place of work, but a home. What Graceland the visitor attraction celebrates is not a musician so much as a farcically successful young man who could buy all the toys he wanted, and did. It retains its fascination because when all's said and done it's a slightly pretentious executive home, such as might have been bought by the owner of a successful car dealership, and it is unsympathetically sited by a main road, which says a great deal about the man who bought it. Graceland, which has extended its footprint remorselessly, moving into car museums and hotels and a venue in order to hoover the maximum amount of cash out of the pockets of visitors to Memphis, attracts not merely Elvis fans; it is actually a magnet for everybody fascinated by death, sex and money – which is another way of saying all of us.

Compared to the home of Elvis, everyone else's offering is thin gruel. Nobody else's estate is throwing open a late star's home in quite such a demonstration of neediness. In Minneapolis it is possible to visit Paisley Park, which was the lair and headquarters but not home of Prince, who died in 2016; however, visitors are kept at a professional distance and the building, which has been unhappily likened to an Amazon warehouse, remains somewhat deficient in charisma. Interestingly Prince, who in life projected the idea that he was all about control and attention to detail, died without leaving a will of any kind, thereby guaranteeing that chaos would ensue. In this he contrasted with Aretha Franklin, who left a whole bunch of wills upon her death two years later, some of which were being unearthed from the depths of soft furnishings and flourished in court years later as her descendants battled over their share of her fortune.

It was only near the end of a lifetime of short change and bad deals that Aretha Franklin began to keep a close eye on her money, going so far as to ensure that her handbag full of that night's fee was on the piano, where she could see it, while she performed on stage. Self-styled hobo Bob Dylan, on the other hand, has always kept his beady eye on the receipts. Dylan actually sold his accumulated treasures in 2016 to the University of Tulsa and a local billionaire for $20 million. Successful visitor centres tend to open in places where real estate is affordable and there is ample room for car parking. (One of the main reasons given for the failure of the UK's National Centre for Popular Music, which opened in Sheffield in 1999 and closed less than a year later, was the fact there was nowhere to park.) The Bob Dylan Center is sited in a former paper warehouse in Tulsa, Oklahoma – the metaphorical heart of the country. Among the relics it has on display is the actual tambourine that it claims inspired 'Mr Tambourine Man'.

When Dylan played down the street in 2022 he didn't drop in to see how it was going, which is standard behaviour for a man whose mystique has never been penetrated by a lifetime of scholarship and stalking. Dylan has however proved himself to be a keen visitor to other sites associated with other names. He visited Graceland in 1987. In 2009, while on tour in the UK, he joined a party waiting to be shown round John Lennon's childhood home in Liverpool and was particularly keen to see the rooms where John and Paul might have composed together. Britain's National Trust, which had historically been associated with acquiring and maintaining stately homes on behalf of the nation, had shown considerable foresight in getting hold of the properties in Menlove Avenue and Forthlin Road and restoring them to the way they would have looked when Lennon and McCartney were teenagers. This has led to speculation that they may in time seek to do the same with the modest lower-middle-class homes in which people like David Bowie and Freddie Mercury did their growing up.

The year before his pilgrimage to Menlove Avenue, Dylan had shown up at the childhood home of Neil Young in Winnipeg. In 1988 he had insisted his tour bus divert and stop in the middle of the night so that he could look at James Dean's high school. It's tempting to speculate that what drew him to all these places was the notion that the view from the bedroom or schoolroom window of a fourteen-year-old with a dream might be one of the more reliable experiences the heritage industry could offer in exchange for a ticket. Here you are gazing upon a world the star had yet to change, which is in many cases more interesting than the gimcrack Xanadu they built for themselves once they could afford it.

Dylan's own mother had sold the family home he had grown up in in Hibbing, Minnesota, back in 1968, when her husband died. The house's new owner discarded Dylan's ice skates and a few other items she had left behind. At the time Dylan was raising his own family in Woodstock and items associated with him were not yet seen as historical artefacts from some lost land of giants. Decades later a more than usually serious Dylan fan called Bill Pagel actually moved to Minnesota in order to pick up whatever items of Dylan-associated memorabilia he could. He had no family and was not motivated by profit. He just wanted to walk in Dylan's footsteps. Some of the items he acquired were distant in their association, such as the ceramic candy bowl that once belonged to Dylan's grandmother and the highchair from which the young Robert Zimmerman may well have launched spoons. By then every car boot sale in the area known as the Iron Range had been combed for material with a Dylan link. There was a brisk trade in copies of the high-school yearbooks in which the seventeen-year-old Bobby Zimmerman says his ambition is to join Little Richard. Pagel had more than one. He even bought old phone books in which Dylan's parents were listed.

Eventually he bought both of the houses in which Dylan had grown up, paying above the odds in both cases. At the time of the purchase of the second one in 2019 he said he had plans to turn both into museums. Since at the time of writing guided tours are available only by appointment it seems reasonable to assume they haven't turned out to be a gold mine. Every year on Dylan's birthday ever more senior fans gather in the road outside and look at the building while some of them play a few of Bob's records. There is a small museum in the basement and Bill's happy to point out where the young Robert Zimmerman wrote his initials on the wall. Even the acquisition of his hero's two childhood homes didn't bring Pagel the peace of mind which all superfans seem to be seeking. When asked what questions he would put to Dylan if he had the opportunity, he said he would like to know which of the two bedrooms in the house was the one Bob slept in. Such are the things that keep a Bobcat awake at night.

It's clear why a person would be keen to spend at least some time in a hero's bedroom. It's a direct and personal link such as anyone can understand. Museums, on the other hand, are for boffins. One exhibit in a glass case is very much like another. It doesn't matter whether it's a Viking warrior's helmet or Syd Barrett's third favourite guitar, an Etruscan vase or Noddy Holder's mirrored hat, Queen Victoria's cradle or the Union Jack tea towel that barely secured the modesty of Ginger Spice. It takes expertise and money to make exhibits seem dramatic and important and not just another item out of the warehouse. This is why proper museums invest so heavily in smoke and mirrors, in order to insure against let-down. In the world of pop there can be a lot of the latter when you get up close. Stage costumes which appeared other-worldly in the glare of a Super Trouper at Wembley Arena all those years ago can easily appear tawdry when draped on a mannequin and inspected at close quarters. Then there are the prize-givings and awards ceremonies to which the legacy media seem so attached. Oscars aside, all prize statuettes seem in retrospect to be ill-advised wastes of metal. In fact, the more fuss daytime TV makes of an item of memorabilia, the less interesting it is bound to appear when it's in a glass case. When you've seen one gold disc, you have most definitely seen them all.

The mass audience is never going to be content gazing at inanimate objects and using their imagination. They will still want to see music and movement even when the people who supplied both have passed away, and a lot of work is going into providing it. The 2022 opening in London of *Voyage*, the 'virtual' show featuring an Abba performance as it might have been in 1979, has proved two things: one, it works, at least in their case; two, it costs a great deal more money than most people are prepared to invest.

For a while now companies have been hungrily eyeing the possibility of being able to keep the show going artificially after the stars have left the stage for the last time. Sometimes this proposed Disneyfication of rock has to start modestly. A company called Eyellusion has experimented with a reborn Ronnie James Dio flashing his devil horns and apparently singing live with a backing band of actual musicians; they have even done the same with Frank Zappa through the cooperation of his son Dweezil. The companies in this space devoutly wish musicians would submit to the full body capture of their movements while alive, pointing out that this is something which has already been done for all living actors working with CGI. The problem is, by the time anybody gets round to doing it with rock stars they no longer move quite like they did in their pomp. Janice Turner in *The Times* in 2023, while admiring the fact that Madonna had not given in to the male critics who thought she shouldn't be prancing around in a basque when she was older than Violet Carson was when she played Ena Sharples in *Coronation Street*, couldn't help noting the 'odd rigidity in her trunk' which indicated her age. All the personal trainers and dieticians in the world can't make a sixty-five-year-old body move with the easy grace of youth.

Often the imagineers are starting with a clean slate. The owners of the copyrights of Edith Piaf, the French singer who died in 1963, have been talking recently about using artificial intelligence to replicate her voice for a film about her life. According to the producers this is so that we may know what messages Piaf would wish to convey to the youth of today or the future. 'Her story is one of incredible resilience, of overcoming struggles and defying social norms to achieve greatness – and is as relevant now as it was then,' they somewhat sententiously pronounce in the distinctive accents of those who would trade in images from beyond the grave. It does not take too great a leap to envisage some future virtual Glastonbury in which Edith Piaf, Lou Reed, Tupac Shakur, Amy Winehouse and Johnny Cash appear out of the darkness to perform their hits, and assuring us that they've always been in favour of whatever happens to be the latest stylish orthodoxy.

It's not impossible that the technology which has worked so triumphantly in realizing Abba's spectacular may not work with anyone else. It could be that the qualities that make it work – the fact that the 'originals' are all still alive, the absence of physical idiosyncrasy in their stage act, the fact that they lend themselves to audience participation in the form of a singalong, and the mysterious fact that the happiest pop music begins to sound poignant once overlaid with the passage of time – are as a package unique to the Swedish group. There's also the technical limitation that nobody seems to have overcome. With all attempts to provide a moving simulacrum of a legendary performer, with whose face we have become almost as familiar as those of members of our family, the imagineers invariably cop out when it comes to the organs with which they used to communicate with us on a million TV shows – the eyes. This may be why one of Eyellusion's first experiments was with Roy Orbison, who kept his behind his shades.

Meanwhile there are the statues. Long before the imagineers began their eerie trade, the makers of graven images had set their sights on keeping pop stars alive for eternity. Where this all started is difficult to pinpoint. While all rock stars are clearly driven by the desire to return in later years to their old school in their home town to ram their success in the faces of the classmates who did them down, the teachers who never thought they would amount to anything and the town worthies who felt they were simply cluttering up the place, there is no recorded example of a young wannabe dreaming of one day having his immortality confirmed via a ton of limestone situated in the town square.

Undeterred, the rock statuary business continues to thrive, driven by commission-hungry sculptors and local bureaucrats convinced it will be good for tourism, despite there being little indication that there is much public appetite for its products. The eight-foot plaster likeness of Michael Jackson, a performer who often seemed to be posing in the hope that a passing sculptor would capture him in mid-flow, was initially sited outside Fulham Football Club in west

London, because the club's owner had commissioned it in honour of the fact that the one football match Jackson ever attended was at Craven Cottage, and presumably because there was nowhere else to stow it. The fans, reasoning that it was hideous and had nothing to do with Fulham, despised it. Consequently, when the club changed hands in 2013 the new owner instantly curried favour with the fans by palming it off on the National Football Museum in Manchester, where its presence would prove to be even more puzzling. They kept it on display for six years before taking advantage of the latest scandal about Jackson's private life and efforts to 'better represent football's stories' to shuffle it off to a back room where it can presumably spend eternity thinking about what it's done.

And yet they keep on coming. There appear to be more statues of rock stars than there are suitable places to put them. The one of American hard rock singer Ronnie James Dio, which is unaccountably sited in Kavarna, Bulgaria, depicts the late front man emerging from an actual boulder. When Michelangelo did this in the sixteenth century it was thought he was seeking to depict the eternal human struggle to escape material trappings. When monumental masons pull the same trick in the twenty-first century they're simply trying to escape their obligation to properly surmount that trickiest challenge to the sculptor's art, a rock star's trousers.

Statues of women performers like the one of Amy Winehouse in Camden Town fare better because the folds of a skirt may safely echo those of classical statuary. However, her image is kept on the far side of a railing to ensure it is safe from any indignities that might be wrought upon it by overenthusiastic members of that section of the public which the tabloid papers always call 'revellers'. This is by no means unusual. The original sculpture of Elvis Presley, which was erected on Beale Street in Memphis, eventually had to be replaced by an image of a younger, hipper King and fenced in, so often had it come in for unwelcome attention from the public. This has also been the fate of the statue of Chris Cornell of Soundgarden in its place outside a museum in Seattle. The statue of blues guitarist Stevie Ray Vaughan in Austin, Texas, has been sprayed with messages in support of local football teams. Andy Edwards' representation of the four young Beatles strolling towards the Mersey is one of the few successful cases of rock statuary: the spacing between the figures allows pilgrims to have their picture taken with the group, and the ton of bronze involved in its making renders it impossible to pinch.

The proliferation of these graven images seems to assume that future generations will be familiar with the people they are intended to depict. Could this faith be misplaced? We can but wonder what a future resident of Dublin will make of the image of Phil Lynott, who died in 1986, leaning on his bass in Harry Street. Will future sons and daughters of Hull look at the image of a guitar in the city's East Park and feel a swell of local pride at its association with Mick Ronson, who once played guitar with somebody called David Bowie? Will the people of Aylesbury understand why their town is the home of a bewildering depiction of Bowie called *Earthly Messenger* merely because he gigged there a few times? Or will future generations shake their heads and wonder where on earth we got the confidence to believe that our passions would be the same as theirs?

AND IN THE END . . .

Ringo Starr and Paul McCartney attend Stella McCartney's show at Paris Fashion Week in March 2024.

36

The train of events I've written about in this book began with Paul McCartney's appearance at Live Aid almost forty years ago. At that point I'd been thinking about him and his old group for a little over twenty years, which seemed a lot at the time. I realize now that I was only scratching the surface. The longer it has gone on, the more our sixty-year relationship has come to mean to me, and the more often I tend to become involved in conversations about all manner of things which inevitably reach a point where somebody will begin a sentence with the words 'it's like the Beatles'. It's possible that in the future people will still be having those kinds of conversations, but they won't be people who lived with them in real time.

People, particularly male people, like to pretend that their relationship with music and those who play it is rational. We like to think that the music we have grown up with will stand the test of time because it is clearly better than what came before and after. We like to think that we found the music which means the most to us when the truth is the music found us. I can't remember precisely when the Beatles entered my life because they seemed to arrive at the same time as adolescence. It was presumably in the latter part of 1962. I was twelve at the time and just beginning to regard myself as a music fan. I was aware of their first single, 'Love Me Do', had probably heard them on BBC Radio's *Saturday Club*, and I feel as though I saw them perform on one of those early evening magazine shows which at the time were broadcast to viewers in the north of England from Granada in Manchester.

From that point forward my teenage years came to be measured out in Beatles records. Not only can I still list from memory their singles in the precise order in which they were released, I actually find it difficult to believe that other people can't do the same thing. The points at which their music seemed to go through a step change placed pins in my memory, enabling me to recall where I was and what I was like. I remember thinking this was a whole new game when 'I Want To Hold Your Hand' was played to a panel of young listeners in late 1963 on the TV show *Thank Your Lucky Stars*. I remember demanding silence from my mother as we sat at the tea table listening to the first radio play of 'We Can Work It Out' and 'Day Tripper' in 1965. It was imperative that this take place in conditions of total silence so that I might absorb every nuance of a record I would probably not hear again for a week. I remember my ears burning with embarrassment as I realized a girlfriend had managed to get a track from *Rubber Soul* played for me on a radio request programme. I can even identify the point in the discography of the Beatles, halfway between 'Penny Lane' and 'Magical Mystery Tour', when I contrived to lose my virginity. I remember the girl I walked across the fields to meet on the very day they did 'All You Need Is Love' on that international telecast in the summer of 1967. My schoolboy life may not have changed very much in that time but these records, all of which had entered my secret heart, seemed to prove that throughout those years I had four older brothers living an unimaginably exciting life on my behalf.

On 31 July 1968 I picked up a yellow-and-purple kipper tie in the closing-down giveaway at Apple's Baker Street store. This was just a few days after my eighteenth birthday, a perfect point at which to place another bookmark. It was as though the Beatles had been there to soundtrack my passage from childhood to the verge of adulthood. I don't remember the death-of-idealism moment which writers invariably associate with the end of the sixties. I always knew they would break up. All groups broke up. In those days there were hardly any examples of bands that didn't. In the years that followed I never took seriously any of the stories that sprang up in the press saying that this or that set of circumstances was going to bring about their reunion. We who had given our hearts to them in 1963 knew there was no going back. Nor did we particularly wish that to be possible. Of all the blessings that flow from being a pop fan born in 1950, none is more precious than the fact that the Beatles never got back together. We even looked down our noses at the people who rushed out to buy the Red and the Blue retrospective albums when they came out in 1973 because we couldn't understand how they could look themselves in the mirror if they didn't still own all the original singles with the name of their owner inscribed in biro on the back just above the ads for Miner's make-up or Morphy Richards hairdriers.

I don't remember thinking about the Beatles all that much in the seventies. There was so much in that time which was new and exciting it made them seem passé. Very little thinking was done about the past at the time. Even the Beatles didn't seem to think about the Beatles very much. This may have had something to do with the fact that the past was not yet easy to access. In December 1976 the thirty-three-year-old George Harrison, visiting Granada Studios in Manchester to talk to presenter Tony Wilson about his latest solo album, was filmed in a back room watching the Beatles perform 'This Boy' in a Granada studio in 1963. The clip is on YouTube. The look on his face, blushing, amused, his eyes filmed with pride, as he sees for the first time his twenty-year-old self and his friends perform this item of juvenilia, is a reminder of how distant even the recent past seemed to be at that time. Four years later John Lennon was dead and there was no longer any prospect of getting back together. After 1980 it seemed the universe was no longer able to listen to the Beatles without experiencing a pang over what might have been, a feeling which was in its way almost as delicious for later generations as the delirium of Beatlemania had been for we who were there.

Paul was never going to discourage the idea of the Beatles as a cult for the ages. Whereas George and John seemed only too keen to cut their old group down to size as though they believed people's obsession with them, which was to grow following Lennon's death, was somehow reducing their freedom to operate in the now, McCartney did the opposite. He was first and foremost a fan. When interviewed for the TV series *Anthology* in 1995, he said of their White Album that the people who think it could be improved by being reduced to a single album should get over themselves. 'It's the Beatles' White Album,' he stated, as though acknowledging the fact that it was bigger than all of us and a piece of history with which even he was simply lucky to be associated. He's remained happy to discharge his duties as their number-one fan, particularly if it happens also to draw some publicity to his latest project. It's no coincidence that he always finds something new to say about his old group every time he is out there plugging his new record.

In the twenty-first century he has reconciled himself to the fact that he is a very powerful symbol, particularly for his compatriots. Very much like the late Queen, with whom he had something in common – she awarded him the MBE, he wrote a song about her, they've both featured on stamps, they both understood the importance of waving – he knew that a large part of his job was simply to raise national morale by being seen, to smile and wave and give people something to go home and tell at least a hundred other people about. When I met him in 2019 to talk about the fiftieth anniversary of *Abbey Road* he had come to his office in London's Soho Square on the train from his place in Sussex, unaccompanied by minders. Sightings of McCartney in the wild are not infrequent. Stopping in Regent's Park to advise somebody doing stretches. Walking past the window of a pizza joint full of lunching diners with a small child on his shoulders. On the tube. On the train. He likes the attention. This contrasts with the likes of Elton John, whose feet never seem to touch the pavement and whose eyes are hidden behind sunglasses in order to avoid contact. Paul McCartney has plainly enjoyed being famous, which is a good thing because he has been very famous for a very long time.

Fame liberated him to move through the world in a way no

previous human could. In June 1966, having realized that his new celebrity granted him permission to do things which mere mortals could not do, he dropped in on the philosopher Bertrand Russell at his Chelsea home. Since the venerable sage was at the time ninety-three and had been raised by a grandfather who remembered the French Revolution first hand and a great-aunt who danced with Napoleon, this was an early indication of the fact that in the fullness of time it would be possible via a couple of steps to link anything on earth with the Beatles. In that 2019 encounter he greeted me, as he had done on other occasions, with a vague reference to previous meetings, which had less to do with his specific memories of talking to me than the realization (which he presumably came to many years earlier) that he was more likely than not already to have met anybody he might ever be called upon to meet. He may or may not be aware that whoever he is talking to is using the lion's share of their mental processing power to remind themselves that they are talking to Paul McCartney and hoovering up impressions of how being Paul McCartney might just be wholly unlike being anyone else on earth. He's certainly the only one who could take my old copy of *Abbey Road* and flip it over in his hands in order to remind himself of what tracks were on it.

This felt like sitting with Thomas Hardy as he leafed through your copy of *Tess of the D'Urbervilles* in order to reacquaint himself with the main characters. The difference being that Paul McCartney seemed to have managed his reputation better than any of the lions of nineteenth-century literature. In fact his stock was higher near the end of his career than it had been at its zenith, largely on the basis of what he had done earlier. The simple things are invariably the hardest, and as time went by, as the tools of the musician's trade became more sophisticated, as bands rose and fell, as movements came and movements went, as recorded music became more dense and more processed, it was those simple things the Beatles had done which seemed to take on the qualities of miracles.

The Beatles story was peppered with quite enough of those during their lifetime. In 2021, fully half a century after they called it a day, they came up with one more, a three-part documentary film called *Get Back*. When it was about to come out, director Peter Jackson told me that he found it amazing that there existed on earth a full, unedited account of any band from the sixties writing, recording and rehearsing their new album. The fact that such a trove existed and that it featured the Beatles rather than Gerry and the Pacemakers or Dave Dee, Dozy, Beaky, Mick & Tich was something along the lines of, yes, a miracle.

McCartney turned up at a London screening at which we were joined by the extended Beatles family, from their children and grandchildren to erstwhile employees and scene makers. Aware of his duties as host, paterfamilias and representative of the Fabs on earth, he welcomed all and declared himself to be rather moved by the sight of his old mates on the big screen. He looked good. He had put his henna period behind him and allowed his hair to go grey. He was dressed as he generally was in his late seventies, in simple clothes that had never been connected to anything so tawdry as a price tag. You had the feeling that he had been closely inspected by one of the women in his life before being allowed out of the door. The outfit had been carefully put together to avoid giving the impression that it had been carefully put together. Everybody in the room raked his appearance head to toe, filing away details to pass on to others who had measured their lives against his since 1962. Around the same time, David Remnick of the *New Yorker* got close enough to see a hearing aid being put back in place. Like every other veteran who has spent a lifetime within range of dangerous levels of volume, McCartney is what the doctors would probably call a high-functioning deaf person.

McCartney probably didn't watch *Get Back* as much as I did that Christmas. If he did, he might have concluded that it was the greatest rock and roll documentary film of all time in that it features the greatest group of all doing the thing that we most desire to see them doing. We don't want to see them playing or giving their opinions to an interviewer. We would far rather just witness them turning up every day in interesting outfits, to drink tea, talk about what was on TV last night, smoke, read snatches out of the paper, arse about, tease each other, ruffle their children's hair, order cheese sandwiches, be familiar and just simply allow us the thing we crave most of any bunch of rock stars – the opportunity to watch them behave.

In the end we like the simple act of looking at rock bands as much as we like any other way of engaging with them. As many people pointed out after watching the film, it was the real people interviewed on the streets of London in 1969 who looked like extras from some gritty period drama, while the Beatles themselves looked as though they could just as easily fit into our time. Which is an indication of the way our time wanted it to be. At the end of 2020 there was not a single actual group in Spotify's list of the most-streamed songs across the world – a significant change. Ever since the Beatles we all have been to some extent invested in the idea of a group being something more than the number of willing hands it takes to create a certain musical sound. A group is more than that. A group contains elements of the boyhood gang, of William Brown and his Outlaws or the Bash Street Kids; it functions the way a family functions, with some members taking responsibility while others evade it; and since it is usually formed with an aspiration to achieve a measure of success which is statistically impossible, any group is a massive bet in which the odds will always favour the house, a conspiracy of hope against the indifference of the world and everyone within it.

The person who pointed out to me that there were no longer any groups in the chart was somebody born in the late eighties, somebody who had grown up in a world dominated by Oasis, Blur and Nirvana, acts that seemed to reverberate to the same root chord as the sounds of the sixties, and furthermore had been exposed to the nineties' promotion of the rock band lifestyle in movies via *Almost*

Famous, and was consequently even more likely to want to regard that life of perpetual escape as more desirable than any other, and the life of a touring band member less as a stage that had to be gone through in pursuit of an objective than as the brass ring itself.

In seeking to account for the disappearance of groups from the 2020 charts he wondered if, like so many things, this could be laid at the door of social media. There was certainly a time when young people, looking to establish their place in the world, would seek out like minds by placing a note on the school's noticeboard in the hope of flushing out a bass player in the year below or a drummer with a driving licence and access to a car. Accomplishing this would be the first step on a journey towards the dream double of having not only blood brothers but also a place to stand.

In the twenty-first century bands may no longer hold sway over the chart, which is dominated by solo acts and duos, but they still have a powerful hold on our imagination. *Get Back*, which was the hit of Christmas 2021, was big enough and rich enough to propose a whole new face of the Beatles, a face with which the twenty-first century could feel entirely comfortable. They were no longer represented by the shiny-faced mop tops of the personal pronoun years or the psychedelic adventurers from Sgt Pepper's arts lab. *Get Back* put in their place another kind of Beatles, an agelessly hip image of everything a band could possibly hope to be. Having cemented their position as the ultimate band with this film it was inevitable that in 2024 Apple should announce a plan to explore their individuality in four interconnected biographical feature films which were slated for release in 2027. The show must go on.

In the late autumn of 1964, Derek Taylor, first and greatest of the spin doctors of pop, was engaged to write the sleeve notes for the Beatles' fourth album, *Beatles For Sale*. In these he offered a prediction. He said it was inevitable that generations not yet born would at some point in the future wish to understand the fuss about the

Beatles. Faced with this question, he advised against trying to explain about the hair or the screams. Instead we should simply play them the records and 'the kids of AD 2000 will draw from the music much the same sense of well-being and warmth as we do today'.

Now the kids of AD 2000 are having kids of their own, but Derek Taylor's words hold good, even if they tell only half the story. What Derek could not have been expected to foresee was just how much people in the future would still yearn for that sense of well-being and warmth. Like a benign inherited condition, Beatlemania has been passed down the decades since, assisted by judicious nudges from marketing, facilitated by advances in technology and informed by a weather eye on the changes in public taste.

The Beatles connected with different generations in different ways. If you grew up in the sixties, if you are so to speak a Fabs OG, you counted out your adolescence in Beatles 45s. If you were a teenager in the seventies you probably know them through the prism of Mum and Dad's copies of the Red and Blue double albums, which stood sentinel alongside so many music centres with their smoked glass lids. For the generation of the eighties the death of John Lennon brought the realization that the *Double Fantasy* chap had once been in a group with the leader of Wings, and the further realization that this group sometimes sounded a bit like ELO. When Britpop arrived in the nineties it came not so much to bury the Fabs' legacy as to raise it to new heights. At around the same time the remaining Threetles told their story in their own way via the TV series *Anthology* and its accompanying DVDs. At the turn of the millennium, at the cresting of the CD boom, they sold thirty-one million copies of a compilation called *1*, which remains the only CD most people under the age of twenty-five can remember. Six years after that, original producer George Martin and his son Giles were tasked with producing a 'mashup' of old Beatles recordings for the Las Vegas show *Love* to be performed by Cirque du Soleil. Over seventeen years later the show is still running in Las Vegas with no end in sight, the business of the Beatles is still being run from a smart townhouse in Knightsbridge, and Giles is still working on new releases bearing the Beatles name.

Giles was born in 1969, the year his father was recording the Beatles on the rooftop and producing *Abbey Road*. Giles wasn't really aware of the Beatles until he was thirteen when he and a friend sat listening to the Red and the Blue albums. For most of his adult life he's been tending to their legacy, while also exploring new avenues for exploiting that legacy which the latest wave of technology throws up. His surname and his background have also imbued him with the diplomatic skills required to operate in the court of such regal figures.

The most active member of this royal family is inevitably Paul, he who never rests, even in his ninth decade. Ringo still says that the reason the Beatles did the number of records they did was because Paul was always on the phone, nagging them back to the studio. Even with the triumphs of *Get Back* and his 2022 Glastonbury appearance behind him, it was Paul who still thought they could use Peter Jackson's Machine Assisted Learning gizmo to get something out of 'Now And Then', the fifty-year-old John Lennon demo they had abandoned almost thirty years earlier while making *Anthology*.

It turned out Peter's magic box could extract Lennon's voice. Once that had been done it was possible to bring in elements of the earlier attempt in order to retain the performance of George, who had died in 2001. Paul and Ringo could re-do their parts remotely; a string section, under the impression they were working on a McCartney record, could be captured in California; and Giles could import the 'oohs' which were the true essence of the Beatles from recordings like 'Here There And Everywhere' made nearly sixty years earlier.

It was a breathtaking example of the lengths the present will go to in order to clone the simplicity of the past.

No matter what the song says, there is never any getting back. In the sixties, all pop music sounded best at a fairground where you could feel the bass. In the seventies, *Abbey Road* became everyone's favourite Beatles album because you could play it alongside Fleetwood Mac. In the eighties, people listening to Beatles CDs were thrilled by the absence of scratches. From the nineties, most music was accessed on headphones. At each stage we have listened in a different way while kidding ourselves it is the same.

In 2011, Giles Martin was hired to mix the sound for Martin Scorsese's film about George Harrison, *Living in the Material World*. 'I was fired because they said "Marty doesn't like your revisionist approach to music". Four weeks later I was called back. I met Marty in a studio, we set up the film and I switched between my mix and the original. He said he preferred my mix and he couldn't understand why. I said, it's because it's never how you remember it being. Our brains adjust. We don't really listen to these things. We recreate them in our heads. My job is to mix a song so that it's how people remember it.'

That may be an impossible job, but it's the task that everybody in the remastering, remixing and reimagining trade sets themselves every time they go back to take something old and try to make it new again. Our relationship with the music that entered our lives when we were young has now lasted a lifetime and inevitably grown more complicated with the passing years. We always want to get back. The performers who have appeared in these pages have simply been doing their best to keep earning their bread and pursuing their trade by ministering to that desire in whatever way they could.

The challenge is that what they've been expected to provide is something which is beyond even music. What we want them to rekindle is a sense of connection that was established at a young age and refuses to entirely let go with the passage of time. We're always reaching back for something which in truth we will never be able to quite grasp. The reality of a live performance given by an old favourite who is now in their senior years will, no matter how accomplished, always be competing with our imperfect memories of the way things were during some performance that they gave decades earlier. A crowd turning up to watch their heroes will be viewing in their mental cinema those same people when they were young. The experience of listening to a decades-old recording, freshly reconditioned as a result of the latest audio miracle, will never be able to quite measure up to the way we feel about the version that remains on permanent repeat on that dusty old jukebox in the attic of our heart.

This is just a stage the pop music of the sixties and seventies is going through. The Giles Martins of the future will no longer have to contend with the memories of a Martin Scorsese, or anybody else, who remembers it the first time around. Nor will they have to spare the feelings of anyone who wrote the song or played on the record. This will pass. During the shelf life of this book most of the music and musicians mentioned in its pages will pass away, dropping out of living memory and into history. If they're lucky, and it suits posterity, a few will be remembered. By the time the promised individual biopics of John, Paul, George and Ringo appear in 2027, the actual individuals will seem every bit as unreal to most people as Elvis Presley and Jimi Hendrix have seemed for the best part of a century.

In the end the most curious feature of pop music, which once celebrated that which is most fleeting and ephemeral, is that its products have remained imprinted inside us far longer than those of any other art form. Therefore, the people who play music remain beloved far longer than actors in our favourite films or the authors of the most treasured books on our shelves. Because their songs are inside us, we want to feel close to the people who made them. That feeling never goes away, which explains why you can count the number of rock stars who retired on your fingers. The overwhelming majority kept going for as long as they were able, and would presumably associate themselves with the sentiment of the ragtime pianist Eubie Blake, who was so enjoying his fame in his nineties that he said, 'If I'd known I was going to live this long, I would have taken better care of myself.'

A Playlist: Songs of Innocence and Experience

I don't believe music is something you should pursue energetically; I tend to think it's best that it comes to you when you're ready to hear it. There are many things in life that you only begin to understand when you get older. Some music seems to spring directly from life experiences people go through only when they're past the first flush of youth. For the older listener some music simply strikes a chord because the singer sounds as though they have some miles on the clock. What follows are thirty recorded performances which have done this for me at one time or another. I don't think any of them could have been done by youngsters.

A PLAYLIST: SONGS OF INNOCENCE AND EXPERIENCE

Southside Johnny, 'All The Way Home' (1991)

It's tempting to read across from incomplete data about a songwriter's personal life to the meaning of their songs, and I won't resist it here. I fancy Bruce Springsteen wrote this song in the wake of the break-up of his marriage. The opening line about knowing what it's like to have failed with the whole world looking on fits too perfectly into such a scenario. Still, songs go where they will, and Springsteen's own version can't touch this slow dance in the singles bar from his New Jersey compatriot John Lyon as he seeks to persuade someone else whose finger bears the shadow of a ring to allow him to escort them home.

Bonnie Raitt, 'Nick Of Time' (1989)

The dominant assumption among younger performers is they have all the time in the world. At some point in middle age they wake up and realize this is not the case. Bonnie Raitt had carved a hellacious path through her twenties and thirties. It wasn't until she was approaching the birthday that begins with a four that she decided to stop drinking and take the wheel. At this point a friend phoned to talk about her body clock. This inspired a song which found a ready ear in Boomer women all over America and provided her first hit.

John Prine and Iris DeMent, 'In Spite Of Ourselves' (1999)

There are a million songs celebrating young love and not nearly enough putting in a good word for the older variety. Since young lovers know nothing about each other while all the older ones could write a book, this seems a particular shame. In the case of this comic masterpiece by Prine, each member of a couple of geezers takes turns to list the noteworthy characteristics of the person they've woken up next to for the last few decades. 'She likes ketchup on her scrambled eggs / Swears like a sailor when she shaves her legs.' That kind of thing.

A PLAYLIST: SONGS OF INNOCENCE AND EXPERIENCE

Kate Bush, 'Mrs Bartolozzi' (2005)

When Kate Bush took a break from the public eye towards the end of the twentieth century it was to raise a child and discover that a life which revolves around laundry will soon find profundity in same. In her song, the housewife of the title watches the disembodied shirts and skirts dancing in the surf and dreams up the only popular song whose chorus is simply 'washing machine'.

Warren Zevon, 'My Ride's Here' (2002)

Zevon lived the first decades of his life as though it would go on for ever. When his health crisis made it clear that it wouldn't, he produced some of his most affecting work. There's 'Keep Me In Your Heart', which glories in the line 'there's a train leavin' nightly called "When All is Said and Done"', and there's this collaboration with the poet Paul Muldoon. Bruce Springsteen performed it live just after Zevon's death in 2003 in a version which seemed to take a grim delight in the idea of a rock star's life ending with the arrival of his final driver.

Neil Young, 'The Needle And The Damage Done' (1971)

If you want to get an inkling of what it's like to live the life of an artist like Neil Young, listen to his Massey Hall concert from 1971 in which he introduces this song, inspired by the death of his friend Danny Whitten, to an audience who are really listening, and then listen to him play it again in 1993 on MTV's *Unplugged* in front of an over-demonstrative audience who are witnessing the re-enactment of this time-honoured ritual of the playing of just another oldie and can't stop whooping to celebrate the fact.

Randy Newman, 'The World Isn't Fair' (1999)

This peerless poet of the unworthy thought has written some of his best songs from the point of view of the divorced and remarried man. These songs must have started some interesting conversations at more than one dinner table. One of the most piercing, addressed to his ex-wife, was candidly called 'I Miss You'. The above song, addressed to the shade of Karl Marx, features a passage describing a parents' evening at the school attended by his second batch of children, at which all the trim and lovely second wives and mothers were accompanied by men like the songwriter, 'froggish men, unpleasant to see'. This description of the way life is could only have been written by an older person.

Loudon Wainwright, 'A Handful Of Dust' (1992)

When writers become parents a door opens to reveal a whole new world of potential material. It then immediately closes when it becomes clear how much trouble it would cause within the family were they to write about it. In his 1992 album, *History*, Wainwright decided it was worth the risk, even writing songs about how he once hit his young daughter, his conflicts with his son and his unresolved feelings about his own late father, finishing with this bleak accounting of what a man's life amounts to put together from lyrics his father left behind.

Aimee Mann, 'Can't You Tell' (2016)

When she was called upon to contribute to an album of songs belatedly protesting the 2016 election of Donald Trump, Aimee Mann avoided the usual route of a withering takedown, such as she might have chosen as a youngster, instead coming up with a song which noted the fact that this was a man running for office in order to slake his fathomless thirst for recognition and to fill the cavernous emptiness inside. 'Can't you tell I'm unwell?' was her refrain.

Steely Dan, 'Things I Miss The Most' (2003)

Back in the era of Nixon, Steely Dan were accused of overdoing the cynicism. In the age of Trump and Putin they seem like sober reporters, which may be why their records seem to be more popular and certainly more revered than ever. Nobody really needed their comeback albums because they were quite happy finding new levels in the fifty-year-old ones. This 2003 song from one of them is delivered from the point of view of a formerly alpha male who has been cleaned out by a divorce settlement, coming to terms with the fact that he misses the companionship almost as much as he misses his Eames chair and his '54 Strat.

Leonard Cohen, 'Tower Of Song' (1988)

One of the many benefits of Leonard Cohen's extended career was that it enabled him to give the lie to the idea that he traded purely in human misery, and that in certain lights it was even possible to regard him as a bit of a comedian. He redefined himself perfectly with this song, to the extent that when he was inducted into the Rock and Roll Hall of Fame in 2008 – which took the word 'inappropriate' into an entirely new dimension – he simply recited all its words, the song making a perfect summary of a life spent standing on the shoulders of everyone who came before, waiting patiently for the next line to arrive, listening to Hank Williams coughing from the floors above, just paying his rent every day in the Tower of Song.

Kate and Anna McGarrigle, 'Matapedia' (1996)

This Kate McGarrigle song always reminds me of a conversation I had with an old friend who described the sharp feeling of watching her daughter growing more beautiful at the same time as she began to feel she would never be desirable again. 'Matapedia' was inspired by an incident when an old flame of Kate's bumped into her seventeen-year-old daughter, Martha, and fleetingly thought he was looking at the young Kate. The record accurately summons those feelings found adjacent to the saying 'if youth but would and age but could'.

Nick Lowe, 'Hope For Us All' (2007)

Bruce Springsteen is fond of observing that rock and roll prolongs adolescence and retards adulthood. In the twenty-first century Nick Lowe made a series of albums exploring that truth through the story of a music businessman who wakes to find himself fully clothed, discovers that the world has moved on and then belatedly finds contentment in marriage and family. All these later records abandoned the box of tricks for which Lowe was once famous in favour of deceptively simple songs in a country/soul idiom. The best of these, he came to recognize, were written by The Bloke, a superior craftsman who was working through him. Since this is the first pop song to use the word 'feckless', we can only assume this is his work.

Lucinda Williams, *Car Wheels On A Gravel Road* (1998)

By the time her belated breakthrough album came out, Lucinda Williams was already forty-five, making an impression had never been harder, and making a record as raw and direct as this one was now so hedged around with unnecessary complications that it had taken the best part of five years and two record companies to make it happen at all. What was never in doubt was the fact that the songs contained therein had a candour and the performances a drive that made her young competitors seem mired in euphemism by comparison. The tragedy was that as soon as she'd painted her masterpiece the record business had up and disappeared and she was left with nowhere to hang it.

James Taylor, 'The Frozen Man' (2007)

James Taylor dealt with maturity well, his vocal range unimpaired, his stage shows marked by his understanding of the fact that the audience were just as happy to hear him talk as they were to hear him sing. Eventually he extended further into a kind of magic lantern show, a high spot of which was his sharing of a picture from the *National Geographic* of an explorer whose body had been preserved in the Arctic permafrost for half a century before being dug up and subjected to the indignity of posthumous fame. The song this introduces is one of his best and, like all the best pop songs, is susceptible to many interpretations.

The Traveling Wilburys, 'Handle With Care' (1988)

If this latter-day Rat Pack project proved one thing it was that middle-aged rock superstars like Bob Dylan, George Harrison, Tom Petty, Jeff Lynne and Roy Orbison were every bit as prone to dreaming about their ideal group as those of us who got no further than doodling the line-up on the back of a school book. If it proved another it was that even lyrics made up on the spot (daycare centres and night schools?) sound both noble and poignant when they're sung by voices we've been listening to for so long.

Norma Waterson, 'Black Muddy River' (1996)

Bands tend to decide when they're ready to feel their age. When Robert Hunter wrote the lyrics for this for the Grateful Dead, he was a mere forty-five yet seemed to be feeling a biblical age. The lyrics refer to Sir Thomas More and Jacob using a stone as a pillow. The Dead's version, which was on their *In The Dark* album, was good but not as good as this version from the veteran English folk singer.

The Orb, 'Little Fluffy Clouds' (1990)

The advent of sampling and its attendant culture of crate digging resulted in a fortunate handful of established names finding themselves popping up decades later, very often on records they had nothing to do with, put there by young artists who were attracted by their relative antiquity. Rickie Lee Jones is now famous for two things: her 1979 hit 'Chuck E's In Love' and the sound of her voice recalling the clouds she remembered from her Arizona childhood on this 1990 hit from the British ambient group.

Gil Scott-Heron, *I'm New Here* (2010)

A year before he died in 2011 the performer poet Gil Scott-Heron ended a sixteen-year silence with this autobiographical album produced by Britisher Richard Russell. Because the latter came from a new tradition informed by hip hop and dance music he was able to frame Scott-Heron's work in a form which would have been inconceivable in any earlier era and hence bring it to the attention of an entirely new public. Since one of the themes of Gil's work is that our forerunners are always audible if we take the trouble to listen out for them, this seemed only right.

Kris Kristofferson, 'The Last Thing To Go' (2006)

Kristofferson, who for decades now has seemed to rather revel in his image as a figure from Mount Rushmore, begins this song with a quote from boxer Willie Pep: 'the first thing to go are your legs, then your reflexes, then your friends'. The song that follows celebrates that since 'every true thing we wrote on the wind is still singing' his legacy is likely to outlive him. That was in 2006. It would be another fifteen years before he announced his retirement.

Johnny Cash, 'Down There By The Train' (1994)

After Johnny Cash had been photographed in that preacher's coat it seemed he could take any piece of material and make it sound as though it emanated from an American Gothic version of the Bible. This applied every bit as much to his version of Nick Lowe's 'The Beast In Me' as it does to this song, in which Tom Waits apparently sees Judas Iscariot carrying John Wilkes Booth as they wait to board the train that offers deliverance.

A PLAYLIST: SONGS OF INNOCENCE AND EXPERIENCE

Willie Nelson, 'Picture In A Frame' (2004)

At the time of writing this book, Willie Nelson has just turned ninety-one and is still touring. What's even more surprising than his willingness to spend his life on a tour bus at this advanced age is that neither the voice nor the majestic delivery seems to have been remotely affected by the passing years. Both are capable of making any old piece of doggerel sound like Strauss's last songs; when they're applied to this declaration of undying love from Tom Waits the results are particularly sublime.

Tom Waits, 'Raised Right Men' (2011)

Traditionally the arc of a musical career bends from youthful noisemaking to a mellow middle age. This has not been the case with Tom Waits, who was raising more Cain in his last album than he had been on his first forty years earlier, complaining on this track of how it took 'a raised right man to keep a happy hen'. If this is his last recording then history will be able to observe that he certainly did not go gentle into retirement.

Bryan Ferry and the Bryan Ferry Orchestra, 'Back To Black' (2013)

Sometimes the indulgences of elderly legends can bear unexpected fruit. Ferry commissioned an album of his Roxy Music compositions done in 1920s style because he simply wanted to hear if they stood up. The success of this led to his being hired to apply the same treatment to twenty-first-century classics for the soundtrack of Baz Luhrmann's *The Great Gatsby*. This jazz version of the Amy Winehouse tune works unexpectedly well.

Bob Dylan, 'The Night We Called It A Day' (2015)

Dylan's decision to use one of his periodic fallow spells as a writer to record an album's worth of songs associated with Frank Sinatra was an obvious move for him if only because it was the last thing his over-reverent fans would ever have predicted. He turned up to sing this selection on the final David Letterman show in 2015, glad that he could play somebody else's retirement party because he had clearly no intention of playing his own.

The Rolling Stones, 'Angry' (2023)

This came from *Hackney Diamonds*, their first record of original material in almost twenty years, which they released in 2023 to prove that they still had some lead in their pencil. It's difficult to maintain that combination of crossness and lust which was always the secret sauce of the Stones when the two front men are grandfathers many times over. But then, as Pete Townshend pointed out, watching Keith Richards on stage trying to do what he used to do is heart-rending but also delightful.

Jimmy Page and Robert Plant, 'Kashmir' (1994)

Whereas Led Zeppelin were a product of the surprisingly eclectic inclinations of the men who formed the band, their boy fans had a very limited idea of what they stood for. If the reformed Led Zeppelin, which was widely thought to be inevitable, could have incorporated an Egyptian orchestra, as Page and Plant did on this 1994 recording for MTV that explored the magnificent variety from which they sprang in the late sixties, then the singer might well have been up for it.

Glen Campbell, 'These Days' (2008)

The song, which was on Campbell's sixtieth album, is all about retirement, regrets and learning to live with your failures. Which is particularly curious when you reflect on the fact that it was written by Jackson Browne when he was fifteen years old, at a time when both his achievements and his failures were all in the future.

A PLAYLIST: SONGS OF INNOCENCE AND EXPERIENCE

Betty Wright and the Roots, 'Old Songs' (2011)
The Clean Up Woman used to resent the way that hip hop acts would lift passages from her seventies hits. In her later years she made her peace with the way black music was going, turning up in the studio to sing live parts that they couldn't lift from an existing recording and even offering 'vocal production' for the likes of Jennifer Lopez and Joss Stone. This celebration of the qualities of old eight-tracks featuring the likes of Stevie Wonder is a rare example of black music permitting itself a wallow in nostalgia.

Joni Mitchell, 'Both Sides Now' (2000)
When in their later years artists revisit the classics of their salad days they tend to take them slower and in a lower key, hoping that greater pathos may result and nobody will notice that they may have lost a step. When Joni Mitchell went back to her signature tune thirty years later it was with the velvety accompaniment of an orchestra, contributions from Herbie Hancock and Wayne Shorter, and a whole new resonance to that line 'something's lost, but something's gained in living every day'.

Bibliography

Banks, Nick, *So It Started There* (Omnibus, 2023)

Birch, Will, *The Life and Music of Nick Lowe* (Constable, 2019)

Blake, Mark, *Pigs Might Fly* (Aurum, 2007)

Bracewell, Michael, *Roxy* (Faber, 2007)

Budnick, Dean, *Ticket Masters* (Plume, 2012)

Dannen, Frederic, *Hit Men* (Muller, 1990)

Davis, Clive, *Inside the Record Business* (William Morrow, 1975)

Duerden, Nick, *Exit Stage Left* (Headline, 2022)

Dyer, Geoff, *The Last Days of Roger Federer* (Canongate, 2022)

Dylan, Bob, *Chronicles* (Simon & Schuster, 2015)

Egan, Sean, *Fleetwood Mac on Fleetwood Mac* (Omnibus, 2016)

Fagen, Donald, *Eminent Hipsters* (Cape, 2013)

Fisher, Marc, *Something in the Air* (Random House, 2007)

Fleetwood, Mick, *Play On* (Hodder & Stoughton, 2014)

Forde, Eamonn, *Leaving the Building: The Lucrative Afterlife of Music Estates* (Omnibus, 2021)

Forde, Eamonn, *1999: The Year the Record Industry Lost Control* (Omnibus, 2022)

Giddins, Gary, *Bing Crosby: A Pocketful of Dreams* (Little, Brown, 2001)

Goodman, Fred, *The Mansion on the Hill* (Random House, 1997)

Greenfield, Robert, *The Last Sultan* (Simon & Schuster, 2012)

Hagan, Joe, *Sticky Fingers* (Canongate, 2017)

BIBLIOGRAPHY

Higgs, John, *Love and Let Die* (Wiedenfeld & Nicholson, 2022)

Holzman, Jac, *Follow the Music* (First Media, 2000)

Hook, Peter, *Unknown Pleasures* (Simon & Schuster, 2013)

Hynde, Chrissie, *Reckless* (Ebury, 2016)

Isaacson, Walter, *Steve Jobs* (Little, Brown, 2011)

John, Elton, *Me* (Macmillan, 2019)

Johns, Glyn, *Sound Man* (Plume, 2015)

Johnson, Wilko, *Don't You Leave Me Here* (Little, Brown, 2016)

Jones, Dylan, *David Bowie: A Life* (Preface, 2017)

Jones, Rickie Lee, *Last Chance Texaco* (Black Cat, 2021)

King, Tony, *The Tastemaker* (Faber, 2023)

Kinney, David, *The Dylanologists* (Simon & Schuster, 2014)

Krueger, Alan B., *Rockonomics* (John Murray, 2019)

Mason, Nick, *Inside Out* (Weidenfeld & Nicholson, 2004)

Rees, Paul, *The Ox* (Constable, 2020)

Remnick, David, *Holding the Note* (Picador, 2023)

Richards, Keith, *Life* (Little, Brown, 2010)

Rogan, Johnny, *Requiem for the Timeless* (Rogan House, 2017)

Simmons, Sylvie, *I'm Your Man* (HarperCollins, 2012)

Sinclair, David, *The Story of ZZ Top* (Virgin, 1986)

Sounes, Howard, *Down the Highway* (Doubleday, 2021)

Springsteen, Bruce, *Born to Run* (Simon & Schuster, 2016)

Stewart, Rod, *The Autobiography* (Arrow, 2013)

Tannenbaum, Rob, *I Want My MTV* (Penguin, 2012)

Thomson, Graeme, *George Harrison: Behind the Locked Door* (Omnibus, 2013)

Thomson, Graeme, *Under the Ivy* (Omnibus, 2012)

Townshend, Pete, *Who I Am* (HarperCollins, 2012)

Wenner, Jann S., *Like a Rolling Stone* (Little, Brown, 2022)

Zanes, Warren, *Petty: The Biography* (Henry Holt, 2015)

Zevon, Crystal, *I'll Sleep When I'm Dead* (HarperCollins, 2008)

Sources

Lyrics on p. 77: Gram Parsons, 'In My Hour Of Darkness' ('the music he had with him so very few possessed') – performer Gram Parsons, lyrics Gram Parsons and Emmylou Harris

Lyrics on p. 160: Joni Mitchell, 'Blue' ('songs are like tattoos') – performer Joni Mitchell, lyrics Joni Mitchell

Lyrics on p. 273: James Taylor, 'That's Why I'm Here' ('pay good money to hear "Fire And Rain" again and again and again') – performer James Taylor, lyrics James Taylor

Lyrics on p. 276: Toto, 'Africa' ('some solitary company') – performers David Paich and Bobby Kimball, lyrics David Paich and Jeff Porcaro

Lyrics on p. 278: Steve Lukather, 'Along For The Ride' ('riding on my bloody coattails') – performer Steve Lukather, lyrics Jeff Babko, Stan Lynch and Steve Lukather

Quote on p. 299: Liz Phair, 'Liz Phair's Songs of Experience' – interviewer Amanda Petrusich, publication *The New Yorker*

Lyrics on p. 382: John Prine and Iris DeMent, 'In Spite Of Ourselves' ('She likes ketchup on her scrambled eggs / Swears like a sailor when she shaves her legs') – performers John Prine and Iris DeMent, lyrics John Prine

Lyrics on p. 383: Warren Zevon, 'Keep Me In Your Heart' ('there's a train leavin' nightly called "When All is Said and Done"') – performer Warren Zevon, lyrics Jorge A. Calderon and Warren Zevon

SOURCES

Lyrics on p. 384: Randy Newman, 'The World Isn't Fair' ('froggish men, unpleasant to see') – performer Randy Newman, lyrics Randy Newman

Lyrics on p. 384: Aimee Mann, 'Can't You Tell?' ('can't you tell I'm unwell?') – performer Aimee Mann, lyrics Aimee Mann

Lyrics on p. 388: Kris Kristofferson, 'The Last Thing To Go' ('every true thing we wrote on the wind is still singing') – performer Kris Kristofferson, lyrics Kris Kristofferson

Lyrics on p. 389: Tom Waits, 'Raised Right Man' ('it takes a raised right man to keep a happy hen') – performer Tom Waits, lyrics Tom Waits and Kathleen Brennan

Lyrics on p. 391: Joni Mitchell, 'Both Sides Now' ('something's lost, but something's gained in living every day') – performer Joni Mitchell, lyrics Joni Mitchell

Acknowledgements

Thanks to: Mark Ellen and Alex Gold, in whose online company many of the matters covered in these pages were first aired; my agent, Charlie Viney at The Viney Agency; Bill Scott-Kerr, Sally Wray, Richard Shailer and Nicole Witmer at my publishers, Transworld.

Picture Acknowledgements

Although every effort has been made to trace copyright holders and clear permission for the photographs in this book, the provenance of a number of them is uncertain. The author and publisher would welcome the opportunity to correct any mistakes.

Chapter openers

Chapter 1, p. 1: © Neal Preston
Chapter 2, p. 11: Bob Riha, Jr./Getty Images
Chapter 3, p. 21: rblfmr/Shutterstock.com
Chapter 4, p. 31: Ebet Roberts/Redferns/Getty Images
Chapter 5, p. 45: Rob Verhorst/Redferns/Getty Images
Chapter 6, p. 57: Michael Putland/Getty Images
Chapter 7, p. 71: Robin Platzer/Getty Images
Chapter 8, p. 83: Snap/Shutterstock
Chapter 9, p. 93: © Dan Burn-Forti via Making Pictures
Chapter 10, p. 101: Richard Young/Shutterstock
Chapter 11, p. 109: Brian Rasic/Getty Images
Chapter 12, p. 119: Erica Echenberg/Redferns
Chapter 13, p. 127: Peter Turnley/Corbis/VCG via Getty Images
Chapter 14, p. 137: Kevin Mazur/WireImage/Getty Images
Chapter 15, p. 147: Spencer Platt/Newsmakers/Getty Images
Chapter 16, p. 157: White House Photograph Office and Sharon Farmer, 'Joni Mitchell,' *Clinton Digital Library*, accessed April 28, 2024 https://clinton.presidentiallibraries.us/items/show/48193
Chapter 17, p. 167: Maximum Film/Alamy Stock Photo

PICTURE ACKNOWLEDGEMENTS

Chapter 18, p. 179: Jorgen Angel/Redferns/Getty Images
Chapter 19, p. 189: Denise Truscello/WireImage/Getty Images
Chapter 20, p. 199: Kevin Mazur/Getty Images
Chapter 21, p. 209: Associated Press/Alamy Stock Photo
Chapter 22, p. 219: David M. Benett/Getty Images
Chapter 23, p. 229: Derek Storm/Everett Collection/Alamy Live News
Chapter 24, p. 239: Philip Vaughan/Shutterstock
Chapter 25, p. 253: The Asahi Shimbun via Getty Images
Chapter 26, p. 261: Kyodo News Stills via Getty Images
Chapter 27, p. 271: Brill/ullstein bild via Getty Images
Chapter 28, p. 283: Stephen Lovekin/Shutterstock
Chapter 29, p. 293: Chris Weeks/WireImage/Getty Images
Chapter 30, p. 301: Kevin Winter/Getty Images for iHeartMedia
Chapter 31, p. 311: Mariah Tauger/Los Angeles Times via Contour RA by Getty Images
Chapter 32, p. 323: Anna Barclay/Getty Images
Chapter 33, p. 331: © David Dixon
Chapter 34, p. 341: Valentina Frugiuele/Getty Images
Chapter 35, p. 353: John Johnson/Alamy Stock Photo
Chapter 36, p. 367: JM Haedrich/SIPA/Shutterstock

Picture section

Page 1: [top] Scott Barbour/Getty Images
Page 1: [centre] Tristan Fewings/Getty Images for Sotheby's
Page 1: [bottom] Amer Ghazzal/Alamy Live News
Page 2: [top] Pete Souza/The White House via Getty Images
Page 2: [bottom] PA Images/Alamy Stock Photo
Page 3: [top] Stefan Rousseau/Pool WPA/AFP via Getty Images
Page 3: [bottom] Sean Dempsey/Pool WPA/AFP via Getty Images
Page 4: [top] Mark Reinstein/Corbis via Getty Images
Page 4: [centre] Jim Ruy/UPI/Alamy StockPhoto
Page 4: [bottom] Alberto Pizzoli/AFP via Getty Images
Page 5: [top] Rahman Hassani/SOPA Images/LightRocket via Getty Images
Page 5: [bottom] Associated Press/Alamy Stock Photo
Page 6: [top] Robert Blomfield Photography/Getty Images
Page 6: [bottom] Alistair Heap/Alamy Stock Photo
Page 7: [top] WENN Rights Ltd / Alamy Stock Photo
Page 7: [bottom] Jeremy Bembaron/Sygma via Getty Images
Page 8: [top] Charles McQuillan/Getty Images
Page 8: [bottom] Dave Benett/Getty Images

Index

A

Abba 232, 361, 362–63
ABC (band), 'All Of My
   Heart' 124
'Abide With Me' 172
Abu Dhabi 187
Acuff, Roy 215
Adams, Gerry 350
Adams, Ryan 298
Ages of Pop 244–45
AIDS 38, 132
Albert, Prince Consort 134
Ali, Muhammad 41
Allen, Marshall Bedford
   305
Allen, Woody 172
Allman, Duane 223
Allman, Gregg 224
Allman Brothers 106,
   223–24
Almost Famous (film)
   170–73, 175–76, 375–6
Alzheimer's disease 212–16,
   249, 255–56
Amara's Law 169
Amazon (company) 358
American Beauty (film) 171
Amis, Martin 313–14
Analogues 232

Anderson, Kelly Dale
   (later Kilauren Gibb)
   160–61
Anderson, Pink 73
Andrew Oldham
   Orchestra 144
Andrew, Prince, Duke of
   York 130–31
Animals 74
Anthology (TV series)
   372, 377, 378
Antigua 89
Apple Corps 112
Apple Inc. 174, 376
Arctic Monkeys 173
Arista Records 97
Arizona 37–38
Armstrong, Louis 266, 347
Aspinall, Neil 112–13
Austin, Texas 365
Australia 232, 276, 355
Australian Pink Floyd 232
Ayers, Kevin 222
Aylesbury,
   Buckinghamshire 365

B

Bach, Johann Sebastian 174
Bacharach, Burt 255

Bachman, Robbie 255
Back Street Crawler 78
Baez, Joan 290
Ballard, Florence 37
Band Aid 13
Bangs, Lester 171–72
Barbarians 77
Barrett, Syd 361
Bash Street Kids (comic
   strip series) 376
Basie, Count 193
BBC 7, 48, 151, 350
   Front Row 226
   Radio One 129
   Radio Two 145
   Saturday Club 369
Beach Boys 36, 38–42,
   212
   'California Girls' 41
   Pet Sounds 170
Beatlemania (show) 112
Beatles 111–17, 369–80
   1 378
   Abbey Road 274, 372,
   373, 378, 379
   'All You Need Is Love'
   370
   Anthology 115–16
   Beatles For Sale 376

INDEX

Beatles – (cont.)
  Blue Album 371, 377–78
  'Can't Buy Me Love' xi
  A Collection of Beatles Oldies 106
  'Day Tripper' 370
  'Free As A Bird' 116
  Get Back (film) 374–75, 378
  A Hard Day's Night (film) 75
  'Here There And Everywhere' 378
  'I Am The Walrus' 106
  'I Saw Her Standing There' 36
  'I Want To Hold Your Hand' 370
  'Let It Be' xi
  The Long And Winding Road (project) 112, 116
  'The Long And Winding Road' (song) 116
  'Love Me Do' 114, 116, 369
  'Magical Mystery Tour' 370
  'No Reply' 115
  'Now And Then' 379
  'Penny Lane' 370
  Red Album 371, 377–78
  Rock 'N' Roll Music 114
  Rubber Soul 370
  Sgt Pepper's Lonely Hearts Club Band 295, 377
  'Something' 274
  'Strawberry Fields Forever' 115
  'This Boy' 371
  'We Can Work It Out' 256, 370

White Album 298, 372
after death of John Lennon 14, 38
Allen Klein and 316
and Beatlemania 112, 314, 372, 377
choice of name 74
covers band 243
and Creedence Clearwater Revival 313
and electric guitars 290
Harold Wilson and 104
and iPod 175
Liam Gallagher on 107
logo 74
Love (show) 196
and newsgroups 152
Noel Gallagher on 106
on *The Ed Sullivan Show* 130, 334
record sales 212
statues of 365
Tony Blair on 105
tribute band 232
and Yoko Ono 59–60
see also Harrison, George; Lennon, John; McCartney, Paul; Starr, Ringo
Beck, Jeff 255
Beckenham, Greater London 329
Belfast 336
Ben & Jerry's, Cherry Garcia ice cream 23–29
Bennett, Tony 255
Bergman, Ingmar 227
Berlin 203
  Brandenburg Gate 67
  East 65
  Wall 65–66, 67
Berlin, Irving 348

'There's No Business Like Show Business' 348
'White Christmas' 348
Berry, Chuck 355
Best, Pete 116
Bhutto, Benazir 249
Biden, Joe 276
Big Shot 233
Billboard (magazine) 201
  chart 256
Billiard Room (studio) 63
Birmingham Mail 227
Birmingham, UK 195, 305
Björk 296
Björn Again 232
Black Crowes 78
Black Sabbath 74
  'The Wizard' 144
Blackmore, Ritchie 141
Blair, Tony 103–7
Bland, Bobby 222
Blockheads 13
Blue Boar cafe, Watford Gap motorway services, Northamptonshire 221
Blue Star Skiffle Group 140
Blue Velvets 314
Blur 107, 111, 376
The Bodyguard (soundtrack album) 97
Bolder, Trevor 222
Bon Jovi 201
Bonham, John 251
Bonnie and Clyde 170
Bono 8, 106, 197, 287, 350
Boomtown Rats 13
Bootleg Beatles 232
Bordowitz, Hank 318
Bowie, David 241–51
  'All The Young Dudes' 250, 329
  Black Tie White Noise 243
  Blackstar 247, 258

INDEX

Earthling 243
Low 243
Never Let Me Down 243
The Next Day 247
Station To Station 243
Tonight 243
childhood home 359
Earthly Messenger
    statue 365
illness and death
    247–48, 251, 349
interviewed by Jeremy
    Paxman 151
at Live Aid 14
on Mick Jagger 242
Nirvana and 88
and Tin Machine 124
on *Top of the Pops* 222
and Victoria and
    Albert Museum
    exhibition 336
Bowie Bonds 245–46
Boyd, Pattie 88, 89
Bradford Singers 250
Branson, Richard 129, 131
Brazil 326, 355
Brinkley, Christie 233–34
Brinsley Schwarz 96
Bristol 279
    The Fleece 226
Britpop 105, 107, 111–12, 377
Brockbank, Neil 98
Brooker, Gary 346
Brother (record label) 40
Browne, Jackson 258
Brussels, Heysel Stadium
    disaster 4
Buckingham, Lindsay 306,
    308
Buffalo Springfield, 'For
    What It's Worth' 144
Buffett, Jimmy 204
Bulgaria 145
Bunyan, Vashti 338

Bush, George 103
Bush, Kate 152
Byrds 74–80
    'Full Circle' 75

C
Cagney, James 334
California 18, 160, 285, 318,
    379
Campbell, Ashley 214–15
Campbell, Glen 211–16
    'Duelling Banjos'
    214–15
    'Gentle On My Mind'
    215
    'Rhinestone Cowboy'
    214
    'These Days' 258
    'Wichita Lineman' 214
Campbell, Kim 213, 215–16
Campbell, Mike 308
Campbell's Soup 305
Canada 141, 161–62, 355
Canterbury scene 222
Canvey Island 227
Carey, Mariah 87–88
    'I'll Be There' 88
Carlson, Tucker 29
Carradine, David 80
Carson, Violet 362
Carter, Carlene 98
Carter, Howard 116
Carter, Jimmy 275
Cash, Johnny 98, 357, 362
    Folsom Prison Blues
    357
Cave, Nick 350
CBS Television 277
CDs (compact discs) 139,
    191, 337, 378, 379
    sales 97, 113, 173
CGI 362
Chamberlain, Neville
    250
Chambers, Martin 250

Charles Kingsley Creation
    248
Charles, Prince of Wales
    (later King Charles III)
    131
Charlesworth, Chris 53
Cher 195
Cheshire, Leonard 67
Chicago 295, 297
Chicken Shack 305–6
    'I'd Rather Go Blind'
    306
Churchill, Winston 26
Cincinnati 4–5
Cirque du Soleil 194, 196,
    377
Clacton 140
    Butlin's 140–41
Clapton, Conor 89–91
Clapton, Eric 13, 66, 75,
    88–91, 287
    'Tears In Heaven'
    90–91
    Unplugged 91
Clark, Gene 75, 79–80
    Firebyrd 76
Clarke, Michael 75, 78–79
Clash 222
Clear Channel
    Communications 203,
    204
Clifford, Doug 314
CliffsNotes 269
Cline, Patsy 357
Clinton, Bill 29, 103, 307
Clinton, Hillary 307
Clooney, George 193
Cobain, Kurt 225, 346
Cocker, Joe, 'Woman To
    Woman' 96, 143–44
Cohen, Leonard 124, 160,
    313
    You Want It Darker 258
Cohl, Michael 48–52,
    63–64, 204–5

INDEX

Cold War 66, 85
Coldplay 173
Cole, Nat 'King' 104
Collins, Judy 160
concert ticket prices 201–5
Conservative Party (UK) 104
Cooder, Ry 313
Cook, Stu 314
'Cool Britannia' 107, 116
Cooper, Alice 212
Cooper, Marc 193
copyright law 344–46
Cornell, Chris 365
Cornwell, Hugh 13
    'Golden Brown' 95
Corona, California 287
Coronation Street 362
Costello, Elvis 77, 96
Coulter, Ann 29
Council, Floyd 73
Country Club, London 327
Country Life 63
country music 357
Coventry 227
Covid-19 pandemic 267, 290, 313, 325, 335
Coward, Noël 192–93
Cream 319
Creedence Clearwater Revival 37–38, 313–20
    'Bad Moon Rising' 315
    'Down On The Corner' 315
    'Fortunate Son' 315
    'Green River' 315
    'Have You Ever Seen The Rain' 315
    'Long As I Can See The Light' 315
    'Proud Mary' 315, 319
    'Run Through The Jungle' 315
    'Travelin' Band' 315

'Up Around The Bend' 315
'Who'll Stop The Rain' 315
Crosby, Bing 343, 347
Crosby, David 75, 78, 79, 151, 152, 255
Crowded House 124–25, 313
    'Don't Dream It's Over' 121
    Farewell to the World show 121–22, 124
    'When You Wish Upon A Star' 121
Crowe, Cameron 170–71, 172, 175
Culture Club 13
Cuomo, Rivers 280
Curtis, Ian 225
Curtiss, Dave (Atkins) 140–42, 145
Curtiss Maldoon
    Curtiss Maldoon 141–42
    'Sepheryn' 141–43
Cypress Hill, 'I Ain't Goin' Out Like That' 144

D
Dadrock 143
Daily Mail 216
Daltrey, Roger xiv, 182, 227
Damned 96
D'Arby, Terence Trent 151–52
'Dark Side of the Rainbow' phenomenon 153
Dartford, Kent 329
Dave Dee, Dozy, Beaky, Mick & Tich 374
David Bowie Is (exhibition) 355
Davies, Ray 106, 315
Davis, Clive 97
Deacon, John 304

Dead & Company 195
Deadheads (fans of the Grateful Dead) 23–27, 289
Dean, James 77, 359
deaths of rock stars 223–27, 247, 251
Deep Purple 141
Deevoy, Adrian 265–66
Def Leppard 50
Defries, Tony 245
Del Santo, Lory 89
Dennis, Carolyn 164
Depp, Johnny 350
Desert Island Discs 104
Desert Trip festival 318
Diana, Princess of Wales 129, 131–34
Dickens, Charles 161–62
Dickins & Jones 305, 307
digital technology 149–54, 164, 173–74
Dio, Ronnie James 361–62, 364
Dion, Celine, *A New Day* (show) 193–94
Dire Straits 305
Disney (The Walt Disney Company) 112, 121, 344
Doc Thomas Group 248
Dolenz, Micky 122
Donegan, Lonnie 290
Donnell, Kenneth 205
Doors 75, 78, 224
    'Light My Fire' 222
Dormieu, Sébastien 355
Dr Feelgood 225, 227
Dragone, Franco 194
Drake, Nick 223, 225
Drifters 36
Dublin 197
    Harry Street 365
Duerden, Nick, *Exit Stage Left* 123
Duluth, Minnesota 329

INDEX

Duran Duran 13, 85
Dury, Ian 13
DVDs 378
Dylan, Bob 263–69,
    358–60
    Biograph 114–15
    Blonde On Blonde 170
    Bootleg Series 112
    'Chimes Of Freedom'
    65
    Chronicles 266
    'Knockin' On Heaven's
    Door' 78
    'Like A Rolling Stone'
    36
    'Masters Of War' 344
    'Mr Tambourine Man'
    75, 358
    'Positively 4th Street'
    163
    albums 161
    Bruce Springsteen on
    36
    cussedness 273–74
    and *Girl from the
    North Country* 267
    and Hall of Fame 36, 42
    and John Fogerty 319
    Joni Mitchell on
    162–63
    at Live Aid 14
    marriage to Carolyn
    Dennis 164
    memorabilia 358–60
    mid-life crisis 124
    Never Ending tour
    265–66
    Nobel Prize 263–64,
    268–69
    recent releases 350
    and *Theme Time Radio
    Hour* 267
    touring xiii
    visits to childhood
    homes of others 359

E
E Street Band 16, 334
Eagles 75, 87, 201
    'Desperado' 87
*The Ecstasy of Wilko
    Johnson* (film) 227
The Ed Sullivan Show 211,
    314, 334
Eddy, Duane 268, 269
Edge, The 214
Edwards, Andy 365
Eisenhower, Dwight D. 285
El Cerrito, California 314
    High School 317
Elektra Records 75
Elizabeth II, Queen 130,
    131, 372
Ellen, Mark 104
ELO 115, 275, 378
Elvis Presley Enterprises
    357
Emberg, Kelly 15
EMI 111, 114, 116
Eminem 326
Entwistle, John 53, 181,
    182–87
Ephron, Nora 19
Epstein, Brian 112
Erasure 232
Ertegun, Ahmet 205
Evans, Chris 105
Everly Brothers 106, 347
Ewens, Hannah 176
Exhibitionism (exhibition)
    355
Extras (TV show) 247
Eyellusion 361–62, 363

F
FA Cup Final 4
Facebook 159, 164
Faces 78
Fairport Convention 13
Family Guy 280
fancy dress 85

Fanning, Shawn 151
Fantasy Records 314, 316,
    317
Faroe Islands 279
Feltham, London 329
Fender, Leo 285–86
Fender Custom Shop
    287–88
Fender guitars 285–86, 287,
    291
    Alligator Strat 289
    Stratocaster 285, 287,
    288–89
    Telecaster 285
Ferry, Bryan 241, 244
file sharing 173
Finn, Neil 121, 125, 308, 313
Finn, Tim 121
Fisher, Mark 67
Fisher, Matthew 346
Fleetwood Mac 113, 306–8,
    379
    'Don't Stop' 307
    'Rhiannon' 344
Fogerty, John 37–38, 313,
    313–20
    'The Old Man Down
    From The Road' 317
Fogerty, Tom 37–38,
    314–16, 318–20
Fogerty, Tricia 319
folk music 290
Forbes (magazine) 27
Ford, Gerald 275
Forde, Eamonn 356
    Leaving the Building
    216
Forster, Robert, *The 10
    Rules of Rock and Roll*
    122
France 60, 61, 355
Franklin, Aretha 346, 358
Freehold, New Jersey 329,
    333
French Revolution 373

INDEX

Friends Reunited 249
Fry, Martin 124
funerals 349–50
Furnish, David 326

G
Gallagher, Liam 107
  'Don't Brother Me' 278
Gallagher, Noel 106, 205
Galveston, Texas 211
Galway, James 67
Garcia, Jerry 23–29,
  288–89
Garcia Family Provisions
  289
gay icons 232
gay performers 163, 192,
  328
Gaye, Marvin 346
Geffen, David 266, 317
Geldof, Bob 4, 131, 181, 350
Genesis 326
Gere, Richard 90
Germany 222, 355
Gerry and the Pacemakers
  374
Gervais, Ricky 247
Giants Stadium, New
  Jersey 203
Gibson Flying V (guitar)
  104
Gilmour, David 62–68, 73,
  205, 232, 335
*Girl from the North
  Country* (musical) 267
Gladiator 171
Glastonbury Festival xi,
  xiii, 106, 227, 318, 327,
  333, 362
Go-Betweens 122
The Godfather 142
Gold Star Studios,
  Hollywood 98
The Golden Girls xv
Google 159

Gore, Al 29
GQ, Genius awards 226
Graceland, Memphis,
  Tennessee 356–57, 359
Graham, Bill 49, 52, 317
Grammys 215
  Lifetime Achievement
    Awards 216
Granada Television 370
Grand Old Opry 211
Grateful Dead 23–29, 74,
  289
  'Black Muddy River' 26
  'Dark Star' 289
  Europe 72 289
  In The Dark 25
  'Not Fade Away' 28
  'Touch Of Grey'
    25–26, 28
Greece 61, 63
Green, Peter 306
Green on Red 76
Griffin, Dale 248–51
Grimes, Hamish 75
Grohl, Dave xiii, 205
Guardian 227
Guildford Town Hall 327
Guilty Pleasures (concept)
  275
Guinness Book of Records
  205
guitars 285–91, 355, 361
Guns N' Roses 77

H
Haggard, Merle 215
Haley, Bill, 'Rock Around
  The Clock' 131
Hall, Jerry 67
Halliwell, Geri (Ginger
  Spice) 361
Hamburg 141, 192
Hammill, Peter 152
Handmade Films 113
Hansard, Glen 350

Hardy, Thomas, *Tess of the
  D'Urbervilles* 373
Harrison, George
  'Something' 113
  and Apple 222
  death 378
  at Granada Studios 371
  and Hall of Fame 36,
    38, 41
  and Handmade Films
    113, 116
  tour of Japan 274
Harrison, Noel,
  'Windmills Of Your
    Mind' 222
Harry, Debbie 13
Harry Palmer films 66
Hartford, John 215
Havens, Richie 222
Hawkins, Ronnie 141
Hay Grammar School 249
Heimann, Betsy 172–73
Hendrix, Jimi 104
  'All Along The
    Watchtower' 36
  Axis: Bold As Love 170
Henley, Don 87
  'Come Rain Or Come
    Shine' 88
Henry's Funeral Shoe 226
Hereford 248
Herman's Hermits 170
Hester, Paul 121, 124–25
Hibbing, Minnesota
  359–60
Higgins, Michael D. 350
Hillman, Chris 78
hip hop 348
Hipgnosis 344
Hodgson, Roger 305
Hoffman, Philip Seymour
  171
Hofner violin bass 243
Holder, Noddy 361
Holly, Buddy 269, 347

INDEX

Hollywood 15, 77, 79, 90, 211
  Roxy Theatre 16
Holzman, Jac 75
Hooters 67
Hornby, Nick, *High Fidelity* 337
Hot Five 347
Hot Seven 347
Houston, Whitney 97, 98
  'Didn't We Almost Have It All' 90
Houston, Texas 64
'(How Much Is) That Doggie in the Window?' 104
Howe, Steve 141
Hudson, Kate 171, 172–73
Hudson, Ola 77
Hull 222
  East Park 365
Human League
  Dare 276
  'Don't You Want Me' 276
Hunter, Ian 250, 251, 329
Hunter, Robert 26, 27
Huyton 104

I
internet 149–54, 191, 343
Internet Archive 29
Internet Underground Music Archive (IUMA) 150
iPod 174–75, 191
Italy 15, 64
iTunes 246, 280

J
Jackson, Michael 85, 349, 363–64
  Bad 64
  Thriller 277
Jackson, Peter, Machine Assisted Learning 378

Jagger, Mick
  She's The Boss 182
  at O2 205
  David Bowie on 242
  eightieth birthday 338
  and Hall of Fame 36
  legal proceedings against 159
  length of career xiv
  at Live Aid 14
  and Michael Cohl 48–52, 205–6
  Mike Love on 41
  solo tour 42
  and Steel Wheels tour 51–52
James, Dick 329
James, Henry 162
Jampol, Jeff 346
Japan 227, 274, 286, 326
Jarre, Jean-Michel 64
jazz, Dixieland 337
Jefferson Airplane 305
Jennings, Will 90
  'Didn't We Almost Have It All' 90
  'Up Where We Belong' 90
Jimmy Kimmel Live 280
Jobs, Steve 174
Joel, Billy 36, 231–37
  'Big Shot' 233
  'Just The Way You Are' 231, 235
  'Miami 2017 (Seen The Lights Go Out On Broadway)' 235
  'New York State Of Mind' 235
  'Piano Man' 231
  'Say Goodbye To Hollywood' 235
  'Scenes From An Italian Restaurant' 235

'She's Got A Way' 231
'Uptown Girl' 234
John, Elton (Reg Dwight)
  'Candle In The Wind' 129
  'Candle In The Wind 1997' 132–34
  Farewell Yellow Brick Road tour 325–26
  Goodbye Yellow Brick Road 328–29
  Lockdown Sessions 325
  The Red Piano (show) 194–95
  'Tiny Dancer' 172
  career 328–29
  and Diana funeral xvii, 129–34
  at Glastonbury 327, 333
  GQ award 226
  and Hall of Fame 36, 38, 41
  knighthood 107
  in Las Vegas 194–95
  at Madison Square Garden 152
  and public attention 372
  and *Q* magazine 15–16
  and Versace funeral 131
  at Wembley Stadium 328
  see also Taupin, Bernie
Johnson, Robert 287
Johnson, Wilko 225–27
Jones, Darryl 54
Jones, Davy 122
Jones, George 222
Jones, Kenney 182
Just William (book series) 376

K
Katrina and the Waves 96
Kavarna, Bulgaria 364

INDEX

'Keep On Truckin''
image 59
Kelly, Gene 15
Kemp, Gary, 'True' 95
Kensit, Patsy 107
Kilimanjaro, Mount 2
King, Stephen 29
King Crimson, '21st
Century Schizoid Man'
144
Kinks 105, 107, 315
Kiss 123
Klein, Allen 112, 316–17
Klym, Mary 280
Knebworth Festival 203
Knopfler, Mark 286, 305
Kung Fu 80

L
Labour Party (UK) 103
LaChapelle, David
194–95
laptops 326
Las Vegas 191–97, 378
Caesars Palace 193
Colosseum 193–94
Desert Inn 192
Hard Rock Hotel 186
Sands Hotel and
Casino 193, 194
Sphere 197
last albums 256–59
Last, James 315
Lauper, Cyndi 4, 67
Leach, Christine 143
Lead Belly 88, 266
Led Zeppelin 7, 74, 77, 88,
175, 202–3, 205–7, 290,
349
'Kashmir' 144
'Stairway To Heaven'
205
'That's The Way' 172
'Through The Out
Door' 203

Lee, Alvin, 'Going Home'
222
Lee, Arthur 123
Légion d'Honneur 263
Lennon, John
Double Fantasy 377
'How Do You Sleep?'
278
'Now And Then' 379
Aunt Mimi on 303
career 191–92
death 14, 191, 225, 334,
349, 371–72
earnings as writer 116
in Germany 222
home in Liverpool
264, 359
on Las Vegas 191, 196
at Madison Square
Garden 192
and Neil Aspinall 112
and Oasis 106
and Tittenhurst Park
187
and Yoko Ono 59–60,
257
Lennon, Julian 38
Lennon, Sean 38
Lennox, Annie 338
'Let It Rock' 34
Levittown, New York 234
Lewis, Jerry Lee, 'Great
Balls Of Fire' 33
Liberace 191
Life of Brian 265
Lipa, Dua 326
Little Richard 360
'Tutti Frutti' 3, 33
Live Aid concert xi, 3–9,
13–14, 15, 34, 64, 67, 121,
131, 174, 182, 326
Live Nation 203
Liverpool 74, 104, 222,
264, 359
Forthlin Road 359

Menlove Avenue 359
*Living in the Material
World* (film) 379–80
Loaded (magazine) 105
Loewenstein, Prince
Rupert 49
logos 74–75
Lomax, Jackie 222
London 184, 285, 305,
334, 375
O2 (formerly
Millennium Dome)
205–7
Abbey Road, St John's
Wood 104, 111,
356–57, 357
Acton 142
Apple Store, Baker
Street 370
Berwick Street 328
Blitz 133
Bond Street 336
Brentford 98
Camden Town 98
Chelsea 89, 141, 373
Crouch End 264
Edith Grove 355
Finchley Road 133
Finsbury Park Astoria
202
Fulham Football Club,
Craven Cottage
363–64
'Gold Top Studios' 98
Hammersmith Odeon
249–50
Haverstock Hill 327
Hyde Park concert
51, 335
Islington 61
King's Road 355
Knightsbridge 378
Met Bar 105
National Portrait
Gallery 355

INDEX

Regent Street 305
Regent's Park 373
Roundhouse 202
Royal Albert Hall 90,
205
Soho Square 372
Speakeasy Club 221
as 'Swinging London'
105
Tate Modern 241
Victoria and Albert
Museum 247, 336,
355
Wembley Arena 361
Wembley Stadium xi,
3–9, 41, 202
Westminster Abbey
129, 132–33
Long Island, New York 231,
232, 234
Expressway 235
long-playing records 343
Lord, Jon 141
Lord, Rob 149–50
Los Angeles 66, 76, 162,
211, 275, 277, 279, 298
Sunset Boulevard
Rainbow Bar and
Grill 79
Whiskey A Go Go
79
Love (band) 75, 123
Love (Las Vegas show) 377
Love, Mike 38–42
Love Story (film
soundtrack) 170
Lowe, Nick 96–99, 313
At My Age 99
The Impossible Bird 98
'(What's So Funny
'Bout) Peace, Love
and Understanding'
96–97
Ludwig drum kit 74
Luhrmann, Baz 347–48

Lukather, Steve 275–76,
278–80
'Along For The Ride'
278
Lydon, John 123
Lynne, Jeff 116
Lynott, Phil 365

M
Ma, Yo-Yo 174
McBean, Angus 111
McCartney, Paul
Give My Regards to
Broad Street 14
'Live And Let Die' 77
at O2 205
awarded MBE 372
and Beatles covers
band 243
and Bertrand Russell
373
career 374–75, 378–79
eightieth birthday xii
enjoyment of fame
372–75
exhibition of
photographs 355–56
in Germany 221
at Glastonbury xi, xiii
and Glen Campbell
215
home in Liverpool 359
knighthood 107
legal action against 38,
41
at Live Aid concert xi,
369
and Neil Aspinall
112–13
and Q magazine 14–15
Ringo Starr on 378–79
at screening of Get
Back film 374–75
sightings of 372–73
tours 201

and Unplugged 88
and Wings 378
MacDonald, Ian,
Revolution in the Head
117
McEnroe, John 250
MacGowan, Shane 349–50
McGuinn, Camilla 76
McGuinn, Roger 75–79
'Ballad Of Easy Rider'
76
'Chestnut Mare' 76
'Mr Tambourine Man'
76
Thunderbyrd 76
Mackay, Andy 244
Mackie, Bob 195
McLachlan, Sarah,
'Building A Mystery' 174
McLean, Don
American Pie 325
Vincent 325
MacLeod, Tracey 98
McNally, Dennis 26, 28
MacNutt, Austin 289
Macon, Georgia, Rose Hill
Cemetery 223–24
McPherson, Conor 267
McVie, Christine (née
Perfect) 305–9
McVie, John 306, 307
Madonna 85, 113, 139, 297,
362
Ray Of Light (album)
139, 142–43
'Ray Of Light' (song)
145
Magic FM 133
Magma 105
Major, John 104, 106–7
Maldoon, Clive 141–43
Manchester
Granada Studios 371
National Football
Museum 364

Mandela, Nelson 66, 277
Manson Family 39
Manzanera, Phil 144–45, 244
Manzarek, Ray 222
Marching Band of the Combined Soviet Forces 67
Margry, Peter Jan, 'The Social Construction of Sacred Space' 224
Marina del Rey, California 40
Marley, Bob 349
    'Could You Be Loved' 174
Marsh, Dave 26
Martin, Dean 193
Martin, George 107, 115, 377
Martin, George R. R. 29
Martin, Giles 377, 378
Marvin, Hank 285
Mason, Nick 60, 62, 63, 73, 335
May, Brian xvii
MC Hammer 78
Meat Puppets 88
Melody Maker 306
Melville, Herman, Moby-Dick 269
memorabilia, rock 355–65
Memphis, Tennessee
    Beale Street 364
    see also Graceland
Mercury, Freddie 7–8, 304, 336, 359
Metallica 151, 290
Michael, George 327
    Bare 163
Michaels, Lorne 112
Michelangelo Buonarroti 364
Mickey Mouse 344–45
Mickey Mouse Protection Act (1998) 345

Mike (musician working with Billy Joel) 231–33, 236–37
Milan 89, 131
millennium bug (Y2K) 169
Miller, Jimmy 78
Miner's make-up 371
Mitchell, Chuck 160
Mitchell, Joni xiii, 67, 159–64, 231, 338, 355
    Blue 160, 170
    Court And Spark 163
    'Little Green' 160
    'Woodstock' 160
    see also Anderson, Kelly Dale (later Kilauren Gibb)
Moloney, Paddy 67
Monkees 122–23
Monroe, Marilyn 129, 132
Montserrat 49, 50
Moon, Keith 182
Morecambe, Eric 327
Morgan Stanley 234
Morissette, Alanis 296
Morphy Richards hair driers 371
Morrison, Jim 224
Morrison, Van 67, 335–36
    'Cyprus Avenue' 336
    'Gloria' 33
Morrissey 105, 249
Moss, Kate 149
Mothers Club, Birmingham 327
Motion, Andrew 264
Mott the Hoople 248–51
    'All The Young Dudes' 250, 329
Mountain, Nantucket Sleighride 105
MTV 15, 25–27, 51, 85, 86, 87, 153, 191, 286
Murvin, Junior, 'Police And Thieves' 222

music newsgroups 152
musical estates 216, 278, 345–46, 356
Musicland, London 328
'My Way' 235

N
Napa County, California, Uptown Theater 216
Napoleon I, Emperor 373
Napster 151, 173
Nash, Graham 151, 160, 288
    Songs For Beginners 288
Nashville, Tennessee 216
    Johnny Cash Kitchen and Saloon 357
    Ryman Auditorium 211, 215
National Trust 359
Needs, Kris 250
Nelson, Willie 305
Nenagh, County Tipperary 349–50
Nesmith, Michael 122–23
New Jersey, Giants Stadium 16
New Wave 13
New York 49, 78, 89, 248
    Madison Square Garden 192, 234–36, 333–34
    Metropolitan Museum of Art 355
    Parker Meridien Hotel 18
    Tower Records 16–17
    United Nations Building 234, 236
    Waldorf Hotel 34, 39
New York Daily News 235
New York Giants 235
New York Times 17, 266
New Yorker 205–6, 263, 374
Newman, Randy, Dark Matter 258

INDEX

Newport Folk Festival 338
Nicks, Stevie 79, 306
Nirvana 88, 251, 347, 376
    'The Man Who Sold
    The World' 88
Nobby's Hobbies Holdings
    327
Nobel Prize xvii, 263–64,
    268–69
Norton Warburg 60
Nudie (Nudie Cohn) 357

O
Oakley, Berry 223
Oasis 105–6, 107, 143, 173,
    290, 376
    Definitely Maybe 105–6
obituaries 221
Ocean's Eleven (1960 and
    2001) 193
O'Connor, Sinéad 67, 255
An Officer and a
    Gentleman 90
Olsson, Nigel 195
one-hit wonders 95–96,
    170, 222
online music 149–54
Ono, Yoko 38, 59, 257
Orbison, Roy 363
Orbit, William 139, 143
Original Dixieland Jazz
    Band 338–39
Orioles 250
Oscars 171, 361
Oxford 103, 104
Oxfordshire 89
Oyster Bay, New York 234

P
Pagel, Bill 359–60
Paich, David 278
Paisley Park, Minneapolis
    358
Paisley Underground 76
Paris 129, 263, 355

Père Lachaise
    Cemetery 224
Parks, Van Dyke 250
Parsons, Gram 77
    'Farther Along' 77
    'In My Hour Of
    Darkness' 77
Patterson, Jeff 149–50
Paxman, Jeremy 151
Peck, Gregory 15
Peel, John 152, 249
Pelosi, Nancy 214
Penn, Sean 113
People magazine 225
Pet Shop Boys 247
Petty, Tom 76–77
Phair, Liz 295–99
    Exile In Guyville
    295–99
    Icon 297
    Soberish 298
Philadelphia 51
    JFK Stadium 3, 6
Philips 141
Phillips, Julianne 18–19
Phoenix, Arizona 211, 288
phones, mobile 4, 191, 326
Piaf, Edith 224, 362
Pike County, Arkansas 211
Pink Floyd 60–68, 73–74,
    152, 232, 335, 355
    'Another Brick In The
    Wall' 61
    The Dark Side Of The
    Moon 60, 153
    The Final Cut 62
    A Momentary Lapse
    Of Reason 64
    The Wall 61, 65, 66, 67,
    73, 87
Pinner, London 328, 329
Pitt, Brad 40, 171, 193
Plant, Robert 88, 206–7
Planters Peanuts 305
Pogues 349

Police 85, 243–44
Porcaro, Jeff 277, 278, 279
Porcaro, Steve 277
Porcaro, Susan 278
Porter, Cole
    'I've Got You Under
    My Skin' 348
    'Night And Day' 348
Prague 246
Presley, Elvis
    Comeback Special 86
    biopic of 347–48
    death 225, 356
    estate 356
    fear of being alone
    186
    and Graceland 356–58
    in Las Vegas 191
    movie songs 211
    and 'Proud Mary' 315
    statues of 364
Presley, Lisa Marie 255
Presley, Priscilla 205
Presley, Reg 221
Preston, Lancashire, Public
    Hall 202
Pretenders 7
Primal Scream, 'Movin'
    On Up' 78
Prince 355, 358
Princeton University 263,
    268
Priscilla, Queen of the
    Desert 232
Probate Court 216
Procol Harum 140, 346
    A Whiter Shade Of Pale
    346
Public Enemy, 'He Got
    Game' 144
Puff Daddy, 'Come With
    Me' 144
Pullman, David 245
punk rock 8, 60, 96, 275
Purple Records 141

INDEX

Q
Q (magazine) 14, 15–16, 104
Quarwood, Stow-on-the Wold, Gloucestershire 184–85, 186–87
Barracuda Inne 184
Queen 7, 182, 203, 251, 304
'Radio Ga Ga' 8

R
Radio City Rockettes 213
Radiohead, 'Creep' 274
Ramones 122, 346–47
Record Store Day 336–37
record stores 336–37
Red Army Chorus 67
Red Hot Chili Peppers 214
Redding, Otis, III 255
Reed, Lou 222, 362
Reid, John 326
Remnick, David 374
Rémy Martin cognac 182
retirement 304–8
Rew, Kimberley, 'Walking On Sunshine' 96
Richard, Cliff 106–7, 242, 285
Richards, Keith xii, 35, 42, 48–50, 53, 204–5, 288
quoted vii, xiv
Richards, Viv 6
Ridgway, Stan 77
Rio de Janeiro 8
Ripley, Surrey 329
'Rob and Jeff' 149–50
Robertson, Robbie 141, 255, 319
Robinson, Chris and Rich 78
Rock and Roll Hall of Fame 33–42, 78, 79, 305, 319, 349
Rock School (film) 290, 303
Rocketman (film) 326

Rolling Rock beer 50
Rolling Stone (magazine) 26, 161, 171, 224, 296–97
Rolling Stones 47–54
'Angie' 347
'Brown Sugar' xvi, 242, 348
Dirty Work 47, 48
Exile On Main Street 295
Forty Licks 243
Hackney Diamonds 338
'Hey Negrita' 348
'Honky Tonk Women' 347
'The Last Time' 144
'Live With Me' 103
'Satisfaction' 273
'Some Girls' 348
'Start Me Up' 347
Steel Wheels 50
Sticky Fingers 103
'Stray Cat Blues' 348
back on the road (1989) 48
and Bill Graham 49
career 107
at Desert Trip festival 318
and fanbase 28
Farewell to Britain tour 202
image of band 24
in Chelsea flat 355
logo 347
longevity of 42, 349
and Michael Cohl 48–53
Mike Love on 41
Pete Townshend on 35
Steel Wheels tour 51–53, 204–5
as 'Stones' 74
Tony Blair on 105

tours 51–53, 201, 202, 204–5, 243, 339
Urban Jungle tour 53
Ronson, Mick 365
Rosen, Jeff 267
Ross, Diana 37
Rossington, Gary 255
Rourke, Andy 255
Rowse, Alycen 186
Roxy Music 144, 244
Royal Command Performance 130
Rundfunk Orchestra and Choir 67
Rush (film) 90
Rush (soundtrack album) 91
Russell, Bertrand 373
Russell, Leon 328
Russia 326

S
Sainte-Marie, Buffy 160
sales
CD 97, 113, 173
charts 241–42
guitar 290
merchandise 28, 51–52, 204, 236, 318, 346
see also T-shirts
record 195, 212, 241–42, 246, 297, 316, 343
tours 201, 203
San Francisco 23
Bay Area 28, 314
Candlestick Park 243
Haight-Ashbury 25, 27
Saturday Night Live 112
Savage, Charlie 153
Scaggs, Boz, Silk Degrees 277
Scarfe, Gerald 67
Schultz, Bill 287
Scorpions 67

INDEX

Scorsese, Martin xv, 379–80
Screaming Abdabs 62
Seattle 365
Second World War 90, 103, 132, 140, 259
Seger, Bob 96
Senegal 141
Sex Pistols 105, 123, 227
Shadows 285
Shakedown Sound 248
Shakur, Tupac 362
  'California Love' 96, 143–44
Shanghai Surprise 113
Shaw, George Bernard xiv
Sheeran, Ed 298
Sheffield 276
  National Centre for Popular Music 358
Sheridan, Tony 222
Shorter, Wayne 255
Silence (band) 248
Sillerman, Bob 203
Simon & Garfunkel 256
  'America' 172
  Bridge Over Troubled Water 256, 257
  'The Sounds Of Silence' 256
Simon, Paul 256–58, 313
  Graceland 257
  Seven Psalms 256, 257, 258–59
Sinatra, Frank 141, 193, 194, 211, 266, 347, 357
Sinn Féin 350
skiffle 192, 290
Slane Castle, Ireland 8
Slash (Saul Hudson) 77–78
Slick, Grace 305
smartphones 191
Smith, Chad 214
Smith, Jean 249
Smith, John 103

Smith, Mandy 47–48
Smiths 105
social media 164, 225–26
Sonny and Cher 211
Sotheby's 336
Soundgarden 365
Southend 226
Soviet Union 65
Spandau Ballet 95
Sparks 274
Spector, Phil 98
Spencer, Charles, 9th Earl 133
Spinal Tap 277
Spirit 346
Spotify 375
Springsteen, Bruce
  'Born In The USA' 334
  'Born To Run' 334
  'Thunder Road' 334
  Tunnel Of Love 18–19
  in Berlin 65
  on Bob Dylan 36
  Live 1975–85 boxed set 16–18
  and fanbase 274
  father's rage over guitar playing 304
  at Giants Stadium 203
  at Glastonbury xiii
  and Glen Campbell tour 214
  guitar as museum exhibit 355
  and Hall of Fame 36, 319
  interviewed for British TV 18
  at Madison Square Garden 333–34
  marriage to Julianne Phillips 18
  Mike Love on 41
  on Nick Lowe 98

  as public speaker 41–42
  on Shane McGowan 350
  at Slane Castle 8
  tour of Britain 333–34
Stainton, Chris 143–44
Star Wars 173
Starcaster guitar 286
Starr, Ringo 38, 41, 74, 112, 114, 116, 378–79
statues 363–64
Steamboat Willie 344
Steinberger 286–87
Stern, Howard 329
Stevens, Cat 175, 182
Stewart, Dave 264
Stewart, Rod 15, 16, 66, 78, 88, 159, 222
  'Every Picture Tells A Story' 172
  Never A Dull Moment 105
Stiff Records 96
Stigers, Curtis 97
Stills, Stephen, 'Love The One You're With' 78
Sting 131
  'Every Breath You Take' 95
Stockholm 263
Stone, Oliver 78
Stranglers 13, 95
streaming economy 343
Styles, Harry 298
Summer of Love 141
Sun Ra Arkestra 305
Super Trouper (spotlight) 361
Supertramp 305
Supremes 37
Sussex 88
Sutherland, Kiefer 287
Swarbrick, Dave 227
Sweden 325

INDEX

Swedish Academy 263
Swift, Taylor 216, 291, 308
Switzerland 250
Sydney
    Harbour 121
    Opera House 124

T
T. Rex 250
T-shirts 4, 18, 51, 52, 172, 231, 306, 318, 328, 346, 347
    slogans 24, 202, 250
Tarantino, Quentin 40, 172
Target 247
Taupin, Bernie 129, 132, 133, 141
Taylor, Derek 376
Taylor, James 160, 273, 313
    'Fire and Rain' 273
    'That's Why I'm Here' 273
teleprompters 215
Temple, Julien 227
Tennant, Neil 247
Testino, Mario 139
Texas 25
TFI Friday 105
Thames, River 307
Thank Your Lucky Stars 370
Thatcher, Margaret 103, 104
Their Mortal Remains (exhibition) 355
Theme Time Radio Hour 267
Thomas, Dylan 227
Thompson, Richard 13
Thorpe, Jeremy 104
Ticketmaster 203
TikTok 335
The Times 133, 176, 362
Tin Machine 124
Titelman, Russ 91

Tittenhurst Park, Berkshire 187
Tolstoy, Leo 39, 40
Top of the Pops 134, 222
Tork, Peter 122
Toronto 63–64, 159
Toto, 'Africa' 275–80
Tower Records 16–17, 150
Townshend, Pete xiv, 35, 53, 151, 182, 186
    Empty Glass 182
Traffic 78
Tremors 140–41
tribute bands 231–37
Troggs 60, 221
    The Troggs Tapes 221
Trump, Donald 247, 276, 344
Tulsa, Oklahoma
    Bob Dylan Center 358
    Tulsa, University of 358
Turkey 150
Turner, Ike 315
Turner, Janice 362
Turner, Tina 14, 255, 315, 319
    Private Dancer 14
    'What's Love Got To Do With It' 14
Tutankhamen 116
Twitter 222, 280

U
U2 8, 85, 105, 196–97, 201, 214, 279
    'Beautiful Day' 197
Ugly Mugs 149–50
Ugly Rumours 103, 104
Ukraine, Russian invasion of 326
Ultravox 13
United Kingdom, leaving European Community 247
United States of America 17, 23, 65, 130, 355

Congress 214
Marines 186
Universe Zero 152–53
'Unledded' (MTV project) 88
Unplugged (music format) 85–88, 91
Urban Outfitters 173
Usenet 152, 153

V
Vampires 140
Van der Graaf Generator 105, 152
Van Halen, Eddie 286
Vanilla Ice 78
Vanity Fair (magazine) 107
Vaughan, Stevie Ray 365
Vega, Arturo 347
Velvet Underground 295
Venice 64–65, 66
    Grand Canal 65
    Piazza San Marco 65
Versace, Gianni 131
Verve, 'Bitter Sweet Symphony' 144
Victoria, Queen 134, 361
Victoria's Secret 267
Vietnam War 327
vinyl 337
Visconti, Tony 247
Voyage (virtual Abba show) 361

W
Waits, Tom, 'Jersey Girl' 18
Walsh, Joe 87
Washington, George 23
Washington Post 153, 290
Washington State 338
Watergate scandal 171
Waters, Roger 61–68, 73, 87, 335
    Radio K.A.O.S. 64
Watford Football Club 134

INDEX

Watts, Charlie 47, 54
Webb, Jimmy 211
Weedon, Bert, *Play in a Day* 140
Weezer 280
Welles, Orson 350
Welsh, Irvine 264
Wenner, Jann 34
West Indies cricket team 6
West, Kanye, 'Power' 144
West, Kanye, and Jay Z, 'No Church In The Wild' 145
West, Keith, 'Excerpt From A Teenage Opera' ('Grocer Jack') 142
West, Leslie 105
White, Clarence 77
White Heat (film) 334
Whiteman, Paul 347
Who, The 4, 53, 181–86, 318
   Live at Leeds 202
   'My Generation' xiv
   Tommy 170
Wichita, Kansas 211
Wikipedia 89
Wilde, Oscar 224
Williams, Hank 265, 266
Williamson, Jane 23-24
Wilson, Bob 7–8

Wilson, Brian 38–40, 163, 212
Wilson, Carl 40
Wilson, Dennis 39–40
   Pacific Ocean Blue 40
Wilson, Harold 104
Wilson, Mary, *Dreamgirl* 37
Wilson, Tony 371
Winehouse, Amy 362, 364
Winger, Debra 90
Wings 115, 378
Winnipeg 359
Winwood, Steve 90
Withers, Bill 304–5
   'Ain't No Sunshine' 305
   'Lean On Me' 305
   'Lovely Day' 305
The Wizard of Oz 153
Wogan, Terry 48
women, as performers 159–60, 161, 192, 296, 298, 305–6, 338, 364
Woodstock, New York 265, 359
Woodstock Festival xiv, 67, 160, 318
Wright, Rick 61, 63
Wycombe Wanderers Football Club 134
Wyman, Bill 47–48, 53–54

Y
yacht rock 279
Yardbirds 74, 75
Yarwood, Mike 98
Yemm and the Yemen 248
Yes 141
Young, Neil 88, 172, 231, 350, 359
   'Heart Of Gold' 344
   'The Needle And The Damage Done' 88
YouTube 164, 246, 371

Z
Zaentz, Saul 317
Zappa, Dweezil 362
Zappa, Frank 345, 362
Zevon, Warren
   'Don't Let Us Get Sick' 258
   'I Have To Leave' 258
   Life'll Kill Ya 258
   'My Ride's Here' 258
   'You're A Whole Different Person When You're Scared' 258
ZZ Top 25

About the Author

David Hepworth has been writing, broadcasting and speaking about music and media since the seventies. He was involved in the launch and editing of magazines such as *Smash Hits*, *Q*, *Mojo* and *The Word*, among many others.

He was one of the presenters of the BBC rock music programme *The Old Grey Whistle Test* and one of the anchors of the corporation's coverage of Live Aid in 1985. He has won the Editor of the Year and Writer of the Year awards from the Professional Publishers Association and the Mark Boxer award from the British Society of Magazine Editors.

He lives in London.

www.davidhepworth.com